W9-BFJ-437

DATE DUE

BRODART   Cat. No. 23-221

DEC — 1993

Acts of Discovery

Acts of Discovery

Visions of America
in the Lewis and Clark Journals

ALBERT FURTWANGLER

University of Illinois Press   Urbana and Chicago

This book is printed on acid-free paper.

Library of Congress Cataloging-in-Publication Data

Furtwangler, Albert, 1942–
    Acts of discovery : visions of America in the Lewis and Clark
journals / Albert Furtwangler.
        p.   cm.
    Includes bibliographical references and index.
    ISBN 0-252-02002-2 (cl).
    1. Lewis and Clark Expedition (1804–1806)   2. Lewis, Meriwether,
1774–1809—Diaries—History and criticism.   3. Clark, William,
1770–1838—Diaries—History and criticism.   4. West (U.S.)—
Description and travel—To 1848.   I. Title.
F592.7.F86   1993
917.804'2—dc20   92-29916
                                                              CIP

Contents

Preface

THE JOURNALS of the Lewis and Clark expedition present the modern reader with many rich descriptions and adventurous narratives, but they are entangled in the tedious, repetitive, and sometimes awkwardly written entries of overlapping daily logs. The past few decades have seen the publication of many new studies that have isolated and clarified the explorers' achievements in geography, natural history, diplomacy, and encounters with the Indians of the Far West. The journals themselves are now appearing in a full and well annotated edition, complete with volumes of maps and illustrations. But the depth and complexity of many moments on the trail remain to be unfolded. And the full, cumulative effect of this project calls for sensitive interpretation and reassessment now that its records are available for everyone to see.

I believe that Meriwether Lewis and William Clark not only carried out the enlightened instructions of Thomas Jefferson but surpassed them, gathering new information with extraordinary perception and intelligence, and helping to achieve a new sense of America, an understanding of this continent that would overturn the science, politics, and even artistic ideals of Jefferson and his age.

This book explores these developments in three fields simultaneously: literature, history, and science. I argue that the journals are a heretofore neglected American literary classic, some of whose features compare in intriguing ways with outstanding works by William Wordsworth, Mark Twain, Wallace Stevens, and others. Chapter 10 explicitly weighs the claim that the journals embody an American epic and have to be understood in epic terms.

At the same time, this book attempts to define the historic achievement of Lewis and Clark in fulfilling and outgrowing the ideals of Jeffersonian science and politics. It examines some ironic outcomes of westward expansion and conquest. And it tries to bring out the peculiar courage of explorers who were the first (and almost the last) to cross the continent by pulling their way up the Missouri.

Finally, this book takes a fresh approach to the idea of scientific discovery by presenting the Lewis and Clark project as a literal, large-scale acting out of experiment and breakthrough: probing into the interior of a continent and finding a way across the Rockies to the Pacific. Many other acts of discovery are also traced here, and I discuss them in light of deep questions about progress posed by Francis Bacon, Henry Adams, and modern physicists, astronauts, and biologists.

I have tried to write chapters that can stand on their own and prove stimulating to readers with special regional or topical interests. I have also tried to make each one inviting for readers who might be put off by a steadily chronological account of the entire expedition. The central idea of the book is discovery, and I have tried not to impose a rigid structure on materials that came from the wilderness and show minds groping to hold on to it. These chapters do, however, follow a coherent sequence as I understand them. The first three show encounters of late eighteenth-century literate science with the surprises of wilderness. The next three show how early statesmen and explorers pressed deeper and deeper into the American interior and into intimate contact with the strange environments and peoples they met there. Chapters 7, 8, and 9 discuss some transforming counterpressures of far western realities, challenges that forced the explorers to make much more reflective and inventive records than their instructions required. The final three chapters question whether these records, taken as a whole, reveal a harmony of American vision—a balance between the futility of western military conquest and the indelible achievement of sympathetic new learning.

Many people have contributed to the development of this book, both in the course of its composition over five years and in its much longer gestation, my learning about the shape and history of North America over the course of a lifetime.

The Lewis and Clark Trail Heritage Foundation has brought much new knowledge to light in recent decades. Its members have preserved and promoted important records and observations on the country the Corps of Discovery explored. Many of their publications are recorded in my notes, for this book has grown atop that wealth. And at their annual meetings dozens of members have proved personally friendly and helpful to me. Meeting with them has been a rare advantage for a prospective author: direct encounter with a large gathering of acute readers from many backgrounds who share a common and deep interest in this subject.

My writing has been done, however, hundreds of miles east of St. Louis and, in fact, outside the borders of the United States. Mount Allison University has once again supported my research and furnished very welcome funds from the Crake Institute, the Dean's Travel Fund, the Marjorie Young Bell Faculty Fund, the faculty research fund, and internally administered funds from the Social Science and Humanities Research Council of Canada. The R. P. Bell Library has proved a mine with rich ores in many subjects; and Anne Ward has again given me many hours of help in securing needed materials on interlibrary loan. My students in an American literature seminar in 1990–91 kept up a lively conversation about many books I mention here, stimulated my thinking about them, and helped me look into others.

The libraries at Harvard and Yale universities have given friendly support during brief visits. Special thanks are due to T. Rose Holdcraft, conservator at the Peabody Museum at Harvard, for showing me many items that were no longer on public display. Peter Hicklin and Tony Erskine of the Sackville office of the Canadian Wildlife Service welcomed me to their library and offered some pertinent suggestions about birds.

Members of my family have joined me in this project in important ways. My wife taught a summer course at Cannon Beach, Oregon, and thus brought us to the West Coast for a week in 1990—right to the place where Clark's party came to see a whale. Our son Tom secured a Dana grant from Vassar College that summer and drove and camped with me all along the trail, from St. Louis to Astoria and Seaside—seeing with fresh eyes and camera lenses and expanding my more bookish attitudes. My wife and our younger son, Andrew, came on the return trip along the Yellowstone—and with him we saw into the High Plains in a new way, especially when he confidently rode an Appaloosa over cattle country near Billings, Montana.

I am grateful for encouraging correspondence and conversations with Leslie Brisman, Sally Bryan, Michael DePorte, Gary Moulton, Richard Penney, Mark Phillips, and James Ronda. Arlen Large and

James Ronda have read the entire manuscript and offered many helpful suggestions. At times I have rejected or ignored good advice; remaining faults are mine alone.

This book has been developing in my mind over the course of decades; in writing it I have been aware of drawing often upon learning that began in much earlier periods of my life.

The discussions of sublimity, Romantic ideals in poetry and landscape, and early American politics owe much to my graduate training at Cornell University, especially in courses taught by M. H. Abrams, Scott Elledge, Geoffrey Hartman, and Cushing Strout.

My interest in relating science to literature stems in part from the rigorous core courses in physics, chemistry, and biology at Amherst College in the early 1960s; in part from life with roommates and close classmates who became physicians, scientists, engineers, and mathematicians; and in part from previous scientific preparation among good teachers and friends in the public schools of West Seattle.

What I know of camping and surviving in the outdoors began during weekend fishing, hunting, and clamming trips with my parents and other relatives during my childhood in the Pacific Northwest, and from small-bore rifle and other training programs sponsored by the West Seattle Sportsmen's Club.

My interest in Lewis and Clark began when I was riding over the route of the Northern Pacific Railway between home and college, eating some of my meals in the so-called Traveller's Rest car of the North Coast Limited, and reading Bernard DeVoto's abridged edition of the *Journals* to create a framework of history for the enormous mountains and plains outside my window.

Finally, I have approached the deepest subject of this book through almost twenty-five years of marriage to a strong partner in discovery.

Abbreviations

The following abbreviations are used in the notes and in the text:

Journals   Gary E. Moulton, ed. *Journals of the Lewis and Clark Expedition.* 7 vols. to date. Lincoln: University of Nebraska Press, 1981–

LCPN   Paul Russell Cutright. *Lewis and Clark: Pioneering Naturalists.* 1969. Lincoln: University of Nebraska Press, 1984.

Letters   Donald Jackson, ed. *Letters of the Lewis and Clark Expedition,* rev. ed. 2 vols. Urbana: University of Illinois Press, 1978.

Ronda   James P. Ronda. *Lewis and Clark among the Indians.* Lincoln: University of Nebraska Press, 1984.

Thwaites   Reuben Gold Thwaites, ed. *Original Journals of the Lewis and Clark Expedition.* 8 vols. 1904. New York: Arno Press, 1969.

Chapter 1 Discovery and Serendipity

"Corps of Discovery" is the name given to themselves by an extraordinary band of soldier-explorers, the party of early Americans who first crossed the continent from the Atlantic seaboard to the Pacific. Their project began in the mind of Thomas Jefferson sometime in 1802, during his first administration as president. His private secretary, Meriwether Lewis, was briefly trained and prepared for this expedition in Washington and Philadelphia; then he embarked from Pittsburgh at the end of August 1803, joined William Clark at the Falls of the Ohio, and with him recruited and disciplined a small military party, which wintered near St. Louis. The following spring they set out to trace the Missouri River from its mouth to its source, cross the Rockies, and follow the Columbia to the Pacific Ocean. After wintering in the plains and near the Oregon coast, they returned safely in 1806. They brought back specimens of what they had found, journals running to several volumes, and memories full of strange sights and adventures. This was the first party of Americans to cross the Rockies, the first to link American claims in the Columbia River country to the newly acquired realm of Louisiana, the first to see many new forms of life in the plants, animals, and indigenous peoples of the Far West. In short, these were the first citizens to know the territory of the United States in its full continental dimensions.

They were always a corps, an interdependent group of disciplined soldiers and officers; they could not have survived otherwise. And they were always making discoveries; they were trained, alert, often brilliant in discriminating among the abundant new things they found and recording them in sharp detail. This combination of official intrusion and perceptive observation gives a nice resonance to their title. The Corps of Discovery helped gain title by conquest to the northern

I

tier of lands between the Mississippi and the Pacific. The Corps of Discovery likewise inscribed the features of this land onto the pages of modern science. And in the main words of its title there hums a happy tension of amateur seriousness. To survive in the unknown West, this corps had to include others—tradesmen, boatmen, interpreters, Indian guides, a black servant, a mother and her infant. To complete their mission of discovery, they had to open themselves to surprises and accommodate them when they occurred. All the while, they kept accurate daily records, even through storms, floods, illnesses, attacks, accidents, and near starvation, and despite fatigue, frustration, swarming insects, and ink freezing in the pen. These records show that Lewis and Clark were highly intelligent in many fields, expert in very few; their men were mainly young, willing foot soldiers with one or two outstanding skills and very ordinary desires. As a band of thirty- or forty-odd members, they could hardly conquer a continent; as scientists, they are almost absurd. Yet this flexible, sometimes loose-knit, sometimes tight-knit character makes the Corps of Discovery still appealing, and still rewarding to readers after two centuries. Their pages lie open to the curious North American who lacks special expertise but would love to recapture the full, rich extent of this land on which we dwell. The entries often end in hasty lines, rudely spelled, but within them stand scores of passages of mind-dilating wonder.

The Corps of Discovery may seem less august and more homely if we consider the source of its name. It probably arose in the first place from an embarrassment between the two leaders. Lewis, who was selected by Jefferson to develop and lead the expedition, was a regular army officer, a captain in the First U.S. Regiment of Infantry. Clark was chosen later, and although he was older and had once been Lewis's superior, his official commission for this task was delayed and disappointing. Lewis had promised him full equality of rank in a shared command. But the War Department and Congress refused to cooperate; they finally delivered a lowly commission as second lieutenant in the Corps of Artillerists. Lewis kept his word by keeping the actual commission terms secret and referring to Clark always as a fellow captain and equal. But captain of what? To cover the need for an honest title for the record, Clark began to sign himself as "William Clark, Capt. on the Missouri Expedition" or "Wm. Clark Captn. on an Expdn. for N. W. Descy" (*Letters* 2:208, 210).[1] Nowhere does this name stick out as pretentious. Clark often signed simply "William Clark, Capt. &c.," and the journal entries usually refer to the exploration group as just "we" or "the party." But soon after the return, one of the sergeants rushed into print with the first book-length account of the expedition. Patrick Gass's title was *A Journal of the Voyages and Travels of a Corps of Discovery, under the Command of Capt. Lewis and Capt. Clarke* (Pittsburgh, 1807). There was the name in print, and it has remained a convenient, shorter alternative to "Lewis and Clark Expedition" ever since.

But in that seemingly simple term "discovery" there is a deep well of meaning. What is a discovery, exactly? How does it begin? When is it complete? How does it compare to other forms of sudden learning? After two centuries of vigorous scientific activity, questions like these trouble us far more than they bothered these explorers, who seem to have plucked the term innocently, as a distinctive bright plume that was just there to be used.

The pages of Lewis and Clark provide abundant and pertinent material for a discussion of the idea of discovery. In fact, Lewis and Clark's direct contact with the geography of America makes them helpful, down-to-earth, comprehensible discoverers. Their travel and reporting is a useful model, much more accessible than, say, the calculations and laboratory work of molecular biologists or astrophysicists. And their peculiar situation nicely reveals the complexities of discovery. Because Lewis and Clark were writers as well as trailblazers, punctilious subordinates to Jefferson as well as wholly independent commanders in the field, hunters and gatherers in a completely foreign realm as well as emissaries from modern civilization, their raw journals expose many of the frustrations and dilemmas of modern searching and researching.

Discovering, for them and us, does not mean just happening upon new things or even recording them. It is rather an elaborate, lengthy process that begins with a directed line of questioning; proceeds through search, confusion, and discrimination; and results eventually in publication and a realignment of general thinking and understanding. It is not done by individuals, in other words, so much as by whole cultures or societies. For to discover something new means to be aware of limitations in the extent of what everyone knows or has known until now. It means deliberately seeking out something alien, and hence bewildering or deceptive at first encounter, and then draw-

3

ing that experience into the enlarged fabric of public common knowledge. Geographical claims—like advances in science—have to be announced and substantiated in print and accepted by others before a discovery is complete.

These stages of directed questioning, experimental observation, and public acceptance and interpretation are neatly broken apart in the story of the Corps of Discovery. The questioning began with Jefferson, who initiated and directed the project and composed a lengthy, detailed letter of instruction for Lewis. Much of the final interpreting fell to Jefferson's scientific colleagues and correspondents, who eventually received what Lewis and Clark brought back. Most of the specimens they had collected were forwarded to Philadelphia: zoological items were displayed in Charles Willson Peale's American Museum; botanical specimens were preserved and arranged at the Academy of Natural Sciences; and most of the journals came to rest at the American Philosophical Society.[2]

This division of personnel between Jefferson as originator and scientific experts as interpreters seems to place Lewis and Clark in a difficult, subordinate, intermediary role, exactly corresponding to their long loop to the West from Washington and back to Philadelphia. But this is not entirely true. The primary task rested on them alone, and in large measure they carried it through to final publication of a very significant discovery. Jefferson directed them to go west, trace the source of the Missouri, and find the most direct route connecting to the Columbia. (Their actual route is traced in fig. 1.) But no one had ever done anything quite like that: Lewis and Clark were to traverse an area that had never before been mapped. There was no telling what they would find at the head of the Missouri; whether they could find any way, let alone any easy way, to cross the Rockies and reach the Columbia; or how they might cross and return safely. It rested with their initiative, their resolve, their observation, their intelligence, and not least their cooperation with native peoples to make this scientific and literal breakthrough across the Continental Divide. They achieved this crossing in August 1805. By the following winter they had reasoned to a further conclusion—that a shorter, easier link between the Columbia and Missouri river systems could be made across the Rockies between their Travelers' Rest camp and the Great Falls. The next summer Lewis led a party across this shorter route. Thus, by reasoning, experiment, adaptation, and revision they

4

worked out a proof that Jefferson's basic hopes could be fulfilled, though not as he had supposed. They denied his assumption that the great western rivers could be linked by an easy portage. They demonstrated that the Rockies were much larger and more complex than anyone had known. And so they redrew the map of the American West. In fact, Clark redrew it with his own hand, composing a master map in 1810 that consolidated his own and others' discoveries. Engraved and published in the 1814 *History* of the Lewis and Clark expedition, it was an outstanding new synthesis of geographical understanding.[3]

In other fields, too, Lewis and Clark's work was the most crucial stage in this project. Jefferson's instructions would have meant nothing except for their diligent practices. Worthwhile evidence for science depended on their acutely intelligent work every day. It was up to them to decide what was, in fact, new and worth collecting and recording. That meant measuring it against their own informed understanding of what was already known and deciding on the spot whether to describe new items in their journal or to preserve and pack them, to fit into the condensed, precious cargo that could be carried back. Insofar as the act of discovery is the act of a single mind, it had to occur on this expedition in the mind of Lewis or Clark. And in large part it had to take place neither in moments of courage or adventure nor in steady, measurable progress from place to place. It happened instead in reflective solitude carved from each day, when a man with a notebook jotted as well as he could, recollecting his experience and making his best first draft of what might later prove telling or worth publishing.

By making these judgments, the explorers had to write themselves into their journals. We may like to think that science is objective or impersonal, and we should always bear in mind that these journals were kept as an official military log. Yet from the nature of this project, each day's entry is also a rough and rather personal composition of place. It is a record of progress and location but also a jotting that might include many incongruous details—weather observations, followed perhaps by a description of a new bird or animal, with later an account of an accident involving one of the men, an altercation, a problem about food supplies, or a curious bit of Indian lore recalled because of some new feature of the geography. There can be no telling whether a detail slighted at one place might prove invaluable after the

5

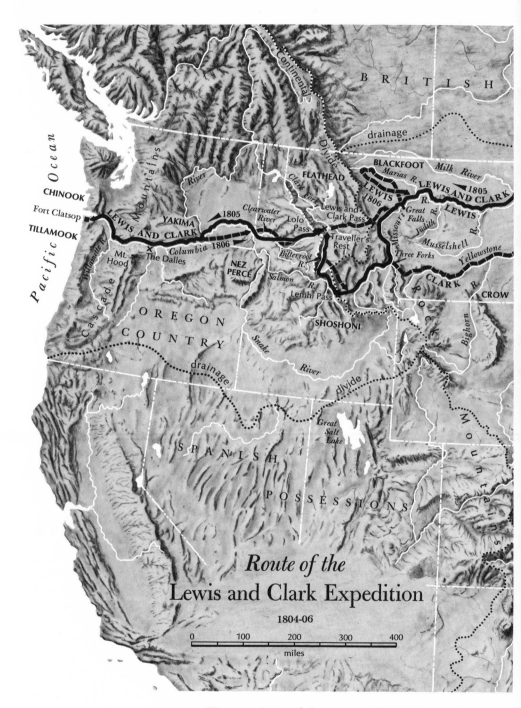

Figure 1. Map of the western United States showing

the routes of the Lewis and Clark expedition, 1804–6.

next bend in the river or in a developing sequence of sightings or events. The writer therefore includes as many oddments as he can and thereby reveals his own peculiar sense of what matters in a day's experience. In fact, Lewis often gives lavish attention to a day's happenings, unashamedly expatiating upon them and even confiding some very personal feelings on occasion. Clark's records are usually sparer, more matter of fact, but nonetheless salted here and there with brief asides and embellishments.

What these records disclose, therefore, is not only information but also a collection of incidents, attitudes, and personal styles or quirks affecting the course of discovery. To bring these out in full detail will be the work of later chapters. For now, we should define discovery more exactly by pointing out how it differs, in general, from other kinds of seeking, especially as these explorers practiced it. To Lewis and Clark, discovery is the work of uncovering or closely observing phenomena as they happen to emerge from each day's experience. At least that is their usual and most consistent attitude. But there are other ways of imagining or explaining the sudden emergence of something new. One way is to assume that powers beyond ourselves disclose meaningful wonders in moments of revelation. Another explanation, for which the decades before 1803 had coined a new term, is that the mind of the seeker may meet with happy accidents, as if a friendly (but reticent, unidentifiable) power were purposely jostling events toward a productive outcome for a well-prepared explorer.

These three distinct patterns show up, for example, as important paradigms in the first paragraph of Samuel Eliot Morison's two-volume work, *The European Discovery of America*. There Morison claims that the discovery and exploration of the New World originated in two separate and quite contrary motives, but before he is done, he accounts for the "success" of Columbus by invoking a crucial third pattern, a meeting point between these two extremes:

> The European discovery of America flows from two impulses. One, lasting over two thousand years and never attained, is the quest for some "land of pure delight where saints immortal reign"; where (in the words of Isaac Watts's hymn) "everlasting spring abides, and never fading flowers." The other impulse, springing to life in the thirteenth century, was the search for a sea route to "The Indies," as China, Japan, Indonesia, and India were then collectively called. This search attained success with the voyages of Columbus and Cabot—who (by the greatest

serendipity of history) discovered America instead of reaching the Indies—and with the voyages of Magellan which finally did reach the Indies and returned around the world.[4]

At one extreme, in other words, is the quest for a land of divinity or immortality—which we might call a realm of revelation. At the other extreme is the mundane, even primal grasping after quicker ways to wealth. Between these two poles lies a quirky, ironic middle ground where searchers set out to find one thing but happen upon something else, something surprising but worth more than their effort, like America instead of the Indies. Morison accurately calls this third way "serendipity," though he does not seem to recognize its full implications and relationship to his two main "impulses" to discovery.

These three distinct explanations of discovery obviously affect our reading of Lewis and Clark. All three stand out in what they have written; they occur as well in later attempts to interpret their work. This should not be surprising, since their crossing of the continent by water routes was the final leg, in effect, in the voyages of discovery that began when Columbus set sail. As we have already noted, their idea of discovery was rather single-minded and ignored the other two possibilities almost entirely. But to understand even that one method or practice aright, we need to develop and illustrate all three.

Discovery, as Jefferson, Lewis, and Clark use the term, refers to a plain, worldly uncovering of things heretofore unseen or unrecorded, with the ultimate aim of turning them to advantage—in this case, for the people and government of the United States. This sense of discovery implies that all the effort or activity is on the part of the discoverers. The things to be uncovered are simply *there*—mountains, bird species, electricity, gold ore, steam power, subatomic particles—to be found, appropriated, and exploited. How such things *got* there is of no particular interest. Whether they are the products or emblems of supernatural powers or intelligences is an entirely separate question, safely disregarded or doubted—a question that can only impede the here-and-now work of discovery. Jefferson appointed Lewis and instructed him very specifically to go west and make discoveries in this way—find the headwaters of the Missouri, locate a route from there to the Columbia, record and bring back samples of plants, animals, and minerals that no one had seen before. Lewis and Clark responded eagerly, without any shadow of hesitation or mental reservation, went

9

west, and energetically gathered things and wrote up descriptions. And, of course, the world beyond Fort Mandan on the upper Missouri was a region abounding in new things to be discovered by these methods. This much and no more seems to be the plain meaning of discovery in "Corps of Discovery."

Revelation is quite another thing. In this sense of discovery the main activity lies elsewhere, in the will of a supernatural power to disclose itself to human beings. Sudden, surprising new phenomena— a burning bush, a heavy stone rolled away from a tomb—are merely preliminary signs that awaken their beholders and prepare them to be drawn into momentous communications with the divine: new laws, covenants, promises, or transfigurations of human identity. People can seek such revelations, individually or collectively, but they do so by efforts of spiritual preparation, discipline, and purification in what Morison calls a "quest" rather than a "search." A quest does not usually begin or find expression in mining excavations, land surveys, the collection of botanical specimens, or what we usually think of as exploration. But it may. In fact, Columbus was certainly driven by both the motives Morison cites. He claimed new lands and their products for Spain (and for himself), and at the same time he carried out a mission he felt was divinely inspired. He was bringing Christianity to the ends of the earth, and he urged that the gold that came to Spain through his discoveries should be used to finance crusades to reclaim Jerusalem.[5]

Morison denies that a quest was ever attained in America, and Lewis and Clark seem hardly conscious of one. They refer to the Bible very rarely and face most Indian beliefs and rituals with either blunt bewilderment or sharp skepticism. Yet it would be overhasty to state that the idea of a quest never influenced them or that it is far removed from the motives that still bring readers back to their journals. A westering idealism runs through the central course of American history, from the Puritans at Plymouth Rock to the Hippies around San Francisco Bay. The Corps of Discovery came as self-avowed peacemakers among the Indians and as emissaries of peculiar American ideals of freedom among the great powers contending for empire along the Pacific. They were loyal directly to Thomas Jefferson, who was as renowned for his declaration of new principles in government as for his innovations through new principles of science. When they finally reached the three forks of the Missouri, they named the most westerly stream Jefferson's River and its two tributaries the Wisdom and the Philanthropy. "We . . . determined that the middle fork was that which ought of right to bear the name we had given to the lower portion or *River Jefferson* and called the bold rapid an clear stream Wisdom, and the more mild and placid one which flows in from the S. E. Philanthropy, in commemoration of two of those cardinal virtues, which have so eminently marked that deservedly selibrated character through life" (*Journals* 5 : 54). Here is an avowal that the landscape in the farthest reaches of the Louisiana Purchase is a place specially blessed. Indeed, by naming two rivers in this way, Lewis and Clark link the sources of western America to ideals of wisdom and caring, to rival what Morison sees as European motives of piety and greed.

And is it necessary that pilgrims or prophets fully understand the meaning of their quests in order to carry them out? In crossing America and laying claim to new regions, the Corps of Discovery was unwittingly anticipating what later generations would develop into a creed called Manifest Destiny. And the accomplishment of nineteenth-century America still sings through voices collected in celebration:

> O beautiful for spacious skies,
> For amber waves of grain,
> For purple mountain majesties
> Above the fruited plain!
> America! America!
> God shed His grace on thee
> And crown thy good with brotherhood
> From sea to shining sea!

The spaciousness of America from sea to sea, the majesty of the Rocky Mountains above the grasslands of the high plains—these are discoveries first made American by Lewis and Clark.

> O beautiful for pilgrim feet,
> Whose stern, impassioned stress
> A thoroughfare for freedom beat
> Across the wilderness! . . .
>
> O beautiful for patriot dream
> That sees beyond the years
> Thine alabaster cities gleam
> Undimmed by human tears!

These verses do not match the reality of any American city, past or present. They sing instead of heaven realized upon earth—precisely of "a land of pure delight," where, if not saints, then people born to equality reign. And the refrain implores God to answer this national quest by crowning natural beauty with "brotherhood," promised by the Revolution, the Civil War, and the active democracy of states freshly carved from the frontier.

> America! America!
> May God thy gold refine
> Till all success be nobleness
> And every gain divine![6]

Discovery by Lewis and Clark may have begun in simple seeking of worldly goods or dominion, but, as a stage of American expansion, inspired by Jefferson, it also has to be measured as a national quest, a refining of material wealth into spiritual gain.

Such a balancing of discovery and revelation was anticipated in the eighteenth century and even named in the term Morison uses to account for the work of Columbus. "Serendipity" was coined and carefully defined by the wealthy British man of letters Horace Walpole, who understood very well that in moments of serendipity there are at least two active beings in the scene, a human seeker and a favorable but surprising and mysterious power. In fact, when he first used this term, Walpole explained that it derived from the story of travelers who kept finding more than they were seeking because of larger designs beyond their knowing.

Writing to his friend Horace Mann on January 28, 1754, Walpole mentioned finding a certain coat of arms in an old book, through a peculiar sort of luck:

> This discovery indeed is almost of that kind which I call *serendipity,* a very expressive word, which as I have nothing better to tell you, I shall endeavour to explain to you: you will understand it better by the derivation than by the definition. I once read a silly fairy tale called *The Three Princes of Serendip:* as their highnesses travelled, they were always making discoveries, by accidents and sagacity, of things which they were not in quest of: for instance, one of them discovered that a mule blind of the right eye had travelled the same road lately, because the grass was eaten only on the left side, where it was worse than on the right—now do you understand *serendipity?*[7]

Such a discovery thus comes about by "accidental sagacity" as Walpole says a line later, "for you must observe that *no* discovery of a thing you *are* looking for, comes under this description." Accident or a force beyond one's seeking throws new phenomena onto the traveler's path. And with sagacity the traveler is able to turn that new information into a discovery. So the prince in Walpole's remembered story notices the appearance of grass on both sides of the road and cleverly reasons that a one-eyed mule has been grazing. So Columbus, "by the greatest serendipity in history," sets off on a new route and sights land, and his contempories eventually discern that he has come upon an entirely unexpected continent.

This single word of Walpole's coining has become the most celebrated item in his voluminous works and correspondence. It has been revived in recent times and pulled off center from this original passage to mean not the process of discovery but a talent, knack, or "faculty" for making such discoveries. To some this has meant the acumen or sagacity for noticing and following up surprising developments in experiments. But for others it has meant a more mysterious power or luck that opens the way for happy accidents to appear on one's path. These seem to be two leanings toward the ideas we have already polarized: the first toward the notion of plain discovery, the application of keen reasoning upon mere accidents; the second toward a reverence for occult powers or divine providences in the careers of the properly disciplined. Several books have been devoted to this subject and the modern yearning that goes with it: if only we could distill serendipity and bottle it, or discreetly pipe it into the lower echelons of modern research centers![8]

But before leaving Walpole, it is worth noticing that his little passage actually anticipates these two distinct interpretations of serendipity. On the one hand he stresses the mental activity of the princes themselves and pooh-poohs their place in "a silly fairy tale." He thus proclaims himself a solid, no-nonsense man of the Enlightenment. Yet on the other hand he coins this word from Serendip, the name of the island near India later called Ceylon or Sri Lanka, and he enlarges his meaning by condensing an Oriental tale. He thus clothes an old idea—"The gods help them that help themselves"—in romantic robes and Eastern perfumes.

Moreover, Walpole may have understood that the tale he cites has a double nature of its own. He seems to have recollected some of its details inaccurately, but the three princes of Serendip conduct a journey of very ambiguous meaning. At first, their accounts of the one-eyed mule (a camel in the actual story) are presented as merely clever ploys, wholly made-up accounts that curiously turn out to match a real animal they are accused of stealing. Later, their startling deductions prove so prophetic that a foreign emperor becomes impressed with their wisdom and sends them to India to recover a magic mirror of justice. At the outset the three young men believe they have been banished and must live by their wits alone. But it turns out that their father has arranged this journey as a quest through the world, to test and perfect their development in wisdom. They return with this quest completed, bearing precious gifts; their father blesses them, and all three become just rulers of great realms.[9]

We should pause a moment, too, to notice a similar strategy in Samuel Johnson's *Rasselas* (1759), another Oriental tale, published just a few years after Walpole's letter. This story again sets travelers on a tour of the world, this time from the depths of far-off Abyssinia, and it shows how they make the most of ironic surprises along the way. At the end of chapter 13, Prince Rasselas and his chosen guide, the older poet Imlac, are trying to dig their way through a mountain to escape from a cloying pleasure palace. They notice that animals have burrowed holes in the mountainside, and they set themselves to working diligently at a long mine. At one point they make a sudden breakthrough, but the wise guide cautions against developing false hopes:

> They returned to their work day after day, and, in a short time, found a fissure in the rock, which enabled them to pass far with very little obstruction. This Rasselas considered as a good omen. "Do not disturb your mind," said Imlac, "with other hopes or fears than reason may suggest: if you are pleased with prognostics of good, you will be terrified likewise with tokens of evil, and your whole life will be prey to superstition. Whatever facilitates our work is more than an omen, it is a cause of success. This is one of those pleasing surprises which often happen to active resolution. Many things difficult to design prove easy to performance."[10]

Is it a quirk of history that modern serendipity is not called "rasselasity"? Here we seem to have an even more sternly matter-of-fact attitude toward fortuitous discoveries. But Imlac speaks with authority as an aged Eastern sage, and his sentiments ultimately reflect the beliefs of Johnson the deeply Christian moralist! The point to be stressed is that in the 1750s, just a few decades before Lewis and Clark, there was a well-developed taste in England for such intricate balancing acts as Walpole's and Johnson's. Between pious Christian faith and a ruthless temper for modern exploitation, more than one conscience was trying to work out an equilibrium that would give meaning to new discoveries.

Such a harmony can be found in—or imposed on—the entire story of the Corps of Discovery. It also fits, or seems to fit, many particular incidents. But when these particular stories are reread in detail they also bring out the very delicate balances in Walpole's fascinating idea and the evanescent nature of discovery as Lewis and Clark actually experienced it. Like many other researchers or explorers, Lewis and Clark could remark strange turns of fortune in a moment, only to lose sight of them again as they released and pursued intersecting threads of exploration.[11] Or they could report many matter-of-fact occurrences that now startle a reader's eye with the fortuitous patterns they make when brought together.

A telling incident of this kind occurred during the portage of canoes and baggage around the Great Falls of the Missouri in 1805. The party camped at a creek below the falls on June 17. Solid timber was hard to find, but they located one tree big enough to use in making rough wheels and so built carts for hauling their canoes across the plains. The appearance of one large tree at just this place seemed noteworthy to Lewis: "We were fortunate enough to find one cottonwood tree just below the entrance of portage creek that was large enough to make our carrage wheels about 22 Inches in diameter; fortunate I say because I do not beleive that we could find another of the same size perfectly sound within 20 miles of us" (*Journals* 4:303). At the end of the portage, another grove of cottonwoods also appeared, which just managed to answer the party's needs at that point, too. There, the explorers required two new canoes to carry surplus baggage; an advance party was set out, and again it located just one grove that would serve. "If we find trees sufficiently large for our purposes it will be extreemly fortunate," Lewis wrote, "for we have not seen one for many miles below the entrance of the musselshell River to this place, which would have answered" (4:370). Yet the next day (July 10) Clark found two trees that were hollow, split, and "windshaken" (cracked by straining in high winds) but could be trimmed to make do.

Between these two points, the men applied some ingenuity to ease the hard labor of dragging heavy weights over a cactus-prickly route. Clark wrote on June 25: "It may be here worthy of remark that the Sales were hoised in the Canoes as the men were drawing them and the wind was great relief to them being Sufficently Strong to move the Canoes on the Trucks, this is Saleing on Dry land in every Sence of the word" (4:333).

The appearance of large, serviceable trees at just these two places on the river still seems astonishing, a remarkably fortuitous accident. The biologist Paul Russell Cutright notes that in visiting the site of the canoe camp in 1965 he found extraordinary trees there still. "By far the largest cottonwoods stand here (five in particular) that I have seen anywhere in my journeyings up and down the Missouri and Yellowstone Rivers" (*LCPN* 166). He also points out that earlier, near Fort Mandan, the party had found canoe timber where ten years before them others had scouted in vain over a distance of seventy-five miles; and later, on his return along the Yellowstone, Clark again found cottonwoods that would just do to make two small canoes lashed together (123, 331). In view of all these timely appearances, the cottonwood seems to Cutright to have been an indispensable resource from nature. "Of all the western trees it contributed more to the success of the Expedition than any other. Lewis and Clark were men of great talent and resourcefulness, masters of ingenuity and improvisation. Though we think it probable that they would have successfully crossed the continent without the cottonwood, don't ask us how!" (332).

The ingenuity of the party stands out here, too, in its rigging of sails to turn the portage into high-spirited play and to harness the otherwise annoying prairie winds. Here, surely, is practical sagacity combined with good fortune—the specific elements of serendipity as Walpole defines it.

But on a second look, we may well question if there is serendipity here at all. For one thing, the three moments that run together in our account of the portage—finding trees for wheels, finding trees for canoes, rigging sails to relieve hard labor—are quite distinct, separate passages in the journals. The explorers themselves do not link these incidents or see their cumulative effect. In fact, Lewis seems to see the operations of "fortune" in the discovery of useful trees, whereas Clark implies that it was the men's cleverness alone that sent them sailing across dry land. For another thing, the results in all three incidents come about from direct searching. The party wants wheels, canoes, and an easier portage, and that is what they get. Such discoveries do not meet Walpole's explicit caveat about serendipity: "*No* discovery of a thing you *are* looking for, comes under this description." They rather underscore the single-minded will of the party to employ every available resource in overcoming obstacles. Finally, there is a fitting illustration here of Imlac's warning in *Rasselas* that bad omens are just as available as good to a mind that is prey to credulity: the party needed two new canoes at the end of the portage precisely because Lewis's darling project for launching a portable boat there had proved an utter failure. He had hauled his carefully designed collapsible iron frame all the way from Harpers Ferry, Virginia, only to meet frustration after frustration at the camp above the falls. Long hours of work to rig a watertight covering from materials at hand ended in soggy collapse. If good fortune was arranging the appearance of some solid cottonwood trunks, bad fortune was just as busy tearing at the skins stretched over these iron frames and seeping into gaps that could not be sealed. Cottonwoods would not yield tar or pitch, and a concoction of charcoal, beeswax, and buffalo tallow, improvised by rather frantic "sagacity," proved worthless.

A second incident in which the search for one thing led to a discovery quite different in kind occurred along the Pacific coast the following winter. Report reached Fort Clatsop, their winter quarters, that a whale had come ashore, and Clark led a party down to the spot where Tillamooks were stripping and rendering the blubber. The avowed purpose of this trip was to obtain meat and oil, of which the men did carry back a considerable load. The appearance of this whale seemed extraordinary in itself. It came just as food supplies were running low. Its size, as Clark measured it (105 feet), still seems incredible to modern science. And in a rare allusion to the Bible in his journal, Clark compared it to the whale that swallowed Jonah: "Small as this Stock is I prise it highly," reads the entry for January 6, 1806, "and thank providence for directing the whale to us; and think him much more kind to us than he was to jonah, having Sent this monster to be *Swallowed by us* in Sted of *Swallowing of us* as jonah's did" (*Journals* 6:183–84). But as an incidental feature of this whale-seeking trip, Clark came upon something else, which his mind developed into a different exclamation of discovery. The path along the coast led over

Tillamook Head and opened a long vista down the coastline, which none of the party would have seen except for this necessity-prompted trek. "We Set out early and proceeded to the top of the mountain next to the which is much the highest part and that part faceing the Sea is open, from this point I beheld the grandest and most pleasing prospects which my eyes ever surveyed" (6:182). Before him lay the boundless ocean; to the north he could see across the mouth of the Columbia; to the south, "the nitches and points of high land which forms this Corse for a long ways aded to the inoumerable rocks of emence Sise out at a great distance from the Shore and against which the Seas brak with great force gives this Coast a most romantic appearance" (6:182). Clark was standing on a high promontory and when he looked south he probably saw Haystack Rock and other formations—which now compose one of the most photographed scenes on the entire Oregon coast.

This is a rare exclamation about scenery from William Clark. And it coincides exactly with the farthest reach of the party outward from St. Louis. The accident of being on a high promontory on the route of a purely mundane search for food, combined with Clark's deliberate scanning of the scene and close description, yields a new—if momentary—mental enlargement. But is this a satisfying example of serendipity? Again problems emerge, especially if we ask in what sense this is a discovery. Clark takes his view from a known path; that night he would obtain from the Indians "a map of the Coast in their way" (6:181). He notes the presence of a "guide" at his side who points out some of the features in the landscape below. This stretch of coastline had been observed and noted before from a different angle—from vessels that had traded and explored around the mouth of the Columbia. What is unique in Clark's record is only his personal feelings in this setting: "I beheld the grandest and most pleasing prospects which *my eyes* ever surveyed" (emphasis added). Thousands of tourists have agreed with Clark's implied judgment that this is a very rare vista. We may agree, too, that his judgment is worth heeding, considering the many spectacular prospects he must have beheld in traveling west. But the stubborn fact remains that what he states is a personal feeling in explicitly personal terms. There is no going behind or beyond his words to find anything either intrinsically new or uniquely observed or deduced.

A third incident is quite different, and perhaps more eligible, because it is massively public and historically significant. This is the sudden opportunity that opened in Jefferson's first term as president to acquire the Louisiana country from France, thereby securing control over the Mississippi River and doubling the geographical size of the United States. It was an unexpected development. Jefferson had sent ministers to France to gain concessions or perhaps control over New Orleans alone; they were surprised by an offer of much grander territory and had to act beyond their instructions. The surprise was also a political puzzle to Jefferson himself, who did not covet so much territory and had to overturn his own constitutional thinking to justify annexation. Here are all the elements of Walpole's serendipity, arranged almost exactly as they appear in the example of the princes and the one-eyed mule.

The Louisiana Purchase also surprised and realigned the developing plans for Lewis and Clark's westward journey. Jefferson had sent a secret message to Congress early in 1803 to acquire money and authorization for this project. He then set about getting passports for Lewis and reassuring jealous European powers that this would be a merely scientific or "literary" expedition into disputed lands. Then in the late spring of 1803 came the news that Napoleon had obtained Louisiana from Spain and would sell it all very willingly to the United States. How much easier that made the prospect of sending an army company into territory across the Mississippi; how very unexpected and fortuitous!

But if Clark's journal entry about Tillamook Head is problematical because it is so very brief and personal, the Louisiana Purchase is problematical because it is so very enormous and complicated in all its ramifications. A full account of this event has to embrace the policies, secrets, motives, understandings, and misunderstandings of scores of officials and political figures in Spain, France, Great Britain, the Caribbean islands, the United States, and Canada, as well as in widely spaced outposts in the Louisiana, Illinois, and Mexican territories. Even if we concentrate on the moves of the United States and oversimplify by imputing them all to the mind and will of Thomas Jefferson alone, the deed called the Louisiana Purchase remains an enigma. It bears on so many contemporary and subsequent political issues that it cannot be stably fixed in a pattern as delicately balanced as serendipity. Rather, the admirers of Jefferson have seen it one way, his critics quite another. Jeffersonians have long argued that he was in entire, masterful control of overarching diplomatic policies that led to European concessions, and that he made the most of them. A recent study traces such claims from Republican pamphlets of the period down to very recent scholarly biographies.[12] At the opposite extreme stands the language of Jefferson's leading adversary, Alexander Hamilton: "Every man . . . possessed of the least candour and reflection," reads Hamilton's lead paragraph in an 1803 editorial, "will readily acknowledge that the acquisition has been solely owing to a fortuitous concurrence of unforeseen and unexpected circumstances, and not to any wise and vigorous measures on the part of the American government." A few paragraphs later, Hamilton goes even further: "Let us then, with all due humility, acknowledge this as another of those signal instances of the kind interpositions of an over-ruling Providence, which we more especially experienced during our revolutionary war, & by which we have more than once, been saved from the consequences of our errors and perverseness."[13]

We need not dwell further on the adequacy, motives, or sincerity of these documents. It is sufficient to note that Jeffersonians abandon serendipity for a view that only brilliant human agency brought about the Purchase, whereas Hamilton gives all credit to a wise and kind "Providence" that had already shaped American destiny in spite of human folly and perverseness. These claims, of course, correspond to notions of plain discovery at one extreme and the workings of revelation at the other.

A fourth example of possible serendipity is doubtless the most fascinating and famous of all that occurred during the expedition. In the winter of 1804–5, Lewis and Clark met a French-Canadian trader at the Mandan villages and eventually hired him as an interpreter on the way west. He was not an appealing character; his ineptitude later proved annoying on many occasions. But Toussaint Charbonneau had somehow acquired two younger Shoshone women who lived with him. That winter one of them bore him a son. And that young woman and her child came along to the Pacific and back. In the course of explorations she sometimes pointed out landmarks in the region from which Hidatsa raiders had abducted her a few years earlier. When the party reached the mountains she recognized the Indians they met there as her own people, and helped weave stronger bonds of friendship and cooperation between them and the white men who needed their horses. To other tribes, her presence with her child was a reassuring sight in this company of armed men, an effective signal that these strangers were coming with peaceful intentions.

This young woman was Sacagawea, as the journals spell her name, or Sacajawea, as she has become transformed in countless place-names, monuments, commercial signs, labels, and works of biography and fiction. Her name is certainly as famous as Lewis's or Clark's; it is among the most widely known in American history. The explorers needed an interpreter, they just happened to find Charbonneau, perhaps they very wisely decided to bring along this particular wife as a native-speaking Shoshone. By this course of events, the explorers combined sagacity with a happy accident to achieve unforeseen benefits weeks, months, and even centuries later.

But it would be improper to call this arrangement serendipity or to ascribe it to the operations of either conscious will or providential intervention. The presence of Sacagawea in the Corps of Discovery was rather a growth and transformation of personal human relations. It would be demeaning to her, to Lewis and Clark, and to us as well to try to reduce her to an adventitious pawn, torn from her people by the gods of Manifest Destiny and placed so as to give birth near Meriwether Lewis after a dose of his rattlesnake powder. Nor was she a mere instrument shrewdly chosen by men to facilitate their Upper Missouri negotiations. She was a person, appearing in the journals sometimes faintly but sometimes very definitely, refracted through experiences of shared danger, need, and decision making. There is no evidence to support her legendary role as an alluring guide across the Rockies. But there is enough to show her being admired for cool courage, thanked for kindly sharing, abused by others' pettiness, sustained by others' attentions through times of debilitation, even pestering to come along to see the whale on the Pacific shore. Did the presence of a woman and a developing infant change the character of this party? Undoubtedly it did, but in ways too subtle to find expression in the journals. In the surviving records Sacagawea is an incidental character, dropped from mention for long stretches, just like many men who also provided indispensable services. They too lie in unmarked graves.

Is serendipity, then, an illusion? Not at all. There are plenty of good examples in the history of science and invention that have withstood close reexamination by serious scientists and readers of Walpole. Many recent books argue that, properly understood, serendipity is *the* form of modern discovery. The sociologist of science Robert K.

Merton once discussed the term extensively and redefined it as "the discovery through chance by a theoretically prepared mind of valid findings which were not sought."[14] This definition leans toward the side of flat discovery rather than revelation. And, framed in this way, it fits a great many of the observations and deductions of Lewis and Clark. They, of course, came west with prepared minds but found themselves in a field so abounding in new things that they often had to be surprised and redirected in their thinking.

But our critical review of their experiences, in light of Walpole's very rigorous definition, brings out a different depth in their work. It shows that there are tricky dilemmas awaiting anyone who tries to pin down an act of discovery with categorical assurance. Exactly where, when, and why it occurs turn out to be controversial, mercurial issues. Discoveries can even evade the eye of the beholder in the moment of being beheld. This problem besets these explorers as well as the modern reader who pursues them. In the act of making their journal entries, Lewis and Clark could not help recording their own complexities of mind—and often of heart—their peculiar slants of vision or blindness, of memory, of powers of expression, of consistency, of bewilderment in facing the unexpected.

For this reason, their outstanding experiences have to be approached by readers who are willing, like them, to ponder sudden surprises. Sometimes this means extracting their accounts from disparate entries and reuniting them with preconceptions we can trace in the language of Jefferson and his era. Sometimes it means tracing the explorers' own quirks of mind. Sometimes it means unraveling our own preconceptions about western progress or American destiny.

The Corps of Discovery disbanded in 1806 at journey's end. Its members dispersed, and within two decades half of them had died. But though their records, too, have been dispersed and have only slowly come to light again in print, they survive as a unique corpus of American discovery. As the records now become available in fully accessible volumes, they invite renewed exploration by readers of American science, history, and literature.

Chapter 2   The American Sublime

ON Thursday, June 13, 1805, Captain Meriwether Lewis set out about sunrise with an advance party to walk across level country in what is now Montana, in search of the Great Falls of the Missouri River. Before noon he had ordered his four companions to separate in search of game. He was therefore alone when the first evidences of the falls appeared to him:

> I had proceded on this course about two miles with Goodrich at some distance behind me whin my ears were saluted by the agreeable sound of a fall of water and advancing a little further I saw the spray arrise above the plain like a collumn of smoke which would frequently dispear again in an instant caused I presume by the wind which blew pretty hard from the S. W. I did not however loose my direction to this point which soon began to make a roaring too tremendious to be mistaken for any cause short of the great falls of the Missouri. here I arrived about 12 OClock having traveled by estimate about 15 Miles. I hurryed down the hill which was about 200 feet high and difficult of access, to gaze on this sublimely grand specticle. (*Journals* 4:283)

Lewis's journal entry continues with a long description of the falls in their setting, composed from a vantage point "on the top of some rocks about 20 feet high opposite the center of the falls" (283). He could see the whole body of the Missouri rushing over a ledge of rocks between perpendicular cliffs:

> Immediately at the cascade the river is about 300 yds. wide; about ninty or a hundred yards of this next the Lard. bluff is a smoth even sheet of water falling over a precipice of at least eighty feet, the remaining part of about 200 yards on my right formes the grandest sight I ever beheld, the hight of the fall is the same of the other but the irregular and some-what projecting rocks below receives the water in it's passage down and brakes it into a perfect white foam which assumes a thousand forms in

a moment sometimes flying up in jets of sparkling foam to the hight of fifteen or twenty feet and are scarcely formed before large roling bodies of the same beaten and foaming water is thrown over and conceals them. in short the rocks seem to be most happily fixed to present a sheet of the whitest beaten froath for 200 yards in length and about 80 feet perpendicular. the water after decending strikes against the butment before mentioned or that on which I stand and seems to reverberate and being met by the more impetuous courant they role and swell into half formed billows of great hight which rise and again disappear in an instant. (4:284)

In short, Lewis placed himself in the midst of this, the grandest sight he had ever beheld, and tried to record it even as it reverberated all around him.

But recording this scene eluded him. His topographical description is plain and full, drawn with the practiced hand of an alert geographer. Yet Lewis is also overcome by feelings and a frustration over his limitations in trying to express them. "After wrighting this imperfect description I again viewed the falls and was so much disgusted with the imperfect idea which it conveyed of the scene that I determined to draw my pen across it and begin agin, but then reflected that I could not perhaps succeed better than penning the first impressions of the mind" (4:285).

Yet as he continues to reflect, Lewis reveals that he knows a great deal about feelings and how they are expressed. "I wished for the pencil of Salvator Rosa or the pen of Thompson, that I might be enabled to give to the enlightened world some just idea of this truly magnifficent and sublimely grand object, which has from the commencement of time been conceled from the view of civilized man; but this was fruitless and vain" (285). He also regrets his lack of a camera obscura apparatus, which would enable him to trace a projected image of the falls. The best he can conclude is that with his recollections and the skill of some artist to whom he can someday impart them, "I hope still to give to the world some faint idea of an object which at this moment fills me with such pleasure and astonishment, and which of it's kind I will venture to ascert is second to but one in the known world" (285).

By appealing in this way for the support of a landscape painter like Salvator Rosa, a poet like James Thomson, or a camera obscura, Lewis identifies himself as a "civilized man," observing this wild and inspiring scene with a firm sense of his connections and responsibilities to "the enlightened world." Yet his regrets and frustrations here turn on his feelings of immediate, spontaneous, lonely awe before a sudden wonder in the wilderness. In a second reading of this long entry in his journal, a reader may well wonder how to take Lewis and his exclamations. Was he really writing on the spot, overcome by a scene entirely new and overwhelming? Or was he doing the expected thing as a man of fashionable taste, even in the roar and rainbow spray of this place he found all on his own? His literary sophistication certainly stands out in sharp contrast to the response of his close partner, William Clark. When Clark reached the falls a few days later, he too "beheld those Cateracts with astonishment" and clambered down over rugged terrain to take a closer look. But to memorialize the moment, he inscribed himself directly into the scene. Finding four cotton willows nearby, he selected one and carved "my name the date, and hight of the falls" (4:304–5). No further flourishes from him for readers or observers far removed!

Lewis's feelings and motives at this scene remain puzzling and paradoxical. If he was overcome by awe, that awe is here nicely shaped and contained by the way he turns upon himself in his reflections. If he was imposing a modish framework on this scene, he was still moved to do it in language that was not only extraordinary for a rough explorer but rare even for Lewis. Nowhere else in his journals does he exclaim like this about a scene, calling up Thomson and Rosa or any other poet or artist.

In this moment of discovery Lewis was no doubt called out of himself. The falls were a striking new phenomenon after months of toil and delay in ascending the Missouri. They were beautiful, vast, and surprising. And at the moment they were deeply gratifying, too. Lewis had been seeking them with apprehension. Just a few days earlier he had separated a few men from the rest of the exploring party to try out this branch of the Missouri after puzzling over two rival forks. Almost everyone in the party was convinced that the true Missouri flowed from the north, but Lewis and Clark agreed that the south fork was the main river and the north fork a deceptive tributary. The discovery of the Great Falls, which had been mentioned by Indians in councils on the plains, now confirmed the truth of the captains' conviction. What is more, the sudden apparition of these high cascades also confirmed a new stage in the party's travels. For months they had been working upstream in the high plains. For at least three weeks they had known they were within sight of the Rocky Mountains. But now the waters came flowing precipitately, dropping at least eighty feet at once. With the river so palpably rugged here, the mountains must finally be at hand—both a new challenge and a new measure of progress in the long trek to the Pacific. These impressions do not come out explicitly in what Lewis writes at the falls, but they are manifest in other journal entries composed as he approached this landmark. To his doubts and seeking, these sparkling, roaring waters gave a refreshing answer—and to him alone, foremost in the van.

Yet if the experience of confirmation gives depth and a ring of truth to Lewis's enthusiasm, there are other influences on his lines and his feelings here. One word stands out in this passage, and he repeats it very precisely—the word *sublime*. "I hurried down the hill," he writes, "to gaze at this sublimely grand specticle"; and later he calls it "this truly magnificent and sublimely grand object." In current American usage, this word can mean simply "noble, exalted, majestic, or grand," but in the eighteenth century, the *sublime* was a particular kind of landscape or situation. The term was reserved for scenes that were vast, rugged, or terrifying; it was opposed to the term *beautiful,* which denoted controlled, harmonious, or even delicate objects and scenery. The next day after discovering the lowest of the Great Falls, Lewis pressed further and came upon other falls in the same system, Rainbow Falls as they are now known.

> Hearing a tremendious roaring above me I continued my rout across the point of a hill a few hundred yards further and was again presented by one of the most beatifull objects in nature, a cascade of about fifty feet perpendicular streching at rightangles across the river from side to side to the distance of at least a quarter of a mile. here the river pitches over a shelving rock, with an edge as regular and streight as if formed by art, without a nich or brake in it; the water descends in one even and uninterupted sheet wher dashing against the rocky bottom rises into foaming billows of great hight and rappidly glides away, hising flashing and sparkling as it departs. (4:289–90)

The regularity of this scene is brought out very clearly. These falls are as regular and uninterrupted "as if formed by art." Again Lewis's mind begins to long for a landscape painter, but he explains a very different design: "I now thought that if a skillfull painter had been asked to make a beautifull cascade that he would most probably have pesented the precise immage of this one; nor could I for some time determine on which of those great cataracts to bestoe the palm, on this or that which I had discovered yesterday; at length I determined between these two great rivals for glory that this was *pleasingly beautifull,* while the other was *sublimely grand*" (290).

Where did a military frontiersman learn aesthetic distinctions like these? The answer is not far to seek. As well as being a military officer and a rough survivor in the wild, Lewis had had plenty of experience in libraries and polite society during his years in Washington as private secretary to President Jefferson. His journal notes were now being kept at Jefferson's order, according to Jefferson's instructions, and presumably for eventual perusal by Jefferson's own eyes. And it was well known that Thomas Jefferson himself was a connoisseur of sublime scenery. In two celebrated long passages he had described it himself in his *Notes on the State of Virginia.*

The first of these passages concentrates on rivers breaking their way through mountains at the confluence of the Shenandoah and Potomac. "The passage of the Patowmac through the Blue Ridge," Jefferson writes, "is perhaps one of the most stupendous scenes in nature. You stand on a very high point of land. On your right comes up the Shenandoah, having ranged along the foot of the mountain a hundred miles to seek a vent. On your left approaches the Patowmac, in quest of a passage also. In the moment of their junction they rush together against the mountain, rend it asunder, and pass off to the sea."[1] What Jefferson sees is evidence that an "ocean" once filled the area behind the Blue Ridge and broke through at just this spot, tearing "the mountain down from its summit to its base" (19). This is a rough, vast, powerful scene, and "the piles of rock on each hand, but particularly on the Shenandoah, the evident marks of their disrupture and avulsion from their beds by the most powerful agents of nature, corroborate the impression" (19). But Jefferson goes on to frame this scene of natural violence with a pleasing contrast. From this vantage point above the confluence and looking through the mountains into the distance where the river flows to the sea, the mind can rise to a scene of beauty beyond this sublimity:

> But the distant finishing which nature has given to this picture is of a very different character. It is a true contrast to the fore-ground. It is as placid and delightful, as that is wild and tremendous. For the mountain being cloven asunder, she presents to your eye, through the cleft, a small

catch of smooth, blue horizon, at an infinite distance in the plain country, inviting you, as it were, from the riot and tumult roaring around,
to pass through the breach and participate in the calm below. Here the
eye ultimately composes itself; and that way too the road happens actually to lead. You cross the Patowmac above the junction, pass along
its side through the base of the mountain for three miles, its terrible
precipices hanging in fragments over you, and within about 20 miles
reach Frederic town and the fine country around that. (19)

Jefferson concludes that "this scene is worth a voyage across the
Atlantic" (19). Lewis seems to echo that it is worth a trek across the
continent. Jefferson's passage, in its design, closely anticipates Lewis's
experience at the Great Falls: a powerful scene of mighty waters in a
precipitous rough setting, followed by a further scene of beauty and
tranquillity, and both experienced not only as something to see but as
a route into a finer country beckoning in the distance.

Jefferson's full-blown praise of the sublime was reserved, however,
for a property he himself owned, the Natural Bridge in Virginia. This,
he declared, was "the most sublime of Nature's works" (24), and for
that reason he forced it into consideration in his section on "cascades" in his *Notes*. Here again he saw evidence of a natural mighty
convulsion and the flow of waters through a rugged and magnificent
scene. For Jefferson, the experience of the sublime had two aspects in
this setting. One was a feeling of overwhelming terror: "Though the
sides of this bridge are provided in some parts with a parapet of fixed
rocks, yet few men have resolution to walk to them and look over
into the abyss. You involuntarily fall on your hands and feet, creep to
the parapet and peep over it. Looking down from this height about a
minute, gave me a violent head ach" (24–25). The other feeling was,
again, a "rapture" at the sight of such a rough and colossal object
framed by distant views and a calm heaven: "This painful sensation
is relieved by a short, but pleasing view of the Blue ridge along the
fissure downwards, and upwards by that of the Short hills . . . ; and,
descending then to the valley below, the sensation becomes delightful
in the extreme. It is impossible for the emotions, arising from the
sublime, to be felt beyond what they are here: so beautiful an arch,
so elevated, so light, and springing, as it were, up to heaven, the rapture of the Spectator is really indescribable!" (25).

Not everyone shared Jefferson's enthusiasm over these scenes. Some
observers pointedly remarked that they were unimpressed. James

Madison passed by Harpers Ferry in August 1786 but could not see what Jefferson had pointed out about the convergence of the rivers there. "I had an opportunity of viewing the magnificent scene which nature here presents," he apologized. "I viewed it however under great disadvantages. The air was so thick that distant objects were not visible at all, and near ones not distinctly so. We ascended the mountain also at a wrong place, fatigued ourselves much in traversing it before we gained the right position, were threatened during the whole time with a thunder storm, and finally overtaken by it."[2] After such a dampening experience it is little wonder that Madison never made a second attempt. And as late as 1809 Jefferson was scolding an author for printing a derogatory account of this wonderful view. Again, he insisted, the observer must have gone to the wrong spot, though he had to admit that "the same scene may excite very different sensations in different spectators, according to their different sensibilities. The sensations of some may be much stronger than those of others."[3]

Jefferson's contemporaries learned to humor his insistence on sublime natural wonders. Even his home, Monticello, seemed purposely designed to show them off. In his eulogy of Jefferson, William Wirt noted the vast views it commanded of the Blue Ridge to the west and of a long curve of horizon to the east: "From this summit the philosopher was wont to enjoy that spectacle, among the sublimest of Nature's operations, the looming of the distant mountains; and to watch the motions of the planets, and the greater revolution of the celestial sphere."[4] But Josiah Quincy used this same vast scene to satirize Jefferson's views of the mob violence necessary in a democracy: "From the top of Monticello, by the side of the great Jefferson, I have watched its sublime horrors."[5]

Jefferson's enthusiasm may therefore seem special or even unique in the America of his time. But as Garry Wills has pointed out very acutely, Jefferson's landscape descriptions follow a well-worn European pattern.[6] A taste for the sublime and the beautiful was commonplace, even an expected flourish to be displayed in the journals of a contemporary gentleman on the Grand Tour. The description of an awesome, rugged, or astonishing natural object regularly fell into three stages: an exclamation of shock or awe, an appreciation of aesthetic fine points, and a scientific account of possible origins of this natural prodigy or of its outstanding possibilities or dimensions. In different sequences these stages can be found not only in Lewis's journals and Jefferson's *Notes* but also in celebrated descriptions of the Alps by many seventeenth- and eighteenth-century writers. Even Jefferson's personal symptom, his headache on the parapets of the Natural Bridge, has its literary antecedents. Lord Shaftesbury, Joseph Addison, and Edmund Burke had written of pain, dizziness, and nausea in similar circumstances. Burke's *Philosophical Inquiry into the Origin of Our Ideas of the Sublime and the Beautiful* (1757) had supplied a thoroughgoing explanation of how such pains coexist with sublime pleasures. If Lewis was echoing Jefferson, in other words, Jefferson was himself repeating a carefully learned formula for landscape descriptions in his time.

Jefferson's admiration for such scenery, however, was more than a matter of taste and training. There was also an edge of patriotism in both the *Notes* and Jefferson's written instructions to Lewis—an urge to show forth the grandeurs of America in particular and so undermine European ignorance and derision. The *Notes* specifically attacked Buffon's notions that there were no life forms in America comparable in size to those in Europe. And we find Lewis and Clark making careful note of an attempted excavation of mammoth bones in Missouri—not long after Jefferson had taken a keen interest in Charles Willson Peale's excavation of a mastodon skeleton in New York State in 1801 (*Journals* 3:340). Hence Jefferson's closing remark about the confluence of the Shenandoah and Potomac: "this scene is worth a voyage across the Atlantic." When he was infatuated with Maria Cosway in Paris in 1786, Jefferson named several attractions that might draw her to America. All of them are scenes that might inspire the painting of Maria or her husband; all of them are sublime. In a letter he wrote to her at the time, Jefferson's "Heart" exclaims over such an idea when it is suggested by his sober "Head":

> I see things wonderfully contrived sometimes to make us happy. Where could they find such objects as in America for the exercise of their enchanting art? especially the lady, who paints landscape so inimitably. She wants only subjects worthy of immortality to render her pencil immortal. The Falling spring, the Cascade of Niagara, the Passage of the Potowmac thro the Blue mountains, the Natural bridge. It is worth a voiage acros the Atlantic to see these objects; much more to paint, and make them, and thereby ourselves, known to all ages. And our own dear Monticello, where has nature spread so rich a mantle under the

eye? mountains, forests, rocks, rivers. With what majesty do we there ride above the storms! How sublime to look down into the workhouse of nature, to see her clouds, hail, snow, rain, thunder, all fabricated at our feet! And the glorious Sun, when rising as if out of a distant water, just gilding the tops of the mountains, and giving life to all nature![7]

From what we have seen so far, then, Captain Lewis's discovery of the Great Falls excited him in personal and particular ways on the spot and yet found expression in terms that evidently echo Jefferson and a long line of European artists and writers. A limit of discipline and even deference seems to control Lewis's spontaneous exclamations. He claims that these falls form the greatest sight he ever beheld. But when he concludes he puts it in second place: he ventures to assert only that this great object "of its kind" is "second to but one in the known world." Perhaps he is referring to Niagara Falls as a greater waterfall, beyond his direct experience. But he might also be directly addressing Jefferson here, whom we have seen lavishing superlatives on Virginia landscapes within his view and even his personal possession.

In any case, we should recall that by coming first on this scene, Lewis was obliged to take possession of it on behalf of the United States by inscribing it in his journal—just as Clark was to do by carving a memorial in a nearby tree trunk, a notice for the eyes of any subsequent explorer. Like Jefferson's, Lewis's sublime has an edge of assertive American patriotism. He lays claim to this new phenomenon of rugged nature and thereby to the grandeur of the whole Louisiana country. He hedges his exclamations with a word of deference to Jefferson. But does he not go the president one better by finding a scene all to himself, one that rivals the already outstanding American wonders back east? Does he not here pen an account of a truly American sublime, one that involves the excitement of discovery as well as the thrill of being surrounded or overwhelmed by natural grandeur?

In the end, it is impossible to know how fully Lewis comprehended the possible nuances in the term *sublime* as he used it in this moment. But by using it at all just here, he gave a new turn to its meaning. Whether he knew it or not, he was redirecting a very ancient term and concept, one that embraced a spectrum of attitudes about nature and art. At one extreme the word suggests a calculated manipulation of words, an ancient rhetorical device for naming or contriving an experience like awe. In a related sense, the *sublime* refers to the tradition of literary taste that Jefferson had inherited from eighteenth-century Europe—a tradition that was already becoming threadbare and suspect by 1803. Yet the concept remained vital and indispensable to a new generation of very precise poets in the early nineteenth century. And, at its other extreme, the word continued to describe a variety of religious or supernatural experiences; feelings that genuinely went beyond words; encounters past, present, and to come with eternal and immutable truth.

These four dimensions of the sublime are evident in the passages we have already examined. All of them appear in Lewis's entry on the Great Falls. All of them touch the ways we still look at vast scenery and try to communicate what we see or feel. They deserve patient review for that reason alone. And through Jefferson's and Lewis's handling of all four possibilities, we can also trace the beginnings of new understanding in a landscape distinctly American.

The ancient authority on the sublime was a short treatise called *Peri Hypsos* in Greek and often translated as *On the Sublime* or *On Great Writing*. For centuries this work was attributed to a third-century A.D. rhetorician named Longinus and so was commonly referred to as "Longinus on the Sublime." (Since the early nineteenth century the questions of date and authorship have become impossible puzzles.) This fragmentary and incomplete treatise contains many telling ideas which we have already touched.

In one aspect it seems to fit among critical works and rhetorical treatises of the ancient world. Its author knows and quotes a number of passages from ancient literature to illustrate his ideas. In one section (chapters 16–29) he catalogs several rhetorical figures that create an effect of grandeur. Behind many of these figures is the suggestion that something is missing and perhaps indescribable. Longinus defines the sublime as a power that "takes the reader [or beholder] out of himself"; it causes an "amazement" from "an irresistible force beyond the control of any audience."[8] Accordingly, Longinus points to well-known rhetorical figures whose power seems to be that they hurry the beholder to imagine something beyond words, either the speaker's or writer's contagious emotion or some astonishing power within the subject at hand. These figures include apostrophe, a sudden oath to the heroic, absent dead; rhetorical questions, with implied but unspecified answers; asyndeton, in which "words burst forth without connectives"; a mingling and varying of figures to give a sense of the speaker's emotional urgency; hyperbaton, a disordering of syntax or usual word order; and sudden shifts of person, for example, to directly address the audience in second person or to interrupt a narrative with a first-person turn of passion.

Such analysis of technical linguistic patterns bespeaks Longinus's concern with rhetorical art and calculation for effect. But he also explains that genuine passions are not "usually random or altogether devoid of method" and that "only by means of art can we perceive the fact that certain literary effects are due to sheer inborn talent" (5). And, indeed, many of these effects show up clearly in the evidently artless prose of Meriwether Lewis before the Great Falls. He interrupts his description to address the reader and express his frustration. He invokes absent artists or poets to do what he cannot in describing the scene before him. His language is not broken or disorderly, but he himself finds it so disgustingly inadequate that he is tempted to draw his pen across it and begin again. Lewis's behavior as a writer exactly coincides with some of the tactics Longinus had codified in antiquity.

Longinus had also seen through these tactics to the fundamental idea of sublimity. In chapter 35 he specifically turns to the ways the human spirit hungers for sublime phenomena in the works of nature:

> What is it they saw, those godlike writers who in their work aim at what is greatest and overlook precision in every detail? This, among other things: that nature judged man to be no lowly or ignoble creature when she brought us into this life and into the whole universe as into a great celebration, to be spectators of her whole performance and most ambitious actors. She implanted at once into our souls an invincible love for all that is great and more divine than ourselves. That is why the whole universe gives insufficient scope to man's power of contemplation and reflection, but his thoughts often pass beyond the boundaries of the surrounding world. Anyone who looks at life in all its aspects will see how far the remarkable, the great, and the beautiful predominate in all things, and he will soon understand to what end we have been born. (47)

The sublime is thus a power that relates the observer to the universe and communicates noble meaning to our lives. Longinus turns to phenomena of nature as incentives to our awe: the fires of heaven, or stars, which dwarf our own little flames; active volcanoes, which also pass our understanding. But first and foremost he mentions mighty rivers: "That is why, somehow, we are by nature led to marvel, not, indeed, at little streams, clear and useful though they be, but at the Nile, the Danube, or the Rhine, and still more at the Ocean" (47). So if Lewis faced the mighty Missouri River crashing down eighty feet at once and resorted to Longinian gestures, he was also responding with proper feelings of natural wonder, which Longinus had specified as genuine and deeply important.

Longinus remained obscure or unknown for centuries and reached a wide public only in the seventeenth century. Thereafter his ideas were not only circulated but also discussed, modified, adapted, and repeated by scores of poets, critics, travelers, and connoisseurs in England and France. By the time of Lewis and Clark, the term *sublime* had become a token of commonplace taste. It was one of three terms—the beautiful, the sublime, and the picturesque—regularly used in discussing landscapes. The full development of these aesthetic terms and their refinements need not detain us here. But it is clear that Lewis knew all these terms and their usual associations when he stood before the falls.

The word *picturesque* shows up in Lewis's entry for June 8, 1805, in which he named Marias River after his cousin Maria Wood and described the surrounding country with a romantic flourish. This river, he writes, "passes through a rich fertile and one of the most beatifully picteresque countries that I ever beheld, through the wide expance of which, innumerable herds of living anamals are seen, it's borders garnished with one continued garden of roses, while it's lofty and open forests, are the habitation of miriads of the feathered tribes who salute the ear of the passing traveler with their wild and simple, yet sweet and cheerfull melody" (*Journals* 4:266). This is dreadfully sticky prose, but it meets the contemporary decorum. In its simplest sense, *picturesque* means "like a landscape painting"—a scene arranged by art. Hence the marks of civilization mentioned here—the "herds," the "gardens" of roses, the "feathered tribes" trilling harmonious melodies. Of course, Lewis is well aware that these are herds of wild animals, surrounded by wild birds and flowers. The picturesque refers to landscape paintings of a certain kind, in which rough textures, craggy rocks, and luxuriant plant life intermingle with evidence of human work or design. It is a compromise between the extremes of the beautiful and the sublime.

Landscape pictures were often categorized in this period by reference to the works of two seventeenth-century painters of Italian landscapes, Claude Lorrain (1600–1682) and Salvator Rosa (1615–73). By the middle of the eighteenth century, these romantic names had become so familiar that exact knowledge of their paintings was no longer required. "Claude" or "Lorrain" represented the beautiful and rural; "Salvator" or "Rosa," the sublime and wild. Well-equipped travelers used a "Claude-glass," for example, to stop and compose a picturesque scene. These glasses were of two types. "A plano-convex mirror, of about four inches diameter, on a black foil, and bound up like a pocket book" was used by the poet Thomas Gray on his tour of the Lake District in 1775. And William Gilpin, the great popularizer of picturesque scenery, seems to have used both that and a different apparatus with colored lenses, designed to "give the object of nature a soft, mellow tinge."[9] As for Rosa, his name became attached to a very different scene, not mellow but striking. Elizabeth Manwaring summarizes the difference with contrasting general descriptions:

> An extended rolling plain, or wide valley opening to the south, traversed by a winding stream, and encircled, amphitheatre-like, by wooded hills; a foreground of plants and trees, richly leaved; a middle distance of plain and hill, adorned with groves, villas, bridges, castles, temples of antique pattern, vine-hung ruins; a far distance of faint blue hills, and often the sea; all this overspread with golden light, preferably of sunrise or sunset: such was the familiar Claudian landscape. The Salvatorial showed precipices and great rock masses of fantastic form, cascades, torrents, desolate ruins, caves, trees dense of growth, or blasted trunks, and shattered boughs.[10]

Lewis uses the terms *sublime* and *picturesque* in just this way. The wide expanses of fertile land with grazing animals, near Marias River, have the golden light of the Lorrain scene—"picteresque," as Lewis spells it. But the Great Falls are a "sublimely grand object," which calls for "the pencil [i.e., painter's brush] of Salvator Rosa." And Lewis furthers his plea by calling for the "pen of Thompson"—evidently James Thomson (1700–1748), the English poet of sublime outdoor scenery in the eighteenth century.

Thomson and Rosa were often mentioned together by contemporary writers. In part, the reason was Thomson's explicit admiration for Italian landscape painting. His poem *The Castle of Indolence* (1748) describes a fantasy gallery of enchanting pictures in a stanza that was often repeated:

Sometimes the pencil, in cool airy halls
Bade the gay bloom of vernal landskips rise,
Or Autumn's varied shades imbrown the walls:
Now the black tempest strikes the astonished eyes;
Now down the steep the flashing torrent flies;
The trembling sun now plays o'er ocean blue,
And now huge mountains frown amid the skies;
Whate'er Lorrain light-touched with softening hue
Or savage Rosa dashed, or learned Poussin drew.[11]

Manwaring comments: "If for sixty or seventy years to come Claude is *soft,* Salvator *dashes,* and Poussin is *learned,* the responsibility is Thomson's." But Thomson also embodied the sublime in his own writings, as many a critic noted. "The scenes of Thomson," wrote John More in 1777, "are frequently as wild and romantic as those of Salvator Rosa." And in a tour guide of 1788, a writer could explain that a region was "such a mixture of the tremendous and beautiful scenery as perhaps no other spot on earth can exhibit. To describe the component parts which form the wonderful whole, would require the genius of a Thomson or a Salvator Rosa."[12] In light of these remarks, Lewis's comments on art at the Great Falls have the hollow ring of a cliché.

By the turn of the nineteenth century, the cult of the picturesque had become widespread and even vulgar. It receives harsh treatment, for example, in Jane Austen's novels, especially when it fills the talk of characters who manipulate their own and others' estates to bring out "natural" effects or "improvements." William Wordsworth also found the practices of landscape architects a dreary business. In 1811 he visited Foxley, the celebrated estate of Sir Uvedale Price, a leading picturesque theorist, and reported that the experience was depressing: "A man by little and little becomes so delicate and fastidious with respect to forms in scenery, where he has a power to exercise a controul over them, that if they do not exactly please him in all his moods, and every point of view, his power becomes his law." Step by step, such an owner does away with seemingly "monotonizing" landscapes, not recognizing that a scene originally dull or impoverished can hardly sustain the new forms of "variety" that result from his efforts at art. "This relish of humanity Foxley wants, and is therefore to me, in spite of all its recommendations, a melancholy spot—I mean that part of it which the owner keeps to himself, and has taken so much pains with."[13] To Austen, Wordsworth, and many others, the picturesque had become a costly form of fastidiousness, sacrificing the abundance of nature or long traditions of local cultivation to the tyrannical whims of rich men's visual taste.

This criticism may seem beside the point in considering Lewis and Clark; they merely looked at western scenery as they passed through it and did not order workmen to go out and demolish groves or redirect rivulets—at least not for the sake of improving the view. But as contemporary critics were coming to understand, the dehumanizing tyranny over nature begins with a tyranny of the eye. And symptoms of that disorder are obvious in Lewis's journal. He not only describes a "picteresque" scene but names and claims it for his cousin, and goes on to prettify its features with herds, songbirds, and roses in an awkward attempt to make it "comport with the pure celestial virtues and amiable qualifications of that lovely fair one" (*Journals* 4 : 266). Later, he records his astonishment and impotence before the Great Falls but concludes by merely ranking the scene among phenomena of its kind.

To find deeper humanity in relation to nature, contemporary poets and philosophers were working out a more precise understanding of the sublime. Edmund Burke's *Philosophical Inquiry* of 1757 began a serious discussion that culminated in Immanuel Kant's *Critique of Judgment* (1790). These works examined not the techniques of rhetoric, painting, and landscape architecture but the physiology and psychology of human perception. They asked how the pain or fear excited by vast, harsh, and terrifying scenes was transmuted into the most deeply satisfying or overwhelming pleasure. The sublime thus came to be understood not as a quality in natural objects, poems, and painting but as an experience of the mind in relation to them.

As Kant explained the sublime, it would apply not only to what Lewis and Clark saw in scenery but also to what they did over the entire course of their expedition. In what he called the "dynamic sublime," the mind struggles to accommodate circumstances that are vast or life-threatening and then breaks through with a recognition of its own infinite power and nobility. In a crucial passage, Kant repeats many of the awesome natural forces that Longinus had listed centuries earlier and turns again to a recognition of infinite powers in the human soul.

Bold, overhanging, and as it were, threatening rocks, thunder-clouds piled up the vault of heaven, borne along with flashes and peals, volcanoes in all their violence of destruction, hurricanes leaving desolation in their track, the boundless ocean rising with rebellious force, the high waterfall of some mighty river, and the like, make our power of resistance of trifling moment in comparison with their might. But, provided our own position is secure, their aspect is all the more attractive for its fearfulness; and we readily call these objects sublime, because they raise the forces of the soul above the height of vulgar commonplace, and discover within us a power of resistance of quite another kind, which gives us courage to be able to measure ourselves against the seeming omnipotence of nature.[14]

Now it does not seem any more likely that Meriwether Lewis pored over the difficult paragraphs of Kant's German than that he spent his spare hours pondering Longinus's Greek. But there can be no doubt that in the Far West he lived out the pattern described here and discovered an inner "power" or "courage" to "measure ourselves against the seeming omnipotence of nature." That kind of inner discovery lay behind the whole enterprise of daring to be first to cross the American Rockies. And, in fact, such inner discoveries are explicitly recorded in Lewis's journals.

On May 26, 1805, Lewis climbed a hill near the Missouri and caught a first glimpse of distant, snowcapped mountains which he took to be the Rockies. "While I viewed these mountains," he wrote, "I felt a secret pleasure in finding myself so near the head of the heretofore conceived boundless Missouri; but when I reflected on the difficulties which this snowey barrier would most probably throw in my way to the Pacific, and the sufferings and hardships of myself and party in them, it in some measure counterballanced the joy I had felt in the first moments in which I gazed on them; but as I have always held it a crime to anticipate evils I will believe it a good comfortable road untill I am compelled to beleive differently" (*Journals* 4:201).

The day before he reached the Great Falls, Lewis took in a similar vista: "We passed a ridge of land considerably higher than the adjacent plain on either side, from this hight we had a most beatifull and picturesk view of the Rocky mountins which wer perfectly covered with Snow and reaching from the S. E. to N. of N. W.— they appear to be formed of several ranges each succeeding range rising higher than the preceding one untill the most distant appear to loose their snowey tops in the clouds; this was an august spectacle and one still rendered more formidable by the recollection that we had them to pass" (4 : 280).

Some weeks later, on August 14, Lewis was to learn just how formidable the barriers would be to further progress beyond the Continental Divide. The chief of the Shoshones "placed a number of heeps of sand on each side [of a river he had drawn on the ground] which he informed me represented the vast mountains of rock eternally covered with snow" through which the Salmon River passed. The chief explained "that the perpendicular and even juting rocks so closely hemned in the river that there was no possibilyte of passing along the shore; that the bed of the river was obstructed by sharp pointed rocks and the rapidity of the stream such that the whole surface of the river was beat into perfect foam as far as the eye could reach. that the mountains were also inaccessible to man or horse" (5 : 88). Giving up on this route, Lewis turned to an old man of that nation for information about a route to the Southwest. But "this he depicted with horrors and obstructions scarcely inferior" (5 : 89): rugged mountains inhabited by fierce, warlike people, leading to a parched desert and a stinking lake, which seemed still far removed from the Pacific coast. Lewis finally determined that there was a rough but passable route farther north, used by the Nez Perces. But the chief "added that the road was a very bad one as he had been informed by them and that they had sufered excessively with hunger on the route being obliged to subsist for many days on berries alone as there was no game on that part of the mountains which were broken rockey and so thickly covered with timber that they could scarcely pass" (5 : 90). All these forebodings proved accurate in the weeks that followed. What Kant called "the seeming omnipotence of nature" was here arranged against any further movement before the following spring, if then. Yet Lewis immediately responds with a force "above the height of vulgar commonplace" to assert his confidence in the greater power of humanity: "Knowing that Indians had passed, and did pass, at this season, . . . my rout was instantly settled in my own mind. . . . I felt perfectly satisfied that if the Indians could pass these mountains with their women and Children, that we could also pass them; and that if the nations on this river below the mountains were as numerous as they were stated to be that they must have some means of subsistence which it would be equally in our power to procure in the same country" (5:90–91).

These passages are not extraordinary but are typical of the cool confidence and determination of Lewis and Clark in the face of daunting challenges from nature. Lewis's approach to the Great Falls, his hurrying alone to gaze at the spectacle, his finding a viewpoint high but directly facing its reverberating power—these actions seem to spring from this same joyful courage. His language may be the hackneyed stuff of guidebooks and garden manuals, but his deeds describe a much richer meaning of the sublime.

As we have seen, the idea of mental sublimity was described by Longinus when he wrote of our "invincible love for all that is great and more divine than ourselves." And the connections between sublimity and divinity were to concern many thinkers in later times. For Thomas Gray in the Alps, scenes of danger were awesome reminders of a dreadful God: "Not a precipice, not a torrent, not a cliff, but is pregnant with religion and poetry," he wrote. "There are certain scenes that would awe an atheist into belief, without the help of other argument. . . . You have death perpetually before your eyes, only so far removed, as to compose the mind without frightening it."[15] Kant would argue in the *Critique of Judgment* that one must have a capacity for ideas, particularly moral ideas, to know the full sublime. We have seen Jefferson at least playing with a connection between sublime scenery and immortality in his letter to Maria Cosway, in which he lists sublime subjects like Niagara Falls and the Natural Bridge because "she wants only subjects worthy of immortality to render her pencil immortal." And at the end of the century the poet William Wordsworth took the sublime as seriously as anyone writing in English ever has.

At almost the same time that Lewis and Clark were ascending the Missouri toward the Rockies, Wordsworth was composing *The Prelude,* the long poem about his own spiritual development, often in the presence of awesome mountain scenery. There and in many other poems, he claimed to have discovered living divinity in relations between the mind and the greatest works of nature. His poetry was an effort to impart such moments of passionate intensity and open the same possibilities for others. He turned again and again to rough crags, high mountains, and flowing waters as images of the beginning and end of time. "Sublimity," he once wrote, "is the result of Nature's first dealings with the superficies of the earth." [16] He thus combined the wonders of nature with a religious awe about Creation and the end of the world.

Behind much of Wordsworth's thought lies a widespread, eighteenth-century understanding of the earth's creation and early history. This theory, developed and popularized by the seventeenth-century theologian Thomas Burnet, held that mountains and other huge irregularities on the earth resulted from an enormous cataclysm at the time of the Flood. Burnet's *Sacred Theory of the Earth* (1681) went through many editions and supplied a tidy, appealing explanation of how a wise and orderly God could have created such wild, irregular things as mountains. It also encouraged hundreds of readers to appreciate the sublime by direct experience of raw scenes in nature. As Burnet understood the Creation, the earth had been formed as a smooth sphere with three layers—a solid core, an outer layer of water, and a delicate crust of earth and stone. At the time of the Flood, this crust was broken. It heaved up to form colossal mountain ranges and to allow waters to pour forth and divide the continents. In a sense, this view of mountains reduced them to mere slag heaps, ruins, and emblems of God's wrath. But in a famous passage Burnet saw them quite differently—as wondrous evidences of divine power: "There is something august and stately in the Air of these things, that inspires the Mind with great Thoughts and Passions; we do naturally, upon such Occasions, think of God and his Greatness: And whatsoever hath but the Shadow and Appearance of INFINITE, as all things have that are too big for our Comprehension, they fill and over-bear the Mind with their Excess, and cast it into a pleasing kind of Stupor and Admiration." [17]

Here is the formula that would soon become familiar for the sublime—pleasing distress or agreeable horror—specifically linked to thoughts on vast nature as the work of an omnipotent God. In the large scheme of Burnet's work, the Christian God was a figure of mercy and redemption even more than one of wrath and destruction. Natural scenes of upheaval retained traces of the perfection of the original earth and the promise of its glorious restoration at the end of time.

For Wordsworth, this theological sublime was an experience he had known in life as well as in poetry. And it had occurred memorably in settings of mountains and mountain waterfalls. He had walked over the Simplon Pass through the Alps between France and Italy in 1790, and in *The Prelude* he recorded this experience and a curious surprise that befell him there. Without being quite aware of it, Wordsworth had passed the summit and begun a descent; a local peasant finally explained that to go on the party should follow a downward stream. At this point in *The Prelude,* the poet records a mysterious power that overcame him either in this moment of disappointment or in recollecting it as he wrote about it. In either case, he describes very exquisitely the experience of the sublime as a Kantian dynamic, a feeling of resistance overcome and of a breaking through into a realm of infinity:

> I was lost,
> Halted without an effort to break through;
> But to my conscious soul I now can say,
> "I recognize thy glory"; in such strength
> Of usurpation, when the light of sense
> Goes out, but with a flash that has revealed
> The invisible world, doth Greatness make abode,
> There harbours, whether we be young or old;
> Our destiny, our being's heart and home,
> Is with infinitude, and only there.[18]

A few lines later in the poem, and through succeeding hours in his Alpine excursion, Wordsworth finds a scene to embody this sense of infinitude, which remains immanent even on a downhill slope beyond the summit of expectation. The travelers must enter a "narrow chasm" or "gloomy Strait" overhung by cliffs and noisy waterfalls. Here Wordsworth perceives time suspended in a confusion of noises, contrasts, and conflicting powers of nature. Yet these tumultuous features come to represent the reassuring presence of a single mind, one face, one power present throughout eternity:

> The immeasurable height
> Of woods decaying, never to be decayed,
> The stationary blasts of waterfalls,
> And in the narrow rent at every turn
> Winds thwarting winds, bewildered and forlorn,
> The torrents shooting from the clear blue sky,
> The rocks that muttered close upon our ears,
> Black drizzling crags that spake by the way-side

As if a voice were in them, the sick sight
And giddy prospect of the raving stream,
The unfettered clouds, and region of the Heavens,
Tumult and peace, the darkness and the light—
Were all like workings of one mind, the features
Of the same face, blossoms upon one tree,
Characters of the great Apocalypse,
The types and symbols of Eternity,
Of first and last, and midst, and without end.[19]

These lines contain the most complex, deeply meditated understanding of the sublime in natural scenery that anyone had achieved by 1805.

Now it would be altogether wonderful if Lewis and Clark, in coming upon fresh vistas in even grander mountains, had had the art to rival this poetry. They did not. Yet there are touches in Lewis's account that relate his perceptions to Wordsworth's. Above all is Lewis's sentence calling the Great Falls "this truly magnificent and sublime grand object, which has from the commencement of time been concealed from the view of civilized man." Is this mere hyperbole, or does Lewis have a glimmer of recollection of Burnet's theory? After all, Lewis had had a few weeks' training for this expedition, including time in Philadelphia with Jefferson's correspondent, the botanist Benjamin Smith Barton, and he carried books suggested by Barton. Barton himself had seen the Niagara Falls in 1798 as a thundering scene of apocalypse: "It is only at the Niagara Falls that the force of that figure made use of in the book of *Revelations* can be fully felt: 'I heard a voice as the voice of many waters.' And what did that voice say? It proclaimed aloud, as if all Heaven spoke, 'Hallelujah: for the Lord God Omnipotent reigneth.' This is the language that has been thundered, for ages, from the Falls of Niagara."[20]

Also, in calling for the pen of James Thomson, just what did Lewis have in mind? Was he merely repeating a catch phrase about Thomson and Salvator Rosa, or could he have known that a long passage in Thomson's *The Seasons* questioned the origins of mountain waters and sought a sublime view through the earth's crust? Thomson's words echo the opening lines of *Paradise Lost*:

Say, then, where lurk the vast eternal springs
That, like creating Nature, lie concealed
From mortal eye, yet with their lavish stores

Refresh the globe and all its joyous tribes?
O thou pervading genius, given to man
To trace the secrets of the dark abyss!
Oh! lay the mountains bare, and wide display
Their hidden structure to the astonished view.[21]

In any event, Lewis's recorded raptures have their limits. To do full justice to his passages, one has to admit that his moments of exclamation are rare, and they are surrounded and even interrupted by much more prosaic observations. His picturesque scene at Marias River sounds almost silly as I have quoted it so far, but it actually occurs as a remark appended to shrewd geopolitical and economic assessments:

> It is a noble river; one destined to become in my opinion an object of contention between the two great powers of America and Great Britin with rispect to the adjustment of the North westwardly boundary of the former; and that it will become one of the most interesting brances of the Missouri in a commercial point of view, I have but little doubt, as it abounds with anamals of the fur kind, and most probably furnishes a safe and direct communication to that productive country of valuable furs exclusively enjoyed at present by the subjects of his Britanic majesty; in adition to which it passes through a rich fertile and one of the most beatifully picteresque countries that I ever beheld. . . . (*Journals* 4:266)

The description of the Great Falls is an exceptional passage of sustained wonder, but it, too, is punctuated by attempts at exact measurements. In a word, Lewis's sense of the sublime is balanced by his scientific interest. Like Jefferson's *Notes on Virginia,* his journal does not work to engage the mind with revelations of the infinite. Rather, it aims, as this passage explicitly states, to report natural wonders from the frontier back to the enlightened, civilized world.

But this aim, in both Jefferson and Lewis, gives its own special flavor to the sublime. It adds an edge of pride in the distinctly American landscape, which is displayed as not only grand and astonishing but superlatively grand and astonishingly new and unreachable. European painters and poets might exclaim, in effect, "Here, too!" as they unfolded a scene in France or England that matched the Italian landscapes of Salvator Rosa; or "Here, I, too!" as they retraced a path across the Alps. But these American writers proclaim, "Here and here alone!" or at least "Here pre-eminently!" and "Here, unfortunately beyond your reach, across the Atlantic and deep in the interior!" By the end of the eighteenth century, citizens of an independent America could proudly identify themselves by pointing to an icon like the Natural Bridge or Niagara Falls. These prodigies of nature came to be not touchstones of taste or emblems of the Christian God so much as signs of numinous power in the continent itself and in the new political order taking shape here. So Jefferson seems to gloat with ownership and patriotism as he lists wonders for the Cosways: "Where could they find such objects as in America for the exercise of their enchanting art?" And whatever scene Lewis had in mind to hold up as superior to the Great Falls, it was surely an American wonder, reinforced by this new report from the Far West.

This new patriotic American sublime does not appear only in the pages of Jefferson and Lewis. It also figures in many paintings of this time. Elizabeth McKinsey notes that if the American subject for painters in the eighteenth century was George Washington, the subject in the nineteenth century was Niagara Falls. At the turn of the century many painters were working to move from images of political sublimity to scenes of natural sublimity, and even to conflate them in the same picture. The very earliest paintings of Niagara Falls embellished the natural scene with details identifying an unmistakable American setting: figures of Indians, enormous beavers, or rattlesnakes. In 1804 the ornithologist Alexander Wilson made a trip to the falls and was inspired to write "The Foresters," a poem of over 2,000 lines, culminating in what became a widely quoted paean to sublimity:

> Above, below, where'er the astonished eye
> Turns to behold, new-opening wonders lie,
> Till to a steep's high brow, unconscious brought,
> Lost to all other care of sense or thought,
> There the broad river like a lake outspread,
> The islands, rapids, falls, in grandeur dread;
> The heaps of boiling foam, the ascending spray,
> The gulf profound, where dazzling rainbows play;
> The great o'erwhelming work of awful Time,
> In all its dread magnificence sublime,
> Rose on our view, amid a crashing roar,
> That bade us kneel and Time's great God adore.[22]

A few years later, Wilson published his *American Ornithology,* in which the falls appeared as the setting for the bald eagle. As Mc-

Kinsey points out, the bald eagle is a powerful indigenous bird and a pre-eminent political symbol of America, but in previous iconography the eagle had stood for St. John the Evangelist, the author of the Book of Revelation.[23] By 1825 Wilson's bewilderment in attempting to catch new wonders in every direction was repeated in one of the folk artist Edward Hicks's canvases: a couplet from Wilson's poem was painted along each of the four border panels to frame a scene of Niagara, which included two tiny human figures plus a rattlesnake, a beaver, a bald eagle, and a moose![24] (See fig. 2.)

In this same period, the patriotic artist John Trumbull was painting the falls, too, and discovering new means for rendering the sublime on canvas. This was the same Trumbull who had already devoted much of his career to recapturing great scenes of the American Revolution—including *The Declaration of Independence, The Surrender of Cornwallis,* and *The Resignation of General Washington.* These heroic historical subjects had fired his ambition after he had served for a time as an aide to George Washington in the Revolution; he eventually executed four of them in life size for the Capitol Rotunda in Washington. As he explained to Jefferson in 1789, this subject matter might well be called sublime in the loose sense of "exalted" or "uniquely noble": his vocation was "to preserve the knowledge and diffuse the Memory of the noblest series of Actions which have ever dignified the History of Man"[25] But in turning to Niagara Falls, Trumbull had to learn new methods for a completely different kind of American phenomenon. His first efforts nicely framed the Falls (and tamed them) in pleasing, picturesque compositions. But he seems to have learned from two novel paintings John Vanderlyn made in 1803 and 1804 that were later engraved and widely circulated. In *View of Niagara Falls,* Vanderlyn captured for the first time the astonishing breadth of the falls in a kind of panoramic view; in *A View of the Western Branch of the Falls of Niagara,* he narrowed his focus to bring out a deep chasm and emphasize a sheer drop of massive waters. Trumbull followed and even exaggerated these possibilities. His two Niagara panoramas of 1808, designed for exhibition on curved walls in London, are fourteen feet wide. And in *Niagara Falls below the Great Cascade* he introduced figures right under a heavy cascade and heightened the prominence of a rainbow above the foam, perhaps to symbolize a new covenant between God and America over this mighty flood.[26]

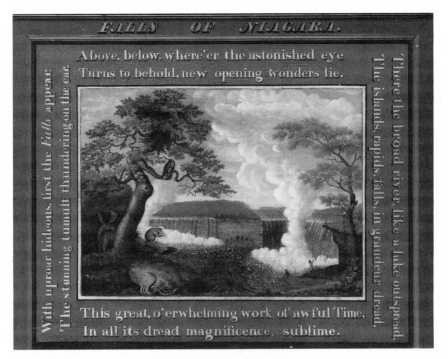

Figure 2. Edward Hicks, *The Falls of Niagara* (c. 1825), courtesy of the Abby Aldrich Rockefeller Folk Art Center, Williamsburg, Virginia.

The merging of landscape with sublime American vision may reach its climax, however, in the folk art of Edward Hicks, the self-taught Quaker preacher and artisan. His most famous work, *The Peaceable Kingdom,* painted in many versions, has emerged from obscurity to wide popularity in this century—in postcards, book covers, and posters on thousands of walls. In its original form, this painting was a companion piece to Hicks's painting of Niagara surrounded by the lines of Wilson's poem. Hicks copied the falls from an ornamental illustration on an atlas map of North America: a print of two American landmarks, Niagara Falls on the right and Jefferson's Natural Bridge on the left. For his earliest versions of *The Peaceable Kingdom* (1825), Hicks joined the Natural Bridge portion of this cartouche to a familiar engraving of a child petting a lion in a wilderness among other wild and domestic animals. This was an illustration of Isaiah 15:6: "The wolf also shall dwell with the lamb & the leopard shall lie down with the kid; & the calf & the young lion & the fatling

47

THE PEACEABLE KINGDOM OF THE BRANCH.

The wolf also shall dwell with the lamb & the leopard shall lie down with the kid; & the calf & the young lion & the fatling together; and a little child shall lead them.

Figure 3. Edward Hicks, *The Peaceable Kingdom of the Branch* (c. 1824–25), courtesy of the Abby Aldrich Rockefeller Folk Art Center, Williamsburg, Virginia.

together; and a little child shall lead them." Hicks copied these words around the four sides of this painting (see fig. 3). By itself this design proclaims an apocalyptic view of America—the Natural Bridge as the setting for the final paradise. But Hicks added one further element to reveal that this peaceable kingdom was already actual in America. Beneath the arch of the Natural Bridge he placed tiny figures of Indians and broad-hatted Europeans (see fig. 4). In later versions these were enlarged to stand out more clearly as William Penn making a peace treaty with the Indians—or, as Hicks put it in the motto of a painting that even shows the wording of the treaty: "Penns Treaty with the Indians, made 1681 without an Oath and never broken. The foundation of Religious and Civil Liberty, in the U.S. of America."[27] Hicks thus joins sublime action with sublime scenery, putting a characteristic American deed in an outstanding American setting as a

48

Figure 4. Detail of Edward Hicks, *The Peaceable Kingdom of the Branch,* courtesy of the Abby Aldrich Rockefeller Folk Art Center, Williamsburg, Virginia.

background to childhood peaceably emerging among colorful lions and leopards.

Hicks's art is a patchwork of copies from widely circulated engravings. But this crude simplicity may heighten the effect of his vision, for sublime American action in sublime American scenery is still the stuff of dreams about a limitless American West. Peace and justice in the form of peace officer or lawman is juxtaposed against the jagged Rockies or Monument Valley. This is the spectacular design of countless Western films, a formula for America that has made larger-than-life folk heroes of Gary Cooper, John Wayne—and Ronald Reagan. It still draws millions of tourists to South Dakota to see the noble brows of Washington, Jefferson, Lincoln, and Roosevelt emerge in gigantic whiteness from Mount Rushmore.

The journals of Lewis and Clark may seem far removed from the paintings of Vanderlyn, Trumbull, and Hicks, for these explorers never saw Niagara directly and were beyond reach of those artists' innovations. But Lewis's sense of the sublime at the Great Falls finally literalizes what they were composing on their canvases. Crossing the continent over the Rockies, meeting and exchanging promises of peace with the Indians, observing and sketching new forms of indigenous animals, asserting American dominion over this vast territory—these explorers were performing the immeasurable American deed in the grandest of American settings. Right here at the Great Falls they were to push on heroically by executing a masterful portage of their canoes and equipment and so breaking through the daunting barrier of high rocks and forceful cascades. And they not only did these things with decisive energy; at the crucial moment, it turns out that Lewis even had the proper words. He could address these falls as sublime and in a way that reawakens many dimensions of that idea.

Wallace Stevens wrote a poem called "The American Sublime" in which he asks how one can find such a thing and enter its communion: "What wine does one drink? / What bread does one eat?"[28] Shame on Wallace Stevens! He should have read Lewis and Clark, for the answers are plainly inscribed in their journals at the Great Falls. For drink, of course, there were not the waters of Helicon at the fount of the Muses but a new fount of sparkling waters that Clark found next to the Missouri on June 18: "the largest fountain or Spring I ever saw, and doubt if it is not the largest in America Known" (*Journals* 4:307). (It still produces about 200 million gallons a day.) As for food, Lewis supplies a hearty answer at the end of his first day at the falls: "my fare is really sumptuous this evening; buffaloe's humps, tongues and marrowbones, fine trout parched meal pepper and salt, and a good appetite; the last is not considered the least of the luxuries" (4:287). And those trout were cut-throat trout, now named *salmo clarkii* in honor of their discovery that day.

Chapter 3   Confronting the Bear

T HE DAY AFTER he came upon the Great Falls of the Missouri, Captain Lewis had an adventure with a grizzly bear. Again he was exploring alone, and he was rather off guard. The bear caught him by surprise. But Lewis tells the story better in his own words:

> I thought it would be well to kill a buffaloe and leave him untill my return from the river and if I then found that I had not time to get back to camp this evening to remain all night here there being a few sticks of drift wood lying along the shore which would answer for my fire, and a few sattering cottonwood trees a few hundred yards below which would afford me at least a semblance of a shelter. under this impression I scelected a fat buffaloe and shot him very well, through the lungs; while I was gazing attentively on the poor anamal discharging blood in streams from his mouth and nostrils, expecting him to fall every instant, and having entirely forgotton to reload my rifle, a large white, or reather brown bear, had perceived and crept on me within 20 steps before I discovered him; in the first moment I drew up my gun to shoot, but at the same instant recolected that she was not loaded and that he was too near for me to hope to perform this opperation before he reached me, as he was then briskly advancing on me; it was an open level plain, not a bush within miles nor a tree within less than three hundred yards of me; the river bank was sloping and not more than three feet above the level of the water; in short there was no place by means of which I could conceal myself from this monster untill I could charge my rifle; in this situation I thought of retreating in a brisk walk as fast as he was advancing untill I could reach a tree about 300 yards below me, but I had no sooner terned myself about but he pitched at me, open mouthed and full speed, I ran about 80 yards and found he gained on me fast, I then run into the water   the idea struck me to get into the water to such debth that I could stand and he would be obliged

to swim, and that I could in that situation defend myself with my espontoon; accordingly I ran haistily into the water about waist deep, and
faced about and presented the point of my espontoon, at this instant he
arrived at the edge of the water within about 20 feet of me; the moment
I put myself in this attitude of defence he sudonly wheeled about as if
frightened, declined the combat on such unequal grounds, and retreated
with quite as great precipitation as he had just before pursued me.
(*Journals* 4:291–92)

Lewis could not explain why the bear retreated. He watched the
animal run off, sometimes looking back as if expecting pursuit; and
going back over his steps, Lewis found "the grownd toarn with his
tallons immediately on the impression of my steps." Yet "the cause of
his allarm still remains with me misterious and unaccountable.— so
it was and I feelt myself not a little gratifyed that he had declined the
combat" (4:293).

The spot where the encounter occurred is now well marked in West
Bank Park in Great Falls, Montana. The story is noted by tour guides
and in popular accounts of the Lewis and Clark expedition. But in its
full details this story also points to other meanings. On the one hand,
it brings out the fragile defenses these early explorers had for the unpredictable world into which they were intruding. Technologically,
they were closer to Christopher Columbus than to pioneers who
would cross the plains and mountains just a few decades after them.
And on the other hand, this story gives historical body to an ancient
legend, the encounter of a hero with a monstrous spirit of the wilderness. How, with such crude implements as he had, could Meriwether
Lewis come to terms with the "misterious and unaccountable"? His
record of confronting the bear provides the answers.

Writing two centuries earlier, in the time of Shakespeare, Francis
Bacon listed three inventions that had transformed civilization since
ancient times:

It is well to observe the force and virtue and consequences of discoveries, and these are to be seen nowhere more conspicuously than those
three which were unknown to the ancients, and of which the origin,
though recent, is obscure and inglorious; namely, printing, gunpowder,
and the magnet. For these three have changed the whole face and state
of things throughout the world: the first in literature, the second in
warfare, the third in navigation; whence have followed innumerable
changes, insomuch that no empire, no sect, no star seems to have ex-

erted greater power and influence in human affairs than these mechanical discoveries.[1]

Bacon was not alone in making such a list in the Renaissance. Elizabeth Eisenstein compares this famous aphorism to other lists of the period, which agreed that these three inventions were most "conspicuous," as Bacon says, but also included the stirrup, the mechanical clock, optical lenses, and advances in metallurgy.[2] Even in expanded form, the total remains small—and corresponds very closely to the inventory of essential instruments Lewis and Clark carried across the continent. Or perhaps, as Bacon implies, these powerful new instruments carried *them* so far from home.

Lewis and Clark's instruments included the compass; the telescope, which Galileo claimed as an invention around the time Bacon was writing; the sextant and octant, invented in the eighteenth century for measuring the angles of the Sun or other stars above the horizon, and thereby calculating latitude; and the chronometer. The chronometer is the mechanical clock that had been refined by the late eighteenth century to keep accurate time even on turbulent voyages—in other words, to mark changes of time as precisely as the other instruments could note locations in space. By various methods, too complex to be summarized here, precise records of time could be combined with celestial observations to calculate longitude.[3] The use of all these instruments, of course, was to determine locations of unknown places in relation to fixed points on the globe—the poles, the equator, a zero meridian in Europe—or in relation to places previously mapped. And the novel force of these instruments was driving explorers around the globe to map it completely.

Keeping records of courses and distances was the daily work of Lewis and Clark. Astronomical sightings were made often, too, when a stable campsite and good weather afforded the necessary conditions. Thomas Jefferson's official instructions were explicit on this point: "Your observations are to be taken with great pains & accuracy, to be entered distinctly & intelligibly for others as well as yourself, to comprehend all the elements necessary, with the aid of the usual tables, to fix the latitude and longitude of the places at which they were taken, and are to be rendered to the war-office for the purpose of having the calculations made concurrently by proper persons in the U.S." (*Letters* 1:62). Records were also to be duplicated to guard against accidental loss. Hence the deep anguish recorded when instruments or papers came into danger. On May 14 one of the boats, the white pirogue, nearly capsized. "In this pirogue," Lewis writes, "were embarked our papers, Instruments, books medicine, a great part of our merchandize and in short almost every article indispensibly necessary to further the views, or insure the success of the enterprize in which we are now launched to the distance of 2200 miles" (*Journals* 4:152). When he saw the boat go over, Lewis was so moved in the instant that he dropped his gun and almost dived into the cold, rough river to swim after it. "There was a hundred to one but what I should have paid the forfit of my life for the madness of my project, but this had the perogue been lost, I should have valued but little" (4:153). The boat and its precious cargo were saved, but it turns out that some of the papers and instruments were utterly worthless all along. Silvio Bedini explains that even the best trained, most practiced hands could not have made reliable astronomical observations on the trail with the equipment Lewis and Clark had procured and studied. Their records proved utterly confusing to the expert mathematician who was finally asked to complete their calculations.[4]

The Corps of Discovery carried many guns and lived by them, too, when there was game. But in many crucial moments this equipment also failed them or proved embarrassing—from the first day of Lewis's journal in 1803, when a bullet from his air gun hit a woman forty yards away, to the return trip, when a hunting accident put a deep wound in the captain's buttock. Lewis himself contributed some innovations to the equipment of the expedition. He had the gunpowder packed in waterproof canisters of lead and nicely balanced the proportions of lead and powder so that they were used up evenly (*Journals* 5:53). And along with one light cannon (or swivel gun), two smaller swivels (or blunderbusses), a few pistols, and many smoothbore muskets, the party seems to have had at least fifteen 1803 Harpers Ferry rifles, the most modern firearms available. These were rifles with much-improved accuracy, even though they had shorter barrels than the long Kentucky rifles many expedition members may have brought from home. Some experts suggest that Lewis himself helped design the 1803 rifle, since it was first manufactured and issued for the expedition.[5]

But even this best modern equipment was none too good: the Harpers Ferry rifle was a muzzle-loaded, single-shot firearm, which required time and presence of mind for reloading. When Lewis stopped to gaze attentively at the buffalo he had shot, he left himself utterly disarmed against the approach of a menacing bear. Even if he had been prepared, it is unlikely that a single shot could have deterred the bear for long. There are many modern stories of grizzlies surviving a dozen direct hits. Already the party had brought down one enormous bear with five balls through the lungs and another five in other parts of the body. Another bear had taken seven balls and still pursued two hunters over a cliff and into the river. A third had run a quarter of a mile after a shot through its heart (*Journals* 4:113, 151, 166). Well equipped, provident, and ingenious as they could be, the explorers still brought very limited firepower to the frontier.

Obviously these men did not carry a big, cumbersome printing press in their canoes. But their journey was surely conditioned by this invention as much as by navigational instruments or gunpowder. Their plans and preparations had sprung from Jefferson's library and from the books, scientific journals, and published maps available in Philadelphia and Washington. When Lewis wrote of the Great Falls that he despaired of communicating their grandeur to the enlightened or civilized world, he could only have meant the print-literate culture of the early nineteenth century in Europe and its outposts. This was the realm of science, of widely and rapidly distributed printed matter in which new discoveries were reported so that they could be tested, confirmed, replicated, criticized, defended, and advanced. It was not merely the voyages of James Cook, George Vancouver, and Robert Gray to the Northwest Coast in the 1790s, or Alexander Mackenzie's overland crossing to the Pacific in 1793, that excited a new itch for western travel. It was the publication of their explorations that had induced Jefferson and Congress to mount an armed excursion up the Missouri and down the Columbia. And it was not merely out of native curiosity and acuteness that Lewis and Clark noticed and described the animals, plants, land forms, minerals, and even peoples they encountered; they organized their observations according to formulas learned among well-read masters. Even their military discipline went by the book.

Still, despite the advantages of print-literate culture, the expedition suffered from manifest weaknesses. A company of soldiers could not memorize all of human knowledge or carry many books in a flotilla of canoes. Their papers were always at hazard in the wilderness, though again the captains seem to have invented some clever means of protecting them: they carried their notebooks in sealed tin boxes. Even so, time and accident intervened between pen and press. Upon Lewis and Clark's return to the United States, the voluminous papers of the expedition were dispersed. Most were eventually deposited at the American Philosophical Society in Philadelphia, but many were kept or entrusted to others by Lewis, Clark, Jefferson, and other members of the party. Plans for publication were not properly coordinated. A much-edited and incomplete *History of the Expedition under the Command of Captains Lewis and Clark* came out in 1814, the same year that the publisher went bankrupt. A full edition of the captains' journals did not appear until 1904, and by then many valuable records, such as vocabulary lists of the Indian languages, had vanished. It is only now that a full edition of all known expedition records is being published (*Journals* 2:8–48, 530–67).

Thus gunpowder, the compass, and the press stand out as determining forces in this expedition, but they also show up as limited, unreliable devices despite centuries of use and refinement. Three hundred and twelve years after Columbus, this party was still naïvely trying to sail across America to the Pacific, even though the Rockies stood in their way. They were popping lead balls one at a time from flintlocks and scratching records with a quill, in a vain hope that their words would soon be hand set and hand printed back in the world of science. Nevertheless, as Bacon had seen and foreseen, these devices were enough to make those who possessed them a different order of human beings. Navigators, shooters, and readers of print were all acculturated to think with a different sense of space and to assert control over larger and larger territories. "Again," writes Bacon, "let a man only consider what a difference there is between the life of men in the most civilized province of Europe, and in the wildest and most barbarous districts of New India [i.e., the Americas]; he will feel it be great enough to justify the saying that 'man is a god to man,' not only in regard to aid and benefit, but also by a comparison of condition. And this condition comes not from soil, not from climate, not from race, but from the arts."[6]

Gunpowder alone may seem the determining, intimidating power by which explorers invaded and conquered the Americas. Lewis and Clark certainly ordered plenty of it shot off in displays at their formal meetings with Indians. But when they came among entirely new peoples, far from other traders, the full force of Bacon's words becomes evident. Here is Lewis on August 17, 1805, discussing the Shoshone people of the Rockies, to whom a gun was one among many wonders: "Every article about us appeared to excite astonishment in ther minds; the appearance of the men, their arms, the canoes, our manner of working them, the b[l]ack man york and the segacity of my dog were equally objects of admiration. I also shot my air-gun which was so perfectly incomprehensible that they immediately denominated it the great medicine. the idea which the indians mean to convey by this appelation is something that eminates from or acts immediately by the influence or power of the great sperit; or that in which the power of god is manifest by it's incomprehensible power of action" (*Journals* 5 : 112).

Meditating on Bacon's aphorism at the end of the nineteenth century, Henry Adams made up other lists of discoveries that had transformed the world, and particularly the American scene, in his own time. To Adams, the devices of the Renaissance were but toys in the history of human control over power. They left the basic means of accomplishing work just where they had been for thousands of years: in sunlight, fire, wind, and the muscles of humans and animals. But in the eighteenth century, Europeans and Americans had learned to harness (and serve) other natural forces, starting with gravity, steam, and electricity. "Evidently a new variety of mind had appeared," Adams writes. "Certain men merely held out their hands—like Newton, watched an apple; like Franklin, flew a kite; like Watt, played with a tea-kettle—and great forces of nature stuck to them as though she were playing ball."[7] In past centuries "the roads were still travelled by the horse, the ass, the camel or the slave; the ships were still propelled by sails or oars; the lever, the spring and the screw bounded the region of applied mechanics. Even the metals were old" (477). But in Adams's childhood in the 1840s, new energies suddenly reached across vast spaces. "Before the boy was six years old, he had seen four impossibilities made actual—the ocean-steamer, the railway, the electric telegraph, and the Daguerreotype" (494). As Adams puts it more vividly, the old universe of his New England parents and ancestors was "thrown into the ash-heap" by these new developments. "He and his eighteenth-century, troglodytic Boston were suddenly cut apart—separated forever—in act if not in sentiment, by the opening of the Boston and Albany Railroad; the appearance of the first Cunard steamers in the bay; and the telegraphic messages which carried from Baltimore to Washington the news that Henry Clay and James K. Polk were nominated for the Presidency. This was in May, 1844; he was six years old; his new world was ready for use, and only fragments of the old met his eyes" (5).

None of these energies were available to Lewis and Clark. They sailed in a keelboat against the Missouri's current, and when the wind failed their men rowed or poled or got out and hauled with a tow rope. When the river finally became impassable even to canoes, at the Great Falls, they effected a portage in crude carts with wheels sawn from logs, expending such brute labor that, as Lewis reports, "at every halt these poor fellows tumble down and are so much fortiegued that many of them are asleep in an instant" (*Journals* 4:328). What was the effect of this forced passage? The wilderness opened before them and closed behind them. Their crossing left hardly a trace on the land—nothing like the changes railroads and electrified wires would bring. A sudden lone bear could still chase a most-civilized captain away from his rifle and into the river, leaving him armed only with sheer courage and his espontoon, like an Indian with a spear. Because of subsequent forms of power, grizzlies now face extinction.

This bear also left Lewis feeling disoriented and perplexed. As we have seen, he could not find a sufficient explanation for the bear's deciding to turn and run. By day's end he was shaken, groping for an explanation, even thinking of occult forces or supernatural powers. For a brief moment, the science that had carried English-speaking explorers from Bacon's London to the ends of the earth collapsed in the captain's mind. To him the bear was as great "medicine" as his air gun would be to the Shoshones ahead of him on the trail—in Lewis's own phrase, "that in which the power of god is manifest by it's incomprehensible power of action."

The eighteenth century had a word for such a bear. It was a *genius loci,* or spirit of the place. It was the embodiment—in this case in animal form—of a power inherent in the land, appearing in order to ward off or attack an intruder from a foreign world. Poets had long been in the habit of drawing personifications into their verses to organize the scenery and give it meaning. Milton's *Lycidas* concludes with words of comfort for a young man drowned in the Irish Sea, envisioning his resurrection and establishment as a guardian spirit over the scene of his death:

Now *Lycidas,* the Shepherds weep no more;
Henceforth thou art the Genius of the shore,
In thy large recompense, and shalt be good
To all that wander in that perilous flood.[8]

(lines 182–85)

A famous *Spectator* paper, one of its most popular and widely reprinted essays, was the Vision of Mirza—an allegory of life and the
afterlife. It opens with the sudden appearance of a mysterious shepherd: "I cast my Eyes towards the Summit of a Rock that was not far
from me, where I discovered one in the Habit of a Shepherd, with a
little Musical Instrument in his Hand. . . . I had been often told that
the Rock before me was the Haunt of a Genius; and that several had
been entertained with Musick who had passed by it, but never heard
that the Musician had before made himself visible."[9] Finally, and
most pertinently, the workings of a spirit of place are at the heart of
Samuel Taylor Coleridge's famous poem *The Rime of the Ancient
Mariner.* William Wordsworth explains the origins of this poem in
later recollections:

> Much the greatest part of the story was Mr. Coleridge's invention; but
> certain parts I myself suggested, for example, some crime was to be
> committed which should bring upon the Old Navigator, as Coleridge
> afterwards delighted to call him, the spectral persecution, as a conse-
> quence of that crime and his own wanderings. I had been reading in
> Shelvock's Voyages a day or two before that while doubling Cape Horn
> they frequently saw Albatrosses in that latitude, the largest sort of sea-
> fowl, some extending their wings 12 or 13 feet. "Suppose," said I, "you
> represent him as having killed one of these birds on entering the South
> Sea, and that the tutelary Spirits of those regions take upon them to
> avenge the crime." The incident was thought fit for the purpose and
> adopted accordingly.[10]

This passage exactly describes the circumstances of Lewis's adventure. He may have been a young explorer rather than an Old Navi-
gator, but he too had violated a new territory by killing one of its
peculiar animals. He had cruelly shot an entire buffalo for his own
dinner and was watching it die a bloody death when the bear charged
him and drove him from the scene.

Lewis's knowledge about the concept of a local genius figures elsewhere in his journals. The white pirogue, for example, had so many
accidents and near disasters that on May 29 he wrote: "it appears

that the white perogue, which contains our most valuable stores, is attended by some evil gennii" (*Journals* 4:215). He repeated the word on May 31: "I fear her evil gennii will play so many pranks with her that she will go to the bottomm some of those days" (4:225). Lewis's spelling suggests a conflation in his mind of the Latin *genius* with the Arabic *jinnie,* the "genie" of the Arabian Nights tales; the idea of tutelary sprit is common to both, and the terms were often confused in this period.

But as a modern man of science, Lewis could only be teasing in these remarks. When put to the test earlier, he and Clark had specifically denied the possibility of local demigods. On August 25, 1804, the two captains had led a party to explore Spirit Mound, in what is now South Dakota. As Clark explains, this was a spot the local Indians—Omaha, Oto, and Sioux—dared not approach:

> In a northerley direction from the mouth of this Creek in an imence Plain a high Hill is Situated, and appears of a Conic form and by the different nations of Indians in this quarter is Suppose to be the residence of Deavels. that they are in human form with remarkable large heads and about 18 Inches high, that they are Very watchfull, and are arm'd with Sharp arrows with which they Can Kill at a great distance; they are Said to Kill all persons who are So hardy as to attempt to approach the hill; they State that tradition informs them that many Indians have Suffered by those little people and among others three *Mahar* men fell a Sacrefise to their murceyless fury not many years Since— So much do the Maha, Souis, Ottoes and other neighbouring nations believe this fable that no Consideration is Suffecient to induce them to apporach the hill. (2:505)

But no fable would deter Lewis and Clark. They approached and found natural reasons to explain the local superstitions. The hill was remarkably regular and stood out in the landscape, but its composition exactly matched the neighboring region and "we Concluded it was most probably the production of nature." As for devils, they could be explained as the workings of wind, insects, and birds:

> The Surrounding Plains is open void of Timber and leavel to a great extent: hence the wind from whatever quarter it may blow, drives with unusial force over the naked Plains and against this hill; the insects of various kinds are thus involuntaryly driven to the mound by the force of the wind, or fly to its Leward Side for Shelter; the Small Birds whoes food they are, Consequently resort in great numbers to this place in

Surch of them; Perticularly the Small brown Martin of which we saw a vast number hovering on the Leward Side of the hill, when we approached it in the act of Catching those insects; they were So gentle that they did not quit the place untill we had arrivd. within a fiew feet of them—

One evidence which the Inds Give for believeing this place to be the residence of Some unusial Spirits is that they frequently discover a large assemblage of Birds about this mound— is in my opinion a Suffient proof to produce in the Savage mind a Confident belief of all the properties they ascribe it. (3 : 10–11)

Despite warnings of occult powers here, the party took no special heed of the facts that their chronometer had inexplicably stopped just after being wound, that the insects swarmed out to bite them sharply, that Lewis's dog turned back early on this excursion, that Clark's slave York was prostrated by it ("he being fat and un accustomed to walk as fast as I went was the Cause" [3 : 8]), that bats appeared for the first time along the Missouri, and that their marksmen's guns could not bring down a large cormorant that day (2 : 506; 3 : 7–12). Sergeant Ordway recorded a day of intense heat: "We was almost famished for the want of warter. The sun beat down verry hot the air Sultry."[11] But without hesitation, the party climbed this hill, admired the scenery, and took compass bearings to other landmarks.

Was the bear, then, an exceptionally potent challenge from powers that loomed beyond nature? It certainly left an impression which deepened as the day wore on, after Lewis had been forced into the river. Around 6 : 30 he came upon another mysterious animal. At first it seemed a wolf; on his nearer approach, "it crouched itself down like a cat looking immediately at me as if it designed to spring on me" (*Journals* 4 : 293–94). Lewis now took time and loaded his rifle, supported it steadily on his espontoon, took careful aim, and fired—and the animal "instantly disappeared" in its burrow. "Whether I struck it or not I could not determine, but I am almost confident that I did" (4 : 294). Yet another strange encounter with animals came almost immediately:

It now seemed to me that all the beasts of the neighbourhood had made a league to distroy me, or that some fortune was disposed to amuse herself at my expence, for I had not proceded more than three hundred yards from the burrow of this tyger cat, before three bull buffaloe, which wer feeding with a large herd about half a mile from me on my

left, seperated from the herd and ran full speed towards me, I thought
at least to give them some amusement and altered my direction to meet
them; when they arrived within a hundred yards they mad a halt, took
a good view of me and retreated with precipitation. I then continued
my rout homewards passed the buffaloe which I had killed, but did not
think it prudent to remain all night at this place which really from the
succession of curious adventures wore the impression on my mind of
inchantment; at sometimes for a moment I thought it might be a dream,
but the prickley pears which pierced my feet very severely once in a
while, particularly after it grew dark, convinced me that I was really
awake, and that it was necessary to make the best of my way to camp.
(4:294)

Was Lewis wearied by the conspiracy of beasts or of the powers
behind them? Or was he exhausted (and exhilarated) by the exercise
of his own powers to stare them down and force three different monsters to retreat? As if he had not had adventures enough, he returned
to camp, slept soundly, and woke to find "a large rattlesnake coiled
on the leaning trunk of a tree under the shade of which I had been
lying at the distance of about ten feet from him" (4:297).

As Lewis and Clark came to learn, tutelary spirits took the forms
of animals in many Indian beliefs and practices. The idea of a genius
did not only derive from books that faintly remembered Roman
shrines and Arabian tales. Rather, it was a living reality for hunters
on the plains and in the mountains, where bears were dangerous adversaries, memorialized in scars. Months earlier, Sergeant Ordway
had noted "Strings of White Bears claws" around the necks of Sioux
warriors—claws "3 inches in length & Strung as close as possable to
each other."[12] Among the Shoshones a few weeks later, Lewis described the same trophies:

The warriors or such as esteem themselves brave men wear collars made
of the claws of the brown bear which are also esteemed of great value
and are preserved with great care. these claws are ornamented with
beads about the thick end near which they are peirced through their
sides and strung on a throng of dressed leather and tyed about the neck
commonly with the upper edge of the tallon next the breast or neck but
sometimes are reversed. it is esteemed by them an act of equal celebrity
the killing one of these bear or an enimy, and with the means they have
of killing this animal it must really be a serious undertaking. (*Journals*
5:135)

Earlier explorers had anticipated this mystery too. Henry Kelsey, who was perhaps the first white man to kill a grizzly bear, sighted one on his lone trek into the Canadian prairies in 1690. The Indians would not let him carry its skin back to Hudson's Bay. He recorded his strange experiences in halting verse:

> [Forest] continues till you leave ye woods behind
> And then you have beast of severall kind
> The one is a black a Buffillo great
> Another is an outgrown Bear wch is good meat
> His skin to gett I have used all ye ways I can
> He is mans food & he makes food of man
> His hide they would not me it preserve
> But said it was a god & they should Starve.[13]

Later anthropologists were to record and link bear myths, rituals, and ceremonies throughout North America.[14] American frontiersmen and hunters would write dozens of stories about mysterious wild monsters who eluded the most skillful marksmen—from before the time of Ahab and the white whale in *Moby-Dick* to after the time of Ike MacCaslin and Old Ben in Faulkner's *The Bear*. There have even been two American presidents who set their hands to tales of bear hunting. Abraham Lincoln wrote a ballad, "The Bear Hunt," around 1846, and Theodore Roosevelt recounted many tales of adventures with bears in the Dakotas. (The stuffed toys called Teddy Bears still memorialize one of his most outrageous experiences, when he refused to shoot a small bear that had been run down and tied for his supposed benefit in 1902.[15]) In ways too numerous to catalog and too complex to analyze here, the bear has long remained a symbol of American wilderness, of a power that killed men of every kind who dared invade its domain.

The Lewis and Clark journals record a step-by-step approach to the edge of this mystery and past it. The climax is the adventure with which we began, between Lewis and the bear that forced him into mid-stream. But it remains for us to trace how Lewis's mind was prepared for this encounter and how it overcame this danger after all.

Between St. Louis and the Mandan and Hidatsa villages where the party wintered in 1804–5, the explorers saw only one "white bear" or grizzly. Peter Cruzatte shot at one in October, but he was so frightened by its formidable appearance that he ran, leaving gun and tomahawk behind (*Journals* 3:188). The following April 13, just a few days after the party had begun moving again, they came upon enormous tracks along the river, near carcasses of winter-drowned buffalo. At this point Lewis recorded the Indian lore he had picked up so far:

> The Indians give a very formidable account of the strengh and ferocity of this anamal, which they never dare to attack but in parties of six eight or ten persons; and are even then frequently defeated with the loss of one or more of their party. the savages attack this anamal with their bows and arrows and the indifferent guns with which the traders furnish them, with these they shoot with such uncertainty and at so short a distance, that they frequently mis their aim & fall a sacrefice to the bear. two Minetaries were killed during the last winter in an attack on a white bear. this anamall is said more frequently to attack a man on meeting with him, than to flee from him. When the Indians are about to go in quest of the white bear, previous to their departure, they paint themselves and perform all those supersticious rights commonly observed when they are about to make war uppon a neighbouring nation. (4:31)

Clark recorded a glimpse of a pair on the next day, running and ascending steep hills with ease, and on April 28 the hunters wounded one. The next day, April 29, Lewis was among a party that brought one down after it had chased Lewis for seventy or eighty yards. His journal contains the first scientific description of this species, and it ends with a sense of conquest: "it is asstonishing to see the wounds they will bear before they can be put to death. the Indians may well fear this anamal equipped as they generally are with their bows and arrows or indifferent fuzees, but in the hands of skillfull riflemen they are by no means as formidable or dangerous as they have been represented" (4:85).

But skilled riflemen soon fired ball after ball into bears that would not die or retreat. Lewis reported on May 6 that the bears' "formidable appearance" and "the difficulty with which they die" were making converts of the curious and brave. He even began to personify the grizzly: "I expect these gentlemen will give us some amusement shotly as they soon begin now to coppolate" (4:118). Four days later: "these bear being so hard to die reather intimedates us all; I must confess that I do not like gentlemen and had reather fight two Indians than one bear" (4:141). On May 14, a bear pursued two men into the river over a twenty-foot bank, and on June 4, Joseph Field narrowly escaped from one after his gun would not fire—almost as if the Company of Gentlemanly Bears was rehearsing and giving fair warning before the lone encounter that forced Meriwether Lewis into the water on June 14.

That encounter came and passed. For a moment, it left Lewis disoriented and puzzled. But the bear and other monsters retreated. He recorded the incidents and thereby got the better of his feelings. What his gunpowder could not accomplish, perhaps his quill pen could. He wrote off the grizzly story, reducing it to an incident. Others were to follow—with more close-call pursuits into the river and sudden discoveries that guns were disabled or useless—on June 18 and 25. But they, too, were briefly noted and so absorbed into the record of daily occurrences.

Eventually, the full record of this period revealed two patterns for Lewis to notice. One was that the party had approached and passed through a zone of many grizzlies. The other was that they were also entering a new geographical region and a zone of many bewildering phenomena. Lewis's cool control in the face of his close encounter is all the more remarkable because it could easily have been the climax of much more severe disorientation.

After months of moving up the Missouri, the party was now at the Great Falls and thus at the threshold between the high plains and the Rockies. They were moving between ecological zones. For months they had been within sight of another large and potentially dangerous North American animal, the bison (or buffalo). But buffalo usually kept their distance, had to be hunted, and were routinely overcome by the developed skills of the Indians. Bears began to appear frequently to Lewis and Clark after the explorers had left Indian communities and entered unmapped territory. Lewis finally noted a good reason for their frequency. Where dead buffalo were plentiful, bears gathered and fed on their carcasses. There were buffalo killed by winter drownings near the first sighting of bears in April. And the Great Falls lay near a buffalo crossing, where many animals were swept away and killed.

> As the buffaloe generally go in large herds to water and the passages to the river about the falls are narrow and steep the hinder part of the herd press those in front out of their debth and the water instatly takes them over the cataracts where they are instantly crushed to death without the

possibility of escaping. in this manner I have seen ten or a douzen disappear in a few minutes. their mangled carcases ly along the shores below the falls in considerable quantities and afford fine amusement for the bear wolves and birds of prey; this may be one reason and I think not a bad one either that the bear are so tenatious of their right of soil in this neighbourhood. (*Journals* 4:303–4)

In that last line, the grizzly remains a person, a gentleman, perhaps even a liberty-loving fellow being, tenacious of rights to his land. But it is also manifest that Lewis here sees through him with a final and decisive superiority. The Missouri flowed through grassland; the grassland fed the buffalo and sustained the whole economies of some plains Indians; the bear now fed on buffalo and frightened the Indians and so asserted its continental supremacy. But Lewis's pen cuts him down to size by explaining his habits and habitat for the civilized reader. It even shows him up as a poor sportsman who merely preys on the already dead.

In the long view, Lewis could place the bear as one among many strange phenomena he found at the Great Falls. It should be remembered that in coming this far from St. Louis the party had already recorded dozens of mysteries and adventures, including an armed confrontation with Sioux warriors, a severe winter on the plains, the death of a sergeant, the disappearance of another man, and a major geographical puzzle over the proper route (at the mouth of the Marias River). Yet the Great Falls seemed to Lewis a place of concentrated wonders. On June 29 he came through a hailstorm to see the Giant Springs and recorded them on "the list of prodegies of this neighborhood towards which, nature seems to have dealt with a liberal hand, for I have scarcely experienced a day since my first arrival in this quarter without experiencing some novel occurrence among the party or witnessing the appearance of some uncommon object" (4:339–40). The Great Falls, the Giant Springs, the grizzly (and its attendant monsters), a previous hailstorm (with hail generally the size of a pigeon's egg), and a mysterious (and still unexplained) noise like distant cannon—all could be listed as prodigies beyond anyone's previous experience. Before this same day was over, Lewis and Clark both were to record a further sudden rain and hail storm that resulted in a flash flood. In Clark's words, "A torrent of rain and hail fell more violent than I ever Saw before, the rain fell like one voley of water falling from the heavens" (4:342). This storm caught Clark, Charbonneau,

Sacagawea, and her child in a ravine, from which they barely escaped before the waters rose to a depth of fifteen feet with an overpowering current. And on the plains it knocked down, bruised, and bloodied the men who were portaging the canoes.

Yet here, as elsewhere, the minds of these explorers remained disciplined with scientific curiosity. Copying Lewis, Clark tried out a number of explanations for the mysterious sound of the Rockies but came to a balanced conclusion. He took compass bearings and wrote an explanation of Indian superstition. "It is probable that the large river just above those Great falls which heads in the derection of the noise has taken it's name *Medicine River* from this unaccountable rumbling Sound, which like all unacountable thing with the Indians of the Missouri is Called Medicine" (4:320). But did it remain unaccountable to Clark? Not at all. "I have no doubt but if I had leasure I could find from whence it issued" (4:320). So with the storms that might have killed them and that did wash away their compass. The captains took them in with numerical measurements: "for about 20 minutes during this storm hail fell of an innomus size driven with violence almost incredible, when they struck the ground they would bound to the hight of ten to 12 feet and pass 20 or thirty before they touched again. After the rain I measured and weighed many of these hail stones and found several weighing 3 ozs. and measuring 7 Inches in circumference; they were generally round and perfectly sollid" (4:348). To which Clark adds a body count: "the men Saved themselves, Some by getting under a Canoe others by putting Sundery articles on their heads   two was kocked down & Seven with their legs & thighs much brused" (4:349).

In approaching and passing the Great Falls and their grizzlies, then, Lewis and Clark bore witness to a modern confidence in European ways of thinking, even when their guns and compasses failed or were slapped away. When monsters and prodigies appeared and even drove them to the brink of death, the explorers were deterred or confused for a moment, perhaps, but not for long. They recorded these phenomena, searched for natural explanations, and explicitly rejected mystery or superstition. They kept their journals for the eyes of civilized readers.

In this way the forces of legend and technology came to a test, and, crude though it was, the technology of gun, compass, and printing press won the day. Just as it had carried explorers from Europe around the globe by sea, so it would now sustain this party over high mountains and, more immediately, over falls that put a barrier to river navigation. Of tribal incantations only a vestige remained—familiar to every reader of Lewis and Clark. "We proceeded on," they wrote as a refrain in scores of their entries. That may seem a rather hackneyed formula (like "Set out early") for recording some movement from day to day. It may echo a sense of camaraderie in steady application to a task that would consume years. But read in full it is an antiphon of Western science and progress. That "we" includes not only the writers and their party but the civilized reading world to which the press ultimately linked them. And "proceeded" means not just that "we" covered ground but also that we made closely measured advances toward a definite destination, undeterred by any threats, and incorporating all surprises into full records that would eventually support their explanations.

Chapter 4   Extending
George Washington's Errand

ALONG THE eastern seaboard of the United States there are dozens of old houses and inns that proudly boast, "George Washington slept here." And from Illinois across Missouri, through the plains to the Rockies, and down the western slopes through Idaho, Washington, and Oregon there are dozens of signs and markers to point out, "Here Lewis and Clark once spent the night." This may seem an odd juxtaposition of historical characters, taking their slumbers east and west. The grim-visaged father of his country does not seem to resemble the energetic young men of 1803–6, nor does the revolutionary general in his headquarters or the president in his mansion fit very well with men in buckskin in rough tents or under the open sky. Besides, Lewis and Clark are usually and rightly identified with a different heroic American. They were Thomas Jefferson's men, his carefully chosen captains for an exploration he had fostered for years and finally set in motion.

But in fact the impulse to memorialize Lewis and Clark's campsites, like Washington's residences, is not at all misplaced, and it is not just a coincidence that all three heroes were military men who slept within reach of arms and a flag. George Washington was himself an important military frontiersman in his youth. In the 1750s he too was commissioned to go into the wilderness. He met danger there with extraordinary courage, skill, and energy. He too kept and published a journal, with very significant results, and his actions brought about important changes on the maps of America and the world. When Meriwether Lewis took command of his keelboat in Pittsburgh in 1803, to begin floating westward down the Ohio River, he was setting sail from the very same western outpost Washington had helped se-

70

cure for what became the United States. And though Jefferson brought wider learning to bear in framing his instructions for western exploration, he could only recast, modify, and embellish a central design Washington had grasped, fulfilled, and outgrown before he was twenty-seven. Washington's adventures even brought on diplomatic embarrassments and international dilemmas, which Jefferson and his captains could escape only by sheer good fortune fifty years later. The Lewis and Clark expedition took shape through Jefferson's will but under Washington's shadow—that is, under a history of imperialist daring and error that Jefferson would have done well to ponder.

Although he later became the great father figure of America, George Washington in his teens and twenties was very much a younger son. What prepared him for the wilderness and then propelled him into it was the necessity of making his way by following the standard procedure for younger sons of good families in the eighteenth century. Two older half-brothers had inherited the better estates his father had developed. So George learned a trade and made the best use he could of family status and connections. The trade was surveying land. The post his connections could supply was a military commission in the colonial forces. In mid-century Virginia, those two callings carried a young man west—to map and defend the lands Virginia claimed beyond the Allegheny Mountains, in the Ohio Valley. Young George took up both tasks with ready ambition.

His training as a surveyor was practical and rapid. He learned geometry and other sciences, not for their intellectual depths, but for their formulas, which he put directly to use. His biographer, James Thomas Flexner, has summarized what those uses were and how they immediately plunged the teenaged Washington into nice problems of law, exploration, and diplomacy.

A surveyor in the wilderness was much more than the word now implies. He was sworn as a government official because, in those unfrequented areas, it was up to him to see that no fraud was done by making surveys larger or smaller than was stated in the deeds, or by laying out land in manners forbidden by the various restrictive laws. On the other side, he served as his employer's agent. When working on a tract already patented, he was an agricultural planner commissioned to divide a large area in the manner that would earn the most money from rent or sale. Or if he were hired to find the land on which to lay out a patent, his role was that of an explorer: he needed to identify and map that acreage which would prove, after the forest had vanished and roads had been built and trade begun, the most valuable. Often his duties as an official and the interests of his clients were in conflicts that it took statesmanship to resolve.[1]

There was a simple formula for what this passage calls "the interests of his clients." Douglas Southall Freeman summed it up years ago: "One verb told the story of the proprietorship for almost a century: it was grab, grab, grab. The rest was detail, always interesting and sometimes amusing but detail only."[2] This may sound like ruthless plundering, but the colonial British interest in land can be compared rather favorably to other forms of exploitation. For one thing, the urge to survey and map land with an eye to imminent settlement distinguished English colonists from their counterparts, the French traders who pursued beaver pelts across Canada, and the Spanish conquistadors who came searching for gold. The figure of the colonial surveyor may well serve as a type for the intellectual cultivator of the land, as opposed to the conquistador or invader who came to take quick profits and carry them far away. Patricia Seed has discussed this distinction in detail. She also notes that continental legal theories of possession were strikingly different from those held in England and were much harsher toward native people in the New World: "The central, most important act legitimating Spanish rights over the New World articulated authority over persons rather than over land or commerce." In its typical records, "Spanish colonialism produced the census, British colonialism the map."[3] Later, the mining industry repeated the worst side of exploitation in the American Far West. Patricia Nelson Limerick has summed that attitude up in a phrase worse than "grab, grab, grab"—if grabbing land implies holding, settling, and inhabiting it, and so taking long-term responsibilities. "The attitude of extractive industry," she writes, "set a mood that has never disappeared from the West: . . . get in, get rich, get out."[4] On the other hand, surveying for permanent agricultural settlement signaled disaster to the Indian peoples of colonial America, for it spelled violent displacement if not extermination.

The "proprietorship" where Washington did his first surveying was also the area where he grew up in Virginia, the tract of several million acres between the Potomac and Rappahannock rivers that was held by the Fairfax family through a grant originally made by Charles II.

Washington was related to this family by neighborhood, by his eldest brother's marriage to a Fairfax daughter, and by employment. It was on behalf of Lord Fairfax that he was sent to the frontier for the first time, at age sixteen, to help survey and claim newly available lands in the Shenandoah Valley. In other words, to survey this world was to explore and extend the boundaries of the homeland Washington knew all his life.

The mental and physical discipline of this work was important training for someone who would become a general officer in America. Washington became very skillful at assessing topography, preparing accurate maps, and estimating relative distances and transport problems over rough terrain. He also absorbed the coarser interests of his neighbors. To the end of his life he made the most of opportunities to claim rich lands. And there was a ruthless edge to this work. To survey on behalf of the rich, who claimed huge American tracts through royal grants and privileged legal maneuvers, was to dispossess the poor, who were squatting on the frontier, clearing their fields, and building their homes. Washington recorded his cold observations of some German immigrants from Pennsylvania on his first surveying expedition: "We did two Lots & was attended by a great Company of People Men Women & Children that attended us through the Woods as we went shewing there Antick tricks. I really think they seemed to be as Ignorant a Set of People as the Indians. They would never speak English but when spoken to they speak all Dutch."[5]

In the 1750s, as a militia major, Washington performed a very similar function when he became an eviction agent between imperial powers on the frontier. Washington's first mission was to cross the Alleghenies in 1753, carrying a message from Governor Dinwiddie to the French commander at a new fort in the Ohio Valley—an order to withdraw from British territory. From then until 1758 Washington was to be engaged again and again in the same theater of what became a world war. On his first mission, he located the French with the help of Indians and trekked almost to Lake Erie, only to receive a firm refusal from the commandant he met there. On his return, he was fired at by Indians in an ambush, then raced back over frozen creeks and snowpacked lands. He hurriedly composed a report, complete with a map, which was printed in Williamsburg and soon reprinted in London and Paris. His adventure resulted in a long effort by British forces to secure the Forks of the Ohio and drive out the

French. The following year, Washington led the first army sent out for this purpose, only to find that the French were already fortifying the junction of the Allegheny and Monongahela rivers. He later came upon a party of about thirty French soldiers and ordered a battle. The French commander and ten others were killed, and their survivors claimed they had come as ambassadors to warn the British off French territory. This was the first blood shed in the Seven Years' War.

For Washington this engagement was high adventure. "I heard the bullets whistle," he wrote his brother in a line that even came to the notice of the king, "and, believe me, there is something charming in the sound."[6] But for two European empires this was the beginning explosion of a major upheaval. When it was over, France had lost all its colonies on the North American continent, and England began to pay for the war by imposing colonial taxes that led to the American Revolution.

Washington remained deeply involved in this contest of empires. His own attempted fortification of an open meadow led to an embarrassing surrender later in 1754 and to his signature on articles that admitted his "assassination" of ambassadors. In 1755 he joined General Edward Braddock's excursion to the Forks of the Ohio and was forced to take command to cope with its disastrous defeat. (He helped get the wounded Braddock off the field and later ordered wagon tracks run over the general's grave to keep the body from being scalped.) Finally, he served with the British army that built a road across Pennsylvania in 1758 and established Fort Pitt on the abandoned ruins of the French Fort Duquesne.

Washington certainly hoped for personal advantages from this service. He made several conspicuous moves to advance his military career and obtain a high rank in the regular British army. From the first he was also serving the plans of his Virginia neighbors in the Ohio Company by fostering a route through the Alleghenies and thus opening the prospects of fur trade, settlement, and land speculation in the western country. At the same time, Washington was being forced to look beyond personal and provincial interests. He was mastering, rapidly and at first hand, his generation's most important lessons in American geopolitics.

Those lessons can be summarized in five points, which later remained vital in Jefferson's thinking and, indeed, still affect deep controversies in the United States and Canada. The first point is that westward expansion would lead directly to dangerous conflict with other imperial powers. The French had claimed a wide arc of lands from the mouth of the St. Lawrence, across the Great Lakes, and down to the mouth of the Mississippi. And once France yielded, Britain and Spain remained to contest the claims of the fledgling United States. Despite explicit treaty terms, the British held onto posts in the region north of the Ohio until 1796. Second, there were already indigenous peoples on the land, and their interests would thoroughly complicate the conflicts between American and European powers. To reach the French on his first mission, Washington had to depend on Indian allies, but the first bullets he heard whistle were directed at him from Indian guns. Third, the key to American empire was control over principal inland waterways. The expansion of Virginia landholding depended on following the Potomac, the James, and other rivers up into the Piedmont and improving those connections between new settlements and the sea. New France had developed directly from control over the St. Lawrence, which led to the Great Lakes and the upper Mississippi. As Washington experienced it, the war was a contest for control over the Ohio, and a fort at the union of the Allegheny and Monongahela was its principal objective.

An important secondary issue was whether Virginia would open the first major route west, linking the Potomac to the Ohio, and so pre-empt developments in Pennsylvania along the Susquehanna or Delaware, or in New York along the Hudson. But a fourth point soon became palpable—that to gain and exploit the interior, the American colonies would have to join forces. The young commander soon found how weak the militia of Virginia could be, even when attached to large expeditions of British regulars. With this experience a fifth point emerged, which the American Revolution would solidly reinforce—that an empire gained might in the end prove too cumbersome to hold, especially as people who actually knew the land learned to evade and defy the ignorant commands of their distant masters.

Washington first crossed to the Ohio as a calculating Virginia surveyor, but he returned as an ambitious young soldier, a rather reckless commander, a chafing subordinate to British authority, and a developing apprentice in large-scale American strategies of war and diplomacy. And if he came to conquer the West, the West began to seize upon him, too. In particular, he took advantage of postwar proclamations and bounties in 1770, made an excursion down the Ohio, and laid claim to a rich tract of 23,000 acres bounded by the Ohio and the Great Kanawha River. For years he made plans of settlement on this tract, even ordered buffalo for domestication there, and had a notion, at the outbreak of the Revolution, that this might be an ultimate refuge of liberty where he and a band of followers might hold out against foreign despotism. "The vision is a fascinating one," Flexner comments: "George Washington, not the beloved master of Mount Vernon, not the august president of the United States, but the buckskinned leader of a band of noble outlaws, the very hero of a favorite eighteenth century romantic dream. Who can doubt that there were in his character and experience potentialities that would have made him effective (if not content) in this role?"[7] But it was not to be. These rich acres were to remain instead a reminder of the precariousness of empire. Washington's title to them was challenged by other speculators. On the eve of the Revolution, the colonial governor threatened to cancel the patents because of irregularities in its surveying. Later, plans for settlement never worked out; two expensive expeditions of slaves and servants were driven away by Indians, and Washington's increasing obligations kept him from ever returning to this land. In his final years he gave a long lease to a smooth-talking trader, with great relief at the prospect of receiving steady cash.[8]

What Washington could not do along the Ohio was achieved, however, by George Rogers Clark during the Revolution. His story reads almost like a pat repetition of Washington's early career. Born in Jefferson's Albemarle County in 1752 and briefly a schoolfellow of James Madison, Clark moved into the central Kentucky region in 1775 as a surveyor for the Ohio Company. With the outbreak of war, he quickly saw the need for preemptive strikes against British-directed Indian raiders in the territory north of the Ohio. Patrick Henry, who was then governor of Virginia, agreed to make him a militia commander, giving him secret orders to invade and take British posts, if possible, from Detroit to Cahokia, opposite St. Louis. Clark reached the high point of his career in 1778 by taking Kaskaskia and other posts along the Mississippi River, then surprising the British fort at Vincennes, forcing a surrender, and taking the hated lieutenant-governor Henry Hamilton prisoner. Thereafter he lacked troops and material support for a further demonstrative blow against the British or the Indians.

Unlike Washington, Clark did not rise from despair to further glory. He fell into debt by securing notes for military supplies and fell into alcoholism and debility after his plans and pleas went unfulfilled. But it was largely through his efforts that Kentucky became a recognized extension of Virginia, settlement greatly increased, and the Old Northwest became part of America at the end of the war. Clark's parents and their other children followed him to settle lands on both sides of the Falls of the Ohio after 1784. His youngest brother, William, was living there, partly to look after this weakened veteran, when Meriwether Lewis's keelboat came down from Pittsburgh in 1803.[9]

Fifty years after Washington's first effort for Governor Dinwiddie, President Jefferson could look farther west for the frontier and envision its exploration with much more sophisticated learning. But the essential problems remained just what they had been in Washington's and the older Clark's time. Jefferson had had his own direct political involvement in the creation of the United States and the planning of new states and territories beyond the mountains Washington had crossed. He had mastered his own private library of lore about the Americas. Although he would never see any western territories himself, he had become renowned as a close observer and interpreter of natural phenomena in America. And he had had years of experience keeping his balance on the shifting sands of international diplomacy. Yet when he looked to the Louisiana country, he faced many of the same prospects and dilemmas that his predecessors had opened by intruding into the Ohio Valley.

The new western territory was much larger and much farther away from the settled eastern seaboard. For the moment, in 1803, it could seem less burdened by threats from foreign powers. The British had withdrawn from the Ohio Valley to territories farther north. Spain had ceded back to France its claims in the Mississippi Valley, and France in turn had just sold those lands to the United States. The deep interior region beyond St. Louis supported just a few trappers and traders; it was unlikely that settlers would disturb such Indian territory for decades, if ever. Yet Jefferson knew very well that the far limit of American territory was now the Pacific coast, where the race for empire was becoming intense. Spanish claims to California had been extended farther up the coast. The British had responded by sending a squadron under George Vancouver in 1791, with resulting explorations around Vancouver Island and into Puget Sound. Then an

American trading vessel had arrived and made a very significant intrusion. The *Columbia Rediviva* of Boston, commanded by Robert Gray, had in 1792 sailed over the bar of a large river Vancouver had failed to notice—and so named and claimed the Columbia River and all adjacent territories for the United States. The same ship had already completed the first American circumnavigation of the world, in 1787–90, making a good commercial profit by carrying sea otter pelts from the Oregon country to the Orient.

A year after the discovery of the Columbia River, Alexander Mackenzie, a British agent of the Northwest Company, crossed the northern Rockies and reached the Pacific. His account, published in 1801, showed that a simple crossing could be made over "a beaten path leading over a low ridge of land," and he seemed to have found the upper reaches of the Columbia.[10] Mackenzie also seemed to grasp the strategic importance of his discoveries: "The Columbia," he wrote, "is the line of communication from the Pacific Ocean."

> It is the only navigable river in the whole extent of Vancouver's minute survey of that coast: its banks also form the first level country in all the Southern extent of continental coast from Cook's entry, and consequently, the most Northern situation fit for colonization, and suitable to the residence of a civilized people. By opening this intercourse between the Atlantic and Pacific oceans, and forming regular establishments through the interior, and at both extremes, as well as along the coasts and islands, the entire command of the fur trade of North America might be obtained, from latitude 48, North to the pole, except that portion of it which the Russians have in the Pacific. To this may be added the fishing in both seas, and the markets of the four quarters of the globe.[11]

The key to empire and even international dominance again seemed to be the mastery of inland waterways. Just as Washington had labored to create a firm, open link between the Potomac and the Ohio, so Jefferson began to plot an American expedition to connect the upper Missouri and the Columbia. He was making official plans to this end as early as 1802, soon after Mackenzie's and Vancouver's books and maps had reached America and well before there was any hint that Napoleon would sell Louisiana. But by this point in life Jefferson could by no means do what Washington had done. Sixty years old and immured in the office of president, he could contribute only political and intellectual leadership to the project. His secret message to

Congress (January 18, 1803) put him in a role like that of Governor Dinwiddie in 1753, a political master sending younger men to brave the frontier. "An intelligent officer," he wrote, "with ten or twelve chosen men, fit for the enterprize and willing to undertake it, taken from our posts, where they may be spared without inconvenience, might explore the whole line, even to the Western ocean, have conferences with the natives on the subject of commercial intercourse, get admission among them for our traders as others are admitted, agree on convenient deposits for an interchange of articles, and return with the information acquired in the course of two summers" (*Letters* 1:12–13). Within a few months Jefferson had not only begun detailed work for the Lewis and Clark expedition but also had outlined military explorations along other major tributaries of the Mississippi.[12]

Jefferson's thoughts about empire did not merely echo Washington's, of course. They have their own depths and subtleties, which stand out very sharply in the planning for Lewis and Clark. Jefferson had been nurturing plans for western exploration over a long period. He had proposed an expedition "from the Missisipi to California" to George Rogers Clark in 1783. From his own reading he summarized what was known of all the major rivers of America in his *Notes on the State of Virginia*. When he was the American minister in Paris in 1787, he met John Ledyard, an American who had sailed on Cook's final voyage, and encouraged Ledyard's plan to set out alone on a journey across Russia to America (Ledyard had hoped to land on the Pacific coast and then travel east across the Rockies, but Catherine the Great had him apprehended in Siberia). In 1793 Jefferson helped raise a subscription for the French botanist André Michaux on behalf of the American Philosophical Society. This expedition "to find the shortest & most convenient route between the U.S. & the Pacific ocean" was aborted within weeks after it began, but Jefferson's detailed instructions for it read like a rough draft of his later instructions to Lewis.[13] And in addition to these armchair explorations, Jefferson had amassed other kinds of knowledge and influence that proved essential to the Corps of Discovery.

He gave this project every advantage from the height of his powers as an intellectual in politics. As president of the United States, he drew upon the expertise of his cabinet; obtained money from Congress; requested passports from England, Spain, and France, and used personal persuasion to deflect the jealousies of those rival empires; commanded supplies and men from the army; and coordinated other ample resources to back a major expedition. As a respected American naturalist, he also turned to personal friends and correspondents for advice and support in preparing Lewis to see and record as much as possible. Lewis even spent a few weeks in Pennsylvania at Jefferson's order, to study directly with America's leading botanist, anatomist, physiologist, and mathematicians—that is, to cram what he could while ordering supplies.

But Jefferson's most insightful action—both political and scientific—may have been his choice of Meriwether Lewis as the leader of this project. Donald Jackson has deflated the idea that Lewis was selected and groomed as Jefferson's aide and private secretary in 1801 with an eye to his becoming a western explorer. He seems to have been chosen instead as a capable young captain with experience in the Ohio country and a good knowledge of the political sympathies of other army officers in a time of troop reductions.[14] Yet his experience as Jefferson's closest companion in the White House gave him incomparable preparation for this mission. He knew the president with intimacy and deep respect—knew his habits of thinking, reading, writing, and decision making so well that he could sustain years of daily record keeping with a sure sense of what his ultimate reader would require.

Many ties developed between these two men despite their difference in age. Lewis was born in 1774 on a plantation a few miles from Charlottesville, and his father died of pneumonia while serving as an officer in the Revolution. The young captain thus qualified for the role of the grown son Jefferson never had. Such circumstances at least guaranteed that the two men spoke the same language from birth and had taken their bearings on America from the same landmarks in Virginia. They also shared long solitudes in Washington. The new Executive Mansion of Jefferson's time was occupied only by the widower and the bachelor for months at a stretch. Dumas Malone concludes that Lewis probably occupied the still-unplastered East Room, which was roughly divided into two rooms; Jefferson's quarters took up several finished rooms in the rest of the building.[15] There were servants to support these two men, and Jefferson wrote out his own papers, but Lewis was charged with carrying official and unofficial messages and attending social functions and political meetings as a confidential aide. Lewis could not help learning from these duties, from intellectual company when Jefferson entertained, and from time alone with the president, when the two men were left (in Jefferson's phrase) like two mice in a church.[16]

Lewis had his own gifts to bring to this situation. In his letters to scientific correspondents in 1803, Jefferson regretted that no better man could be found for the expedition—but in words that express how rare Lewis's qualifications really were:

> It was impossible to find a character who to a compleat science in botany, natural history, minerology & astronomy, joined the firmness of constitution & character, prudence, habits adapted to the woods, & a familiarity with the Indian manners & character, requisite for this undertaking. All the latter qualifications Capt. Lewis has. Altho' no regular botanist &c. he possesses a remarkable store of accurate observation on all the subjects of the three kingdoms, & will therefore readily single out whatever presents itself new to him in either: and he has qualified himself for taking those observations of longitude & latitude necessary to fix the geography of the line he passes through.[17]

When Jefferson expanded this portrait for a biographical sketch in the 1814 *History* of the expedition, he noted that from boyhood Lewis had been a minute observer of plant and animal life. He also recalled that when the Michaux expedition was being formed in 1792, "Capt. Lewis being then stationed at Charlottesville on the recruiting service, warmly sollicited me to obtain for him the execution of that object" (*Letters* 2:589). At the first mention of a new expedition in 1803, "he renewed his sollicitations to be the person employed. My knolege of him, now become more intimate, left no hesitation on my part. I had now opportunity of knowing his character intimately" (*Letters* 2:589). Acquired learning, natural curiosity, a solid constitution, reliable character—to all these qualifications Lewis added tested respect for Jefferson and a devoted eagerness to go west. Even these latter qualities stand out in Lewis's journals. When he set out from Fort Mandan in 1805 he wrote of his "most confident hope of succeading in a voyage which had formed a darling project of mine for the last ten years" (*Journals* 4:10). And, as we have seen, when the white pirogue overturned and all the chief goods and records seemed about to go under, Lewis could barely hold back from plunging headlong after them (4:153).

When the expedition began, Lewis was still in his twenties. His high intelligence had had some schooling, some training and experience in the army, some polishing in Jefferson's official household, but nothing like Jefferson's intellectual formation with mentors at William and Mary or his long experience in government, diplomacy, and science in America and Europe. Jefferson would always remain the authority behind this work, while Lewis was the devoted subordinate, who even shared his command willingly with his former superior William Clark. Still, youth gave Lewis one final, important advantage—not only strength and stamina but also freshness for discovery.

Jefferson's mind looked west and projected patterns ingrained by years of comprehensive study. Part of what makes Jefferson an inexhaustible fascination is a double attitude that beriddles his most conspicuous achievements. With one eye he saw the world in ideal orders and patterns. With the other he paid close attention to minute particulars and oddments. As Charles A. Miller has brilliantly shown, he focused on Nature, a key concept in the Enlightenment, with an intense application of these very different (and sometimes contradictory) attitudes. He was a conscious intermediary between what Miller calls "universal" and "particular" nature. The latter kept Jefferson busy for a lifetime as an amateur botanist, zoologist, or "naturalist" in the New World. But "universal nature" was preeminent in his thought about politics; his revolutionary principles were derived from what he believed were natural laws that should be established in the institutions of an uncorrupted continent. Miller describes Jefferson's unique mentality as a balance in these terms: "As much as anyone of his generation, whether in America or Europe, Jefferson was devoted to both the scientific and the social concerns of nature. In America he was the most European-minded man of nature. When in Europe he was the most nature-minded American. No other American statesman matched his interests in natural history. None other matched his reliance on natural law and natural right in politics."[18]

The balance between universal and particular nature never reaches explicit resolution in Jefferson's writings. His career did not lead him to a final philosophical synthesis, which would in fact have mediated between absolute idealism and encyclopedic practical observation and resolved the ancient tension between Plato and Aristotle. Instead Jefferson favored one and then another point of view and left behind odd monuments to both. With the pen of a revolutionary philosopher, he drafted the Declaration of Independence, deriving free and independent foundations of government from "the laws of nature and of nature's God." With the pen of a naturalist, he composed *Notes on the State of Virginia,* cataloging details of plant life, animals, geography, geology, population, and climate. He won international renown for inventing an improved plow, the most practical device for keeping a farmer in productive contact with the soil, yet he perfected this design in the abstract quiet of his study by determining the most advantageous curve by principles of geometry. He built and rebuilt Monticello in order to live on a lone mountaintop within sight of productive fields and experimental gardens, with expansive vistas of mountains and far horizons. Yet he leveled the mountaintop to make a beginning and designed his house by imitating the geometrical balances of Palladian architecture. He even erected a large dome for which no one has ever found a justifying practical use—though practicality dictated his invention of gadgets in room after room.

The list could go on and on, and that is a good part of the point. By the time he framed instructions for Lewis, Jefferson had lived out decades of pondering nature, both universal and particular. And he was manifestly stuck between those poles. He was stuck physically in the eastern United States, where it was incumbent upon him, as president, to balance political idealism with practical compromises. And he was stuck intellectually between the orderliness of his library and the hazards and variety of growth in his fields and gardens. Comprehensively informed as his mind was, it was informed with ideas and categories that now seem provincial to his time and place—to the early America that lay east of the Mississippi, in constant correspondence with Europe. He had no way of imagining the immense, open plains, high mountains, and tangled evergreen forests to which he was committing three dozen lives. What he did instead was project patterns based on what he knew—including geometry, empirical science, and sheer fantasy. And he gave orders for Lewis to discover what he expected.

Part of what Jefferson expected turned out to be a tissue of wishful thinking. Like many another explorer or imperialist, he allowed desire to run ahead of doubt. Because of his reading and his direct knowledge of the Blue Ridge and the links that could be made between the Potomac and the Ohio, he gave instructions to seek out the headwaters of the Missouri and make a connection with a principal river flowing to the Pacific. He followed widely accepted notions that the American continent was symmetrical, that the Rocky Mountains would not be higher than the Alleghenies, and that rivers on one side would flow from near the sources of those on the other, so that there would be easy commerce between them. Indeed, many writers thought, and continued to think for many decades, that there was a single, pyramidal height-of-land in the west from which the Missouri, the Columbia, the Colorado, and other great rivers all took their source. Jefferson's message to Congress in 1803 confidently predicted that the Missouri traversed a moderate climate, was navigable to its source, and was within "possibly a single portage" of fully navigable streams flowing westward. He supposed that an expedition could cover this route easily "in the course of two summers" (*Letters* 1:12–13). What optimism! John Logan Allen has devoted a long book to the disillusionments Lewis and Clark underwent as a result. They not only had to force their way through severe conditions, over unnavigable rivers, and across range after range of mountains, but they also had to go through mental contortions trying to reconcile the geographical authority of Jefferson's library with the harsh realities staring them in the face and stabbing them in the feet. Allen demonstrates that they were so well indoctrinated with what they should be seeing that their records and maps preserved and furthered some long-standing misconceptions of the American West.[19]

Jefferson imposed a more reasonable but still strenuous demand when he instructed Lewis to take exact observations of longitude and latitude all along the route and record and transmit them with great care. This information would be essential for constructing accurate maps and guiding later travelers. But implicit in Jefferson's thinking was another notion, which again set abstract ideas higher than concrete experience. In Congress, Jefferson had been the ultimate author of two major bills that determined the development of federal lands in the West as far as the Mississippi—the Land Ordinance of 1785 and the Northwest Ordinance of 1787. These acts provided for an exact rectangular survey of lands into townships six miles square and set out the steps by which governments could be organized in new territories and eventually form states equal to the original thirteen. Thus Jefferson thoughtfully anticipated western expansion and provided a new principle of colonial development, not for the benefit of the mother country over its colonies but for the balanced equality of diverse states in a growing federation. Yet the full design Jefferson set out in the proposed Ordinance of 1784, from which these later acts

Figure 5. Map of the Old Northwest showing boundaries and names for new territories proposed by Jefferson (and others) in 1784. From Julian P. Boyd, ed., *The Papers of Thomas Jefferson*, vol. 6 (copyright ©1952, renewed by Princeton University Press), reprinted by permission of Princeton University Press.

derived, reveals an intellectual colonialism that time could not overthrow. Before many new settlers had a chance to move onto the new federal lands and discover by experience what their political contours should be, Jefferson had decided for them, even sketched a map of fourteen new states arranged in two tiers with very rectangular boundaries, and assigned many of them names in jawbreaking academic Greek: Assenisipia, Polypotamia, Metropotamia, Cherronesus, Pelisipia (see fig. 5).

Miller points to this map as a prime example of universal nature displacing particular nature in Jefferson's thinking. That is not quite fair, because in 1784 Jefferson was acting as chairman of a committee of Congress, which was groping to develop a reasonable and acceptable plan immediately after the Revolution. As Julian Boyd sees it, the map is "a curious combination of what Jefferson and the committee privately intended, what they actually reported, and what Congress finally approved—plus a variation not attributable to any of these." Nevertheless, the map and surviving documents do show that, along with many others in power, Jefferson was looking west from a great distance and making extraconstitutional plans based on very abstract considerations rather than a feeling for geographical detail.[20] It seems he might have wished that the Mississippi River ran due north and south without any curves, so as to preserve uniformity along the boundary of the westernmost tier. In any case, he helped establish a way of thinking about the Far West that survives in many a long rectilinear boundary. And if his thoughts at one time focused on symmetrical river systems connecting across balanced ranges of gentle mountains, at other moments he blanked out such geographical nuisances as much as possible to see the continent as a uniform political grid.

Finally, Jefferson stipulated to Lewis that the details of nature should be observed and classified in further intellectual grids. To his mind, there was really nothing new under the sun. His science rested on the assumption that all forms of nature—mineral, vegetable, and animal—had existed since the dawn of creation; that nothing had become extinct, though some species had migrated far from where their relics now were found; that nothing new had evolved. The labors of the naturalist were collection and arrangement. This was orderly Enlightenment natural history, the aim of which was to amass all knowledge and arrange it in enormous, complete tables. If pressed to a logical conclusion, this way of thinking implied that Lewis and Clark could really *discover* nothing, in our modern sense of that term. They could encounter nothing that was wholly unpredictable or beyond ready comparison to things already well known, nothing that could challenge accepted patterns of thought. Jefferson left to others the work of synthesizing data; nor did he see much use in speculative science or conceive of revolutions in thought. He spent most of his scientific effort simply observing, recording, and collecting.[21] And he sent Lewis and Clark out to observe, describe, and collect. Take note, he wrote, of soil, plant life, animals (and the remains or accounts of those too rare to be seen), minerals, volcanoes, weather patterns, and the life cycles of living things—precisely the kind of data he accumulated himself in lifelong records at Monticello and on his travels (*Letters* 1:63).

In another long list of prescribed observations, Jefferson even implied that human customs were to be noted and tabulated. Clark carried an extensive list of questions for the Indians, which resulted in long tables of tribes, customs, practices, diets, tools, possessions, houses, and trade goods. Lewis and Clark labored over these tables through the cold winter of 1804–5, even before they set out beyond the Mandan villages. Hence, too, the Indian vocabulary lists (now lost), which Jefferson had designed and used earlier, and which the explorers assiduously completed—as if the voices of America could be condensed into orderly tables of different-sounding synonyms.[22]

As a direct result of Jefferson's energetic brilliance, Lewis and Clark were sent off on a predetermined errand. Their journals bear witness day after day to a tension between deeply indoctrinated order and the effort to find new terms for new realities. The explorers were caught in strict subordination to the president. They were junior army officers, following explicit written instructions, keeping and revising daily journals in which full reports were expected of every move and its consequences. They were responsible for recruiting, training, and managing a company of infantry soldiers. They were accountable for supplies and wages for these men and for others hired later as boatmen and interpreters. It was their specified duty to follow a certain route, seek out particular landmarks, assert some definite claims in the face of opposition by other nations, refrain from making others, gather and transmit samples and reports, and return.

Of course, Lewis and Clark were willing partners in Jefferson's plans, sprung from the same Virginia soil, honored by personal acquaintance with this president, eager for the excitement and advancement (personal, national, and scientific) that it promised. Were they setting off to do the impossible? Their youth might have laughed away such a question. Did not Jefferson's expectations of universal learning, along with heroic hardihood, demand talents and strengths beyond human capacity? They could turn to Jefferson himself for authoritative expressions of confidence, backed by his own political energies to facilitate this venture, and his formidable intellectual example.

But whatever their apprehensions or expectations, the Corps of

Discovery set out—and disappeared. From April 7, 1805, when they sent back their keelboat from Fort Mandan, until they returned to St. Louis in late September 1806, they were beyond direct reach. Jefferson's orders might still hover over their shoulders and command their pens, but the new realm they entered exerted powerful forces, too, which left their marks on their own pages. As well as strict discipline, the captains observed new relations of interdependency with their men. To reach Fort Mandan the band of soldiers had been expanded to include French-speaking boatmen and engagés; then it grew a different way, to include a Shoshone woman and her newborn son, and, later, other Indians who came as guides. Together these people had to face dangers, get lost and bewildered, starve, feast, explain themselves to tribes none of them had met before, invent means of survival, and return. They went away long enough and far enough to escape some of the formalities of official instructions. They had to do so if they were to live, and live together, and honestly set down what they actually experienced.

Instead of being wholly Jefferson's men, in other words, they sometimes became Washington's followers—just young officers again, sent into unsurveyed wilderness to meet with Indians and establish a claim to empire. Perhaps Lewis's one exchange of gunfire can be best understood in these terms.

It took place on July 27, 1806. After the entire party had returned across the Rockies, Lewis led a group that retraced the Missouri while Clark and the others went a different way to explore the Yellowstone. Beyond the Great Falls, Lewis split off further to explore the extent of the Marias River. But he began to travel very warily when he found fresh signs of Indian encampments. He wanted to get an accurate reading of his northernmost latitude, but he dared not linger for the skies to clear. On July 26 he gave up and rode on from a spot he named Cape Disappointment. Later that day one of the men, George Drouillard, rode apart, and Lewis along with Joseph and Reuben Field surprised a band of Piegan Blackfeet as they were watching Drouillard approach. Lewis saw that his party was outnumbered by a hostile force, even though the Indians exchanged friendly signs and turned out to be only eight strong by the time the two parties made camp together. Through the evening, Lewis communicated with them, aided by Drouillard, an expert in signing. He learned that they were part of a larger band who met British traders at the Saskatchewan

River and traded pelts for guns, blankets, and liquor. In return, he explained that he was sent by a great power from the East, that he had traveled across the continent and back, and that he had come to open new trade and make peace among all western peoples. He urged them to send their chief to a council at the mouth of the Marias— where his own forces would by now be anxiously awaiting his return. At last all the Indians fell asleep, and Lewis slept soundly, too—after rousing Reuben Field to watch against theft.

But at daylight that sleep was torn open by violence. According to Lewis's journal, the Indians tricked Field, seized the party's guns, and were overcome only by the sentry, who ran after the first thief and stabbed him through the heart. The soldiers recovered their guns and Lewis ordered them to hold their fire. But the Indians made a countermaneuver to drive off all the horses, and after pursuing and shouting warnings, Lewis fired at one of the Indians, who was hit, fell, and fired back. The day ended with two Indians dead and four soldiers galloping at full speed across country toward the Missouri— a ride of a hundred miles before they stopped at two in the morning (Thwaites 5 : 223–26). The next day they were reunited with the others at the mouth of the Marias, opened their caches there, and began the secure voyage downriver to St. Louis.

James Ronda has weighed this version of the fight at Two Medicine River against later accounts transmitted by the Blackfeet survivors (Ronda 238–44).[23] The details of bloodshed do not differ, but the reasons for it do. Lewis's journal reveals many apprehensions that these Indians were hostile, that they were bent on theft if not murder, even before they could exchange signs. But in Ronda's understanding of this encounter, Lewis's approach frightened these people, and his explanations in camp that night deeply alarmed them.

Although what Lewis heard from the Piegans worried him, what he said frightened them. Explaining that he came from the East and had been beyond the mountains to the great ocean, Lewis unwittingly dropped a geopolitical bombshell by declaring that the Blackfeet's traditional enemies—the Nez Perces, Shoshones, and Kutenais—were now united by an American-inspired peace. Even more shocking to Piegan ears was word that these united tribes would be getting guns and supplies from Yankee traders. If Lewis thought the Blackfeet would receive such news with glad hearts and then join an American alliance, he gravely misjudged western realities. That night along the

Two Medicine the explorer, in effect, announced that the clash of empires had come to the Blackfeet. After more than twenty years of unchallenged power on the plains made possible by Canadian guns, the Blackfeet now faced a profound threat to their power and survival (Ronda 241).

The clash of empires had come, and there was no turning back. In fact, this clash had come twice within fifty years, played out by young soldiers and Indians in scenes thousands of miles apart. French forces had come into the Ohio Valley from Canada in the 1750s. Young George Washington was sent to meet and deter them and undo their evident trade and influence with the Mohawks. Before his first mission was over Indians had shot at him, and he dashed back to Virginia at breakneck speed. Now in 1806 British outposts had reached across the continent from Montreal to the Rockies. Young Meriwether Lewis was sent out to rival them, to establish claims to lands in high latitudes and draw away the trade of the plains Indians. Before his mission was over Indians had shot at him, too, and he galloped for a hundred miles to make his escape. And at this point the contest of empires had reached its final global extent. "I had come," Lewis told the Blackfeet, "a great way from the East up the large river which runs toward the rising sun, [and] I had been to the great waters where the sun sets and had seen a great many nations" (Thwaites 5:222).

Washington's military mission left even a literal echo of violence for Lewis to hear. The young militia officer has his famous line about French gunfire on the frontier: "I heard the bullets whistle and, believe me, there is something charming in the sound." Here is Lewis's record of a dying adversary's courage: "He fell to his knees and on his wright elbow from which position he partly raised himself up and fired at me, and turning himself about crawled in behind a rock which was a few feet from him. he overshot me, being bearheaded I felt the wind of his bullet very distinctly" (Thwaites 5:224–25).

Chapter 5   Ingesting America

To GET A feeling for the daily life of the Corps of Discovery, take note of what they were eating. Food is a constant preoccupation in the journals. Finding it, capturing or procuring it, preparing it, preserving it, sharing it, eating it, and, not least, coping with the results of eating it—these processes stand out prominently on page after page. These were the primary, essential tasks of daily survival. For the most part, these explorers lived off the land. They hunted, fished, and foraged, or they traded with local peoples. As a result, they took in the country they explored not only with their eyes and ears and intelligence but also with their guts and their wits. They sampled whatever grew in their immediate surroundings and learned to appreciate what others had discovered ahead of them to make food abundant, to make it more palatable, to make it portable, or to make it last.

It would be tedious to list all the plants, animals, and other substances that at some time or another got between the teeth of Lewis or Clark. The curious reader may prefer, anyhow, to discover these things in full detail throughout their writings. But it may be useful to sketch here the general outline of their experience. The course of their travels along the Missouri and Columbia rivers took them through three distinct regions of North America, all different from the eastern woodlands they had known. These were the flat, dry, and treeless Great Plains; the rugged, steep, and heavily timbered Rocky Mountains; and the cool, moist Northwest Coast. Each region stood apart with its distinctive climate and topography and hence its different species of plants and animals. The explorers had to move slowly upstream and uphill for most of their time on the trail. They also spent the winters stalled on the plains and on the coast. So they were forced to adjust their metabolisms to different foodstuffs while passing through different regions or dwelling at one spot through a change of seasons. And as a large party, expending lots of energy in traveling and working (or just keeping warm in winter), they were always faced with the risks of scarcity and malnutrition.

From the beginning, the commanders made sensible provision for the party. While he was still in Philadelphia in the spring of 1803, Lewis had a local cook prepare 193 pounds of "portable soup," probably according to a standard army recipe. It was packed in canisters to be carried across the continent and used many months later (*Letters* 1:81).[1] In addition, the men of this party were practiced hunters, and the packing lists included plenty of trade goods for barter with the Indians. In case of an encounter with trading vessels on the coast, Jefferson also provided an official letter of credit, asking the "Consuls, agents, merchants & citizens of any nation with which we have intercourse or amity to furnish you with those supplies which your necessities may call for, assuring them of honorable and prompt retribution" (*Letters* 1:106).

Once under way on the Missouri, the party was divided into five messes of soldiers and boatmen, and provisions were issued daily to each mess—varied combinations of meat and grain (*Journals* 2:254–55, 258). Yet problems about food began almost immediately. Lewis's accounts include an expenditure for 300 pounds of "Voyagers grease," which Donald Jackson explains as "lard, deer tallow, or bear fat used as a staple in the diet of French watermen" (*Letters* 2:424, 431n). And those hardworking boatmen not only ate different food, they also wanted more. "The French higherlins Complain for the want of Provisions, Saying they are accustomed to eat 5 & 6 times a day," Lewis noted on June 17, 1804, about a month after leaving St. Charles. The captains would hear no such complaints: "they are roughly rebuked for their presumption" (*Journals* 2:306).

Entries for the same date show that "the country about abounds in Bear Deer & Elk," and that the hunters were bringing in fresh meat, which was being "jerked" or cut in thin strips and dried (2:306). But the party was already experiencing boils and dysentery, probably the results of poor nutrition. Dr. E. G. Chuinard comments:

> The occurrence of boils and dysentery so early in the trip was a warning of the precarious balance between diet and infection that would plague the men throughout the journey. They were living mainly on a high protein diet, and the jerked meat probably was always contaminated

with bacteria. The meat jerked by themselves probably was cleaner than the meat and grease which they bought from the Indians and other traders. Knowledge of bacterial infection was a half-century in the future. They probably accepted their meat as being clean and edible unless it was crawling with maggots or so spoiled as to be repugnant to the nose as well as to the mouth. The lack of fresh fruit and vegetables also contributed to a lowered resistance to infection, as did the lack of frequent bathing and the wearing of soiled and unwashed clothing. Undoubtedly they developed considerable resistance to these bacterial infections, but not total immunity, as the future would show. They were to have repeated and occasionally almost fatal episodes of intestinal infection.[2]

Differences in dietary habits, rough practices in food preparation, and ignorance about sanitation all combined with sharp hunger to make food a danger and a point of constant concern from here on.

Fortunately, the route ahead was not merely a wilderness abounding in game and bacteria alone. Eons of biological adaptation had produced a variety of plants as well as animals. And centuries of human ingenuity had produced lore and practices for making the most of these resources. The Plains Indians had mastered an economy based on the hunting of buffalo. The Columbia River Indians had an economy based on salmon. Tribes in the mountains migrated between the buffalo plains and the salmon rivers and gathered plants on which they survived when game was scarce. And on the plains and the Far West coast, where the party wintered, there were Indian settlements that traded a variety of foodstuffs with other tribes.[3] After leaving Fort Mandan, where they were still within reach of white traders, the party had to learn as well as observe Indian ways. Their journals record elaborate lessons in the arts of being human, through feast and famine in a wholly new world.

The land of the buffalo proved as fascinating to Lewis and Clark as it ever has to any of their followers. Game was abundant on the plains, and it could be seen over long distances. Many an entry exclaims over a prospect of thousands of animals grazing peacefully under the sun. The hunters brought in deer, elk, antelope, buffalo, and occasionally squirrels, beaver, and other small animals. Catfish could be caught at any time. Joseph Fields killed the party's first buffalo on August 23, 1804; soon they were being hunted almost daily. And before the year was out fifteen members of the party had joined the

Mandans in a winter hunt and come back frostbitten and exhausted from a chase over snow up to ten inches deep. Still, they did see the Indians "Killing the Buffalows on horseback with arrows which they done with great dexterity" (*Journals* 3:254). Much later, Clark reported the Indian hunting methods in more detail (*Letters* 2:531).

The Mandans and the neighboring Hidatsas were settled in villages and grew crops through the summer months—corn, beans, tobacco, squash—which they exchanged with other tribes and European traders. They hunted when they could, but always with caution against other Plains Indians who claimed the buffalo ranges. Lewis and Clark were wintering at a place where international trade had been long established and where buffalo was, therefore, one of many available goods. René Jusseaume and Toussaint Charbonneau, traders who were there ahead of them, sometimes served as their interpreters. The Indians were glad to trade food for expert repairs to their guns and tools, as well as new-made battle-axes. Clark sums up that winter's "peculiar Situations as to provision &c. &c" in a few lines:

> We by the aide of our Black smiths precured Corn Sufficient for the party dureing the winter and about 70 or 90 bushels to Carry with us. we Soon found that no Dependance Could be put in the Information of our Interpreter Jessomme's Information respecting the Supplies of meat we were to recive of the Indians, and Sent out hunters and frequently went ourselves to hunt the Buffalow Elk & Deer, and precured a Sufficency dureing the winter—, also Skins for our mens Shoes— The Indians being without meat half the winter—fearfull of going out at any great Distance to hunt for fear of the Sioux who are Continually harrassing the mandans &c. We had at one period of the Winter Buffalow in great numbers near us the weather being excessively Cold we Could, we found it imprackable to precure at that tinme a Sufficiency of Meat without the riesque of friesing maney of our men, who frequently, were Slightly frosted. (*Journals* 3:486)

Nevertheless, they laid in food of sufficient variety that no one that winter suffered a nutritional disorder. And if, as seems likely, they stowed away pemmican—jerked buffalo, pounded and packed with tallow and wild fruit—they were also well prepared with a balanced diet for weeks ahead. It was at Fort Mandan, too, that they became involved with three further novel experiences of buffalo hunting and secured the services of Charbonneau, the guide and interpreter who was to prepare fresh buffalo in unforgettable style.

Two of the hunting experiences were religious, and James Ronda argues that the explorers did not fully understand them. One was the Indians' offering of smoke or food to buffalo heads to propitiate dead animals and prepare for the hunt. The other involved the active participation of some men in the party, who joined a sexual dance with young women. This ceremony was described briefly by Clark on January 5, and years later he dictated a more extensive description. But the best he could make of it was that husbands presented their wives to old men or white men "to cause the buffalow to Come near so that they may kill them" (*Journals* 3:268). It actually was meant to channel hunting prowess, by means of intercourse, from the old or the powerful to the women's husbands (Ronda 107, 131–32).

The third experience was observation of the Indians harvesting drowned buffalo from the frozen Missouri when it broke up in late March. "I observed extrodanary dexterity of the Indians in jumping from one Cake of ice to another, for the purpose of Catching the buffalo as they float down," Clark wrote on March 29; "maney of the Cakes of ice which they pass over are not two feet Square" (*Journals* 3:322). At the same time he noted that the Indians were setting the plains on fire "to induce the Buffalow to come near to them" (3:322). And it was probably during this winter that Lewis learned of the *pishkun* method of hunting buffalo by stationing a human decoy dressed in robes with a buffalo head at the edge of a cliff and then driving a herd toward him and over the precipice. The expedition never witnessed such a hunt, but Lewis described it in detail in his entry for May 29, when he came upon a pile of carcasses near a cliff (*Journals* 4:216–17, 221). (Modern studies conclude that this particular kill was more likely another result of spring drownings as herds crossed on thin ice.)[4]

The outstanding (and hence often quoted) experience with buffalo came later, however, when the party was on the trail again far from any group of Indians. The corps had hired Charbonneau as an interpreter, and he proved himself a superb culinary artist. He is chiefly remembered now as Sacagawea's husband—a rather inept trader in his mid-forties who somehow picked up a teenaged Indian wife. The journals often point to his bungling, especially in handling the white pirogue, and especially in contrast to his wife's quiet competence (4:29, 152, 157). Lewis's final line on him is an epitaph no one could envy: "a man of no peculiar merit."⁵ But no vexation appears in Lewis's entry for May 9, 1805, which must be quoted in full:

> I . . . killed one buffaloe which proved to be the best meat, it was in tolerable order; we saved the best of the meat, and from the cow I killed we saved the necessary materials for making what our wrighthand cook Charbono calls the *boudin blanc,* and immediately set him about preparing them for supper; this white pudding we all esteem one of the greatest delacies of the forrest, it may not be amiss therefore to give it a place. About 6 feet of the lower extremity of the large gut of the Buffaloe is the first mosel that the cook makes love to, this he holds fast at one end with the right hand, while with the forefinger and thumb of the left he gently compresses it, and discharges what he says *is not good to eat,* but of which in the squel we get a moderate portion; the mustle lying underneath the shoulder blade next to the back, and fillets are next saught, these are needed up very fine with a good portion of kidney suet; to this composition is then added a just proportion of pepper and salt and a small quantity of flour; thus far advanced, our skilfull opporater C—o seizes his recepticle, which has never once touched the water, for that would intirely distroy the regular order of the whole procedure; you will not forget that the side you now see is that covered with a good coat of fat provided the anamal be in good order; the operator sceizes the recepticle I say, and tying it fast at one end turns it inwards and begins now with repeated evolutions of the hand and arm, and a brisk motion of the finger and thumb to put in what he says is *bon pour manger;* thus by stuffing and compressing he soon distends the recepticle to the utmost limmits of it's power of expansion, and in the course of it's longtudinal progress it drives from the other end of the recepticle a much large portion of the [*blank*] than was previously discharged by the finger and thumb of the left hand in a former part of the operation; thus when the sides of the recepticle are skilfully exchanged the outer for the iner, and all is compleatly filled with something good to eat, it is tyed at the other end, but not any cut off, for that would make the pattern too scant; it is then baptised in the missouri with two dips and a flirt, and bobbed into the kettle; from whence after it be well boiled it is taken and fryed with bears oil untill it becomes brown, when it is ready to esswage the pangs of a keen appetite or such as travelers in the wilderness are seldom at a loss for. (4:130–31)

If Charbonneau "makes love to" his various morcels in these lines, Lewis also makes up to Charbonneau. And between them they transform the gross stuff of guts and their contents into playful dips, bobs, and flirts of good clean fun. The powers of buffalo and appetite make the hapless Charbonneau over into "our wrighthand cook" and "skil-full opporater," muttering half to himself in euphemisms as he promises and delivers something new and artful, to distend to their utmost limits the open receptacles of the hunters and the imaginations of hundreds of readers. And apparently this chef did it again and again. Lewis noted a pang of regret when the end came in sight. The Indians had predicted that the buffalo country would end at the Great Falls. When they got there, Lewis wrote that "this I much regret for I know when we leave buffaloe that we shal sometimes be under the necessity of fasting occasionally. and at all events the white puddings will be irretreivably lost and Sharbono out of imployment" (4:354).

"Fasting occasionally" turned out to be a terrible understatement. Through late June and early July men were assigned to dry meat while it was still available and to pack pemmican. But the Rockies lay ahead, where game was scarce, and beyond them would be a winter of damp cold with meager rations. A stark contrast to Charbonneau's leisurely preparations is Lewis's description of the Shoshones devouring a fresh-killed deer. These were hunters in the foothills, kept from the plains by fear of larger, fiercer tribes. Their near-starved condition in August was an omen of hard months ahead:

When they arrived where the deer was which was in view of me they dismounted and ran in tumbling over each other like a parcel of famished dogs each seizing and tearing away a part of the intestens which had been previously thrown out by Drewyer who killed it; the seen was such when I arrived that had I not have had a pretty keen appetite myself I am confident I should not have taisted any part of the venison shortly. each one had a peice of some discription and all eating most ravenously. some were eating the kidnies the melt and liver and the blood runing from the corners of their mouths, others were in a similar situation with the paunch and guts but the exuding substance in this case from their lips was of a different discription. one of the last who attacted my attention particularly had been fortunate in his allotment or reather active in the division, he had provided himself with about nine feet of the small guts one end of which he was chewing on while with his hands he was squezzing the contents out at the other. I really did not untill now think that human nature ever presented itself in a shape so nearly allyed to the brute creation. (5:103)

By September 12 Clark was noticing the bark peeled from Ponderosa pines, which the Indians "eate at certain Seasons of the year";

and he added a note of his own hunger: "our hunters Killed only one Pheasant this after noon" (5:201). Two days later the party killed a colt because there was no other meat. They were now across the Continental Divide, roughly following the Lochsa River across steep country with fallen timber. The men were working hard and needing food just when supplies ran low. September 18: "We dined & suped on a skant proportion of portable soup, a few canesters of which, a little bears oil and about 20 lbs. of candles form our stock of provision" (5:211). September 19: "Several of the men are unwell of the disentary. brakings out, or irruptions of the Skin, have also been common with us for some time" (5:215). At last, on September 20, Clark and six hunters reached the Weippe Prairie, where the Nez Perces gave them food: "a small piece of Buffalow meat, Some dried Salmon berries & roots in different States, some round and much like an onion which they call quamash the Bread or Cake is called Pashe-co Sweet, of this they make bread & Supe they also gave us the bread of this root all of which we eate hartily" (5:222). They were now in the great camas-root center of the Pacific Northwest, and they would be eating this staple food for months to come. But its first effects were awful. "I find myself verry unwell all the evening from eateing the fish & roots too freely"; and the next day: "I am verry sick today and puke which relive me" (5:223, 227).

Whether it was overeating, change of diet, or some organism in the food, the result was widespread. Almost everyone became sick and stayed sick for days, while dried fish and roots remained their main diet for lack of game. Still "unwell," the explorers nonetheless managed to fell trees, hollow out canoes, load them, and launch themselves on October 7, thus beginning an easier ride. They also began to buy dogs from Indians along the shore, though Clark could not bring himself to relish dog meat.

At the end of ten days they had floated into the Columbia, into salmon country. It was now fall and the salmon were rushing upriver to spawn, in numbers as countless as the buffalo had been on the plains. In his entry for October 17, Clark noted the abundance of salmon, the way the Indians prepared them, and some likely results of a fish diet. He had explored upstream on the Columbia and found an island where "two large Mat Lodges of Indians were drying Salmon, (as they informed me by Signs for the purpose of food and fuel, & I do not think it at all improbable that those people make use of

Dried fish as fuel[).] The number of dead Salmon on the Shores & floating in the river is incredible to Say and at this Season they have only to collect the fish Split them open and dry them on their Scaffolds" (5 : 287). Clark also noted that in the clear waters salmon could be seen to a depth of twenty feet. There were many other lodges along the river, where numbers of Indians who lived by salmon watched him and set out in canoes for a closer look. Clark took a closer look in return:

> One of those Mat lodges I entered found it crouded with men women and children and near the enterance of those houses I saw maney Squars engaged Splitting and drying Salmon. I was furnished with a mat to Sit on, and one man Set about prepareing me Something to eate, first he brought in a piece of a Drift log of pine and with a wedge of the elks horn, and a malet of Stone curioesly Carved he Split the log into Small pieces and lay'd it open on the fire on which he put round Stones, a woman handed him a basket of water and a large Salmon about half Dried, when the Stones were hot he put them into the basket of water with the fish which was Soon Sufficently boiled for use. it was then taken out put on a platter of rushes neetly made, and Set before me they boiled a Salmon for each of the men with me, dureing those preperations, I Smoked with those about me who Chose to Smoke which was but fiew, this being a custom those people are but little accustomed to and only Smok thro form. (5 : 288)

But this wonderful fresh food seemed to have its price, evident in the blind eyes and worn teeth of many Indians. "Those people as also those of the *flat heads* which we had passed on the Koskoske and Lewis's rivers are Subject to Sore eyes, and many are blind of one and Some of both eyes. this misfortune must be owing to the reflections of the Sun &c. on the waters in which they are continually fishing, during the Spring Summer & fall, & the Snows dureing the, winter Seasons, in this open country where the eye has no rest" (5 : 289). Modern science casts cold doubt on that explanation; Chuinard and Cutright trace the cause of blindness to diseases such as glaucoma, trachoma, and gonorrhea.[6] But Cutright (*LCPN* 224) agrees with Clark's further speculation: "I have observed amongst those, as well in all other tribes which I have passed on these waters who live on fish maney of different Sectes who have lost their teeth about middle age, Some have their teeth worn to the gums, perticelar those of the upper jaws, and the tribes generally have bad teeth   the cause of it I cannot account   sand attachd. to the roots &c the method they have of useing the dri'd Salmon, which is mearly worming [warming] it and eating the rine & Scales with the flesh of the fish, no doubt contributes to it" (*Journals* 5:289–90).

Within a few days the canoes were negotiating the falls of the Columbia through the Cascade range. The explorers were also negotiating, in a different sense, with sharp traders who lived along the banks. The explorers had found it hard to obtain salmon, though they could buy dogs for food from the Indians. At the Columbia Falls they reached a natural trading center of this region. Here was the dividing barrier between the coastal climate and the very different interior, and the narrows and falls of the river also formed a splendid trapping place for leaping salmon. (They remained a center of Indian fishery until they were flooded by high dams in the mid-twentieth century.) Clark observed "great numbers of Stacks of pounded Salmon neetly preserved" (5:323), and he described how the fish was dried, pounded between stones, and layered in tightly woven baskets: "Their common Custom is to Set 7 [baskets] as close as they can Stand and 5 on top of them, and secure them with mats which is raped around them and made fast with cords and Covered also with mats, those 12 baskets of from 90 to 100 w. each form a Stack. thus preserved those fish may be kept Sound and Sweet Several years, as those people inform me, Great quantities as they inform us are Sold to the whites people who visit the mouth of this river as well as to the nativs below" (5:323, 325). In short, the explorers were dealing with wholesale salmon packers who had large, well-developed markets, including other white traders. They were not about to exchange their valuable goods for trinkets.

Beyond this point, in the Columbia estuary, the Corps of Discovery would spend a long, wet winter. And for a number of reasons they had to be watchful in managing their supplies. For one, the party was large and never showed any particular liking for salmon or any other fish as a steady diet. When it came to making a campsite for several months, they established Fort Clatsop near the mouth of the Columbia, where the hunters could find elk and where a few men could be sent out to the coast to make salt from sea water. For another, their stock of trade goods was now low—and it would have to see them through the winter and the return trip. The local Indians were used to trading with European vessels; they asked high prices and did not bargain easily. Finally, mild rain meant rot. The men's leather clothing fell apart in the fog and drizzle of the Northwest marine climate; they turned elk and deer skins into new coverings and moccasins.

Their diet grew painfully lean. Until they killed their first elk on December 2, the party subsisted for many days on dried fish boiled in salt water. Many became ill. Clark was deeply grateful for a morsel of bread that Sacagawea shared with him, "it being the only mouthfull I had tasted for Several months past" (6:97). Hawks and ducks were prized as "fat and delicious." Once the fort was established, the elk still proved poor in quality and frequently hard to find. Hunters had to seek game farther from the fort and pack it back, and it often spoiled in the mild weather (*LCPN* 250–51). Lewis and Clark moved into their quarters on December 23, but Clark reported a miserable Christmas: "We would have Spent this day the nativity of Christ in feasting, had we any thing either to raise our Sperits or even gratify our appetites, our Diner concisted of pore Elk, So much Spoiled that we eate it thro' mear necessity, Some Spoiled pounded fish and a fiew roots" (*Journals* 6:138).

Every new berry and root became a welcome novelty thereafter, and the captains turned to making long journal entries about all the plants and animals in the region—as if they would digest every possible resource with their pens if not their stomachs. Again they were eating dog meat and learning to like it. "It is worthy of remark," Lewis wrote on January 3, "that while we lived principally on the flesh of this anamal we were much more healthy strong and more fleshey than we had been since we left the Buffaloe country. for my own part I have become so perfectly reconciled to the dog that I think it an agreeable food and would prefer it vastly to lean Venison or Elk" (6:162). Many men became sick during the winter and recovered slowly "in consequence of the want of a proper diet, which we have it not in our power to procure" (6:384). The captains were brought a dog for these convalescents on their last day at this fort.

As Lewis recorded these virtues of dog meat, he also noted another bountiful source of food that would soon lure the party right to the ocean. Some Indians who had brought for sale "some roots buries and three dogs" had also brought "a small quantity of fresh blubber" (6:162). Two days later Lewis learned that a whale had washed ashore many miles to the south. The salt makers sent some blubber to the fort, and Clark and a dozen men set out to get more—taking

Sacagawea, too, who insisted on seeing the Pacific at last after traveling so far across the continent. According to Lewis, the blubber "was white & not unlike the fat of Poark, tho' the texture was more spongey and somewhat coarser. I had a part of it cooked and found it very pallitable and tender, it resembled the beaver or the dog in flavour" (6:166).

Clark traveled over a rough trail across Tillamook Head and found that the whale was already picked clean. He recorded a skeleton 105 feet long—which implies either that Clark mismeasured or estimated, or that nature prodigiously threw up a blue whale, the largest living animal on earth, to meet the hunger of this party (*LCPN* 253; *Journals* 6:185n).[7] In any case, Clark found the local Indians handling the blubber:

> [They boiled it] in a large Squar wooden trought by means of hot Stones; the oil when extracted was Secured in bladders and the Guts of the whale; the blubber from which the oil was only partially extracted by this process, was laid by in their Cabins in large flickes for use; those flickes they usially expose to the fire on a wooden Spit untill it is prutty well wormed through and then eate it either alone or with roots of the rush, *Shaw na tâk we* or diped in the oil. The *Kil a mox* [Tillamooks] although they possessed large quantities of this blubber and oil were so prenurious that they disposed of it with great reluctiance and in Small quantities only; insomuch that my utmost exertion aided by the party with the Small Stock of merchindize I had taken with me were not able to precure more blubber than about 300 wt. and a fiew gallons of oil. (*Journals* 6:183)

Yet hunger made this load well worth the hard work of hauling it back to camp. It even provoked the meager joke mentioned in chapter 1, which remains a rare example of both levity and Bible reading at Fort Clatsop: "Small as this Stock is I prise it highly; and thank providence for directing the whale to us; and think him much more kind to us than he was to jonah, having Sent this monster to be *Swallowed by us* in Sted of *Swallowing of us* as jonah's did" (6:183–84).

Providence provided one final harvest from the sea in late February. Candlefish, a variety of smelt, began to run on the Cowlitz River, a tributary of the Columbia. The Columbia also yielded a few sturgeon. Lewis describes in his entry for March 4 how Indians smoked their candlefish and steamed fresh sturgeon (6:378). The oily, tender candlefish remain vivid in our memories of this expedition if only because they are sketched, life-size and handsome, across the journal pages where they are reported (Lewis for February 24, 1806; Clark for February 25). But they also seemed remarkably delicious to these very hungry writers. "We have th[r]ee days provision only in store and that of the most inferior dryed Elk a little tainted" (6:351). In comparison, these little fish were an effortless delicacy to Lewis:

> I find them best when cooked in Indian stile, which is by roasting a number of them together on a wooden spit without any previous prepe-ration whatever. they are so fat they require no additional sauce, and I think them superior to any fish I ever tasted, even more delicate and lussious than the white fish of the lakes [i.e., Great Lakes] which have heretofore formed my standart of excellence among the fishes. I have heard the fresh anchovey much extolled but I hope I shall be pardoned for beleiving this quite as good. the bones are so soft and fine that they form no obstruction in eating this fish. (6:344)

Is there a little ostentation here in the reference to the much-extolled European anchovy? Or is this passage just a tiny scale's breadth this side of destitution—with a writer who had recently feasted on whale now exclaiming with relief ("they are so fat . . . the bones are so soft") over fish not much bigger than his finger? If candlefish were something to write home about, how much better it would be to deliver the message in person—and get back into buffalo country on the way!

From a land of plenty on the plains to a land of starvation in the mountains, from the openhanded Nez Perces with their fields of camas bulbs to the close-trading salmon packers on the Columbia, from feasts of elk and whale to cherished tastes of a few fresh berries and candlefish—the Corps of Discovery learned to eat and appreciate.

In two important entries at Fort Clatsop in January, Lewis expati-ated on the meaning of hunger and of shared effort in meeting the needs of sheer subsistence. As he often does rewardingly, Lewis here pushes from the bare facts of a report into a few lines of penetrating second thoughts. They are not finished reflections, but they carry the force of hard-earned experiences freshly refracted through a keen mind.

The entry for January 5 describes the taste of whale blubber (a passage quoted earlier), then reports that "these lads" who brought it in from the coast also brought some good salt. Lewis's reflection turns on that essential mineral from the sea:

They brought with them a specemine of the salt of about a gallon, we found it excellent, fine, strong, & white; this was a great treat to myself and most of the party, having not had any since the 20th ultmo.; I say most of the party, for my friend Capt. Clark declares it to be a mear matter of indifference with him whether he uses it or not; for myself I must confess I felt a considerable inconvenience from the want of it; the want of bread I consider as trivial provided, I get fat meat, for as to the species of meat I am not very particular, the flesh of the dog the horse and the wolf, having from habit become equally formiliar with any other, and I have learned to think that if the chord be sufficiently strong, which binds the soul and boddy together, it dose not so much matter about the materials which compose it. (6:166–67)

Some of this same learned indifference is echoed, but with a different turn, a few weeks later in the entry for January 29: "Our fare is the flesh of lean elk boiled with pure water, and a little salt. the whale blubber which we have used very sparingly is now exhausted. on this food I do not feel strong, but enjoy the most perfect health;— a keen appetite supplys in a great degree the want of more luxurious sauses or dishes, and still render my ordinary meals not uninteresting to me, for I find myself sometimes enquiring of the cook whether dinner or breakfast is ready" (6:245). Lewis is neither ascetic nor particular about food. What he suggests is that he has come to know himself, to have a clear sense of the difference (for him) between necessity and luxury. There is a trace of amusement, too, in that understanding. He watches himself calling to the cook as hunger makes his food grow more interesting. And in a wonderful flash of boatman-woodman-frontiersman language he gives life and meaning to an old metaphor, as food becomes the hemp or rawhide "cord" that holds body and soul together. (It was by means of a cordelle, or "chord"—a heavy towrope made of elk skins—that the boats were often hauled upstream by men pulling through shallows or along the shore.) It seems almost worth the long struggle to get from Jefferson's parlor to a rough-hewn hut in the West, to be able to throw off this line the way Lewis does: "I have learned to think that if the chord be sufficiently strong, which binds the soul and boddy together, it dose not so much matter about the materials which compose it."

That is the wisdom of solitude. But the next day's entry reflects on social patterns in facing hunger. Clark's party had gone off to find the whale, and Lewis takes time this day to notice customs of the local

Clatsops, Chinooks, and Tillamooks, especially the way men and women share responsibility for providing food:

> In common with other savage nations they make their women perform every species of domestic drudgery. but in almost every species of this drudgery the men also participate. their women are also compelled to geather roots, and assist them in taking fish, which articles form much the greatest part of their subsistance; notwithstanding the survile manner in which they treat their women they pay much more rispect to their judgment and oppinions in many rispects than most indian nations; their women are permitted to speak freely before them, and sometimes appear to command with a tone of authority; they generally consult them in their traffic and act in conformity to their opinions. (6 : 168)

Again an observation grows into a provocative reflection. Lewis ventures to assert "as a general maxim that those nations treat thier old people and women with most difference [deference] and rispect where they subsist principally on such articles that these can participate with the men in obtaining them; and that, that part of the community are treated with least attention, when the act of procuring subsistence devolves intirely on the men in the vigor of life" (6 : 168– 69). Very clearly Lewis is here weighing the perceived life patterns of these Pacific fishing and root-gathering peoples along with the ways of Indians on the plains, where men were the hunters. He goes on to mention the Plains practice of abandoning the old and infirm:

> Among the Siouxs, Assinniboins and others on the Missouri who subsist by hunting it is a custom when a person of either sex becomes so old and infurm that they are unable to travel on foot from camp to camp as they rome in surch of subsistence, for the children or near relations of such person to leave them without compunction or remose; on those occasions they usually place within their reach a small peace of meat and a platter of water, telling the poor old superannuated wretch for his consolation, that he or she had lived long enough, that it was time they should dye and go to their relations who can afford to take care of them much better then they could. (6 : 169)

Lewis reports a more generous attitude among the Hidatsas and Arikaras, who were farmers as well as hunters. But it is also evident that he sees in these peoples a new reflection of his own social values—both here at Fort Clatsop and back in the "civilized" world to which his journal is addressed. The crucial evidence is a single sentence—another casual but penetrating remark—nestled between his formal maxim statement and his discussion of the hunters on the plains: "It appears to me that nature has been much more deficient in her filial tie than in any other of the strong affections of the human heart, and therefore think, our old men equally with our women indebted to civilization for their ease and comfort" (6:169). This is a complex sentence that can stand some close explication. By the filial tie, Lewis means the bond of affection of children toward their parents; he looks forward to his next remark about how the Plains Indians "without compunction" abandon a "poor old superannuated wretch." But by stressing this bond of society, Lewis tacitly lets go of the tensions he noticed earlier between men and women. The contrast is still between strong and weak, but young and old have now replaced male and female as the focus of attention—but for just a moment, because instantly Lewis brings both supposedly weaker groups together and claims that they are protected not by natural affection but by artificial conventions. "Our old men equally with our women"—old or young—are seen as "indebted to civilization for their ease and comfort" (as opposed to abandonment and starvation).

Perhaps this one extraordinary sentence should not be weighed too heavily. But it is hard not to be arrested by the suggestions in its language. Lewis evidently sees strong and weak separated by the way their societies provide subsistence—by which he here means food. He sees that different regions put different demands on their peoples and that societies answer them differently, with different social roles and values for men and women, old and young. Yet he has traveled through all these regions himself and shared many tasks with others. Is he merely repeating a commonplace male prejudice of his time? Is he a man gloating in the assertion that women owe their survival to the conditioned indulgence of naturally stronger but "civilized" men?

There is good reason to doubt that. In the first place, Lewis seems suspended here, needing to write out these newly perceived cultural variations, and he tries, at least, to compose a neutral maxim for determining who is strong or weak. His most value-laden phrases—"treat . . . people . . . with respect," "filial tie," "strong affections of the human heart"—all point to an implied criticism of the male-dominated Plains hunters. So does his remark on the hunter-farmers who are also reported to abandon their old: "In justice to these people I must observe that it appeared to me at their villages, that they provided tolerably well for their aged persons, and several of their feasts appear to have principally for their object a contribution for their aged and infirm persons" (6:169). Finally, this is the same Meriwether Lewis who a day earlier was reflecting on his own long hungers on this expedition, who had known privation in company with others and known relief with others as well, and in fact had often depended on better hunters for *his* survival. Not a week would pass before he would write of George Drouillard: "I scarcely know how we should subsist were it not for the exertions of this excellet hunter" (6:200). Earlier Lewis had known the "domestic drudgery" involved in preparing food as well as hunting it.[8] During the portage around the Great Falls of the Missouri he had established an advance camp and assigned himself the duty of cooking while others hauled canoes and baggage overland and worked on preparing his (unsuccessful) portable boat. For some days after June 26, 1805, he had to assign and supervise many tasks at once, but he took on the kitchen work willingly: "I collected my wood and water, boiled a large quantity of excellent dryed buffaloe meat and made each man a large suet dumpling by way of a treat" (4:333–34). Bearing this background in mind, I read Lewis's reflections on the strong, the weak, and the provision of subsistence as a genuine questioning of his own culture as well as others', another flash of learning on his part over the mystery of food as the cord binding body and soul.[9]

With the benefit of leisure to read these journals, we can see further fortuitous results of what the Corps of Discovery ate. By depending on the land for their provisions, they escaped many dangers of food that other explorers suffered then and later. They had their times of malnutrition, but no prolonged disorder like scurvy or other vitamin deficiencies of the kind that plagued seafarers on poor rations. They also escaped poisoning. Sir John Franklin's Arctic voyage in the 1840s (in further search for the Northwest Passage) came to a mysterious end: the ships were found years later in the ice, intact but empty. A recent study has pointed to lead poisoning from food containers as a possible cause of erratic behavior by crew members and consequent disaster.[10] The portable soup Lewis had prepared in Philadelphia traveled for months in thirty-two canisters. If those canisters were made of lead, as the gunpowder containers were, we can be very thankful that they were so few and that the soup was so awful it was tapped only as a last resort and abandoned in favor of horse meat or camas bulbs or any local alternative. The soup is mentioned as late as May 26, 1806, when it was given as a medicinal dose to a lame Nez Perce man. There is no mention of the party's consuming it then, even though at this time the captains were cutting the buttons off their coats to trade for roots.

By eating local foodstuffs the party also brought themselves into more open, direct contact with the land and its indigenous people. In a sense, this exploration was driven by the pursuit of luxury, just as countless earlier voyages had been set in motion to find gold or beaver pelts or tea or spices. Its principal aim was to open profitable new trade routes and claim land for America. But in its daily operations it had to find necessities, not luxuries, gather food and prepare it for three dozen hungry bellies, and make provision for coming days, if possible. In encounters with the Indians this need made the white- and black-skinned strangers comprehensibly human. Sharing food was an immediate and obvious way of establishing trust; sharing the hunt, sharing food preparation, paying attention to different food customs, exchanging recipes, and sharing lean times or feasts were all ways of deepening intimacy. At one point on the upper Columbia, Clark entered a mat lodge and found the people terrified: "They said we came from the clouds &c &c and were not men &c. &c." (*Journals* 5:305). In this case, the Indians were relieved by the arrival of Sacagawea and her baby. But such illusions could not last long, once the explorers showed that they became hungry, ate meat, got indigestion, hunted, fished, had pressing bodily needs, and relieved those needs just like everybody else.

Finally, to put it as delicately as possible, they passed through America as America was passing through them. These explorers went from coast to coast as no one had done before them, wintering in the woodlands, on the plains, and in the Far West and thus dwelling long enough to become acclimated to very different possibilities of land, weather, shelter, and subsistence. When they returned they brought samples and written records. They also brought flesh and blood—generated from buffalo and elk meat, salmon and whale, beaver tails and camas bulbs, corn, squash, berries, squirrel and prairie dog meat, and dozens of other, half-forgotten experiments with root, fruit, fish, flesh, and fowl. Their track left hardly a scratch on the long trail they followed, hardly a thing that was not biodegradable, as we now say. But the trail had become part of them. John Colter found it so satisfying that he would not return all the way. At the Mandan villages on the way home, he met two trappers headed west. They invited him to join them, and he did. And his plan must have appealed to many. Clark wrote, "We agreed to allow him the privilage provided no one of the party would ask or expect a Similar permission to which they all agreed" (Thwaites 5 : 341). If the captains had not been so forceful, the American West might have ingested other men.

Chapter 6 Signals of Friendship

FROM THE TIME they left the Mandan villages in April 1805 until just before they first touched the Continental Divide on August 12, the Corps of Discovery traveled alone, without directly meeting or seeing any new people. They found Indian camps and other signs from time to time, but they were wary of meeting a large party of armed hunters and relieved to make progress upstream without such a threat. Yet as they approached the Rockies they became anxious to find friendly Indians from whom they might learn what lay ahead and obtain horses for making the crossing from the Missouri to the Columbia. That first contact came on August 11, when Lewis spotted a young Shoshone man far ahead on horseback and tried to signal him to halt and come closer. All in vain. For here, far up the Missouri where no white-skinned explorers had ever come, Lewis and his party had no adequate words or gestures for completely foreign human beings. This first Indian fled, and the next encounters, two days later, also began very poorly. The expedition eventually succeeded in developing friendly relations with the Shoshones, gaining information they needed, acquiring sufficient horses, and even securing a guide across the mountains. It turned out that Cameahwait, the chief of these people, was related to Sacagawea, who was here reunited with her people many years after her abduction. But in its first stages this incident was an encounter between people wholly alien to each other. It called up unforeseen resources in Lewis's mind and temperament as he struggled to make himself understood and trusted, both immediately and in anticipation of the approach of his armed and sometimes clumsy followers.

Making gestures across a barrier of language was not new to Lewis or Clark. Much earlier in their excursion they had become practiced at communicating and even securing some firm understandings with people who spoke words they could not make out and who practiced very puzzling customs. James P. Ronda's perceptive study *Lewis and Clark among the Indians* discusses many of their methods in detail. The explorers could rely on interpreters, but they also had to trust their own judgment and intuition in exchanging meaningful gestures. French, British, and Spanish predecessors in the Upper Missouri region had learned and developed many practices well understood on both sides: smoking a common pipe; presenting medals, certificates, and other showy symbolic items to powerful chiefs; distributing food, tobacco, and trinkets to whole tribes; making a show of firepower; exchanging feasts and speeches. Lewis and Clark became adept at these procedures as they worked their way to the outer reaches of previous trade, safely passed through a confrontation with the demanding Teton Sioux, and wintered peacefully near Hidatsa and Mandan villages.

Yet as Ronda points out, they could not help blundering, and sometimes they escaped the consequences of their ignorance through sheer blind luck—or the patience and better prudence of the tribes they met (149–50). They came without knowing any Indian languages, and they could not master any in the time they had. They were puzzled or offended by some customs (such as offers of women as bedfellows). And they never fully saw the intricacies of intertribal warfare, alliance, and trade on which their attempted diplomacy would depend. They saw and recorded present appearances very sharply, but as they kept moving they could not see into much history or into extensive networks of economic and geographical interdependence. And they had their own crude assurance as American officers sent west by Jefferson himself. They sometimes supposed that their arrival and speeches made lasting impressions and had significant effect, when to the ears of their beholders they were incomprehensible, confused, or fleetingly entertaining.

In the long view their chief assets may well have been qualities in their personal dispositions, which strangers could read apart from their words and conventional actions. Between them, Lewis and Clark shared reserves of three such gifts: good will, unwavering authority, and willingness to learn.

These officers had everything to lose by making a critical offense against any Indians. Jefferson had explicitly instructed them to avoid trouble. "In all your intercourse with the natives," he began his in-

structions on this point, "treat them in the most friendly & concilia-
tory manner which their conduct will admit; allay all jealousies as to
the object of your journey, satisfy them of it's innocence, make them
acquainted with the position, extent, character, peaceable & commercial dispositions of the U.S.[,] of our wish to be neighborly,
friendly & useful to them" (*Letters* 1:64). Jefferson encouraged the
captains to invite chiefs to come to Washington at public expense. He
authorized them to promise education to their young people. He
asked them to introduce inoculation against smallpox. And in a further paragraph he cautioned against any risk of life through hostility:
"We wish you to err on the side of your safety, and to bring back your
party safe even if it be with less information" (1:64). The clear message was to develop and enlarge friendly relations wherever possible.
And there was a measure of truth to the idea mentioned here that the
object of the expedition was "innocent," even though its primary purpose was imperial exploration. There was no immediate gain the
party could take. They did not come to settle or to establish any ventures for their own profit, nor could they envision others coming in
large numbers in the future. The Upper Missouri region seemed destined to remain under Indian domination for decades, if not centuries.
These intruders did come mainly for "information."

Besides, it ran against the grain for either of these captains to be
inflictive. It was characteristic of Clark to like Indians and be helpful
to them. The trust he developed among them led them to bring him
their sick at Fort Mandan and at the Long Camp on the western
slopes of the Rockies, and later to bring him their troubles during his
decades as superintendent of Indian affairs in St. Louis. Lewis was
probably more reserved. But he too had generous impulses, as when
he found Shoshone hunters unwilling to share meat with all their
people and immediately ordered three of his own hunters' deer distributed among the destitute (*Journals* 5:149).

There were a few times when the explorers felt forced to take things
from Indians, but these were recorded with a sense of wrong. "We
have made it a point at all times not to take any thing belonging to
the Indians," Clark wrote on October 14, 1805, on the upper Columbia. But one of the canoes had overturned on a rock late that day,
spilling its clothing, bedding, and food into the water—all as the sun
was going down. On a nearby island there was split timber to be
found, "the parts of a house which the Indians had verry Securely

covered with Stone" (5:272). No Indians were there; there was no
telling how long the timber had been left there; but it still seemed a
violation to take even part of it. "But at this time we are Compelled
to violate that rule and take a part of the Split timber we find here
bured for fire wood, as no other is to be found in any direction"
(5:272). There was apparently less compunction about taking a large
canoe from a friendly tribe near Fort Clatsop when the party had to
pack up again and head upstream in 1806. The captains again
pleaded necessity (no more could be got by trade; the trade goods
were almost exhausted anyhow), and they trumped up a hollow ex-
cuse and imputed it to others: "We yet want another Canoe as the
Clatsops will not Sell us one, a proposition has been made by one of
our interpt and Sever[al] of the party to take one in lieu of 6 Elk which
they Stole from us this winter &c." (6:428). This act of theft was
aggravated because the canoe was hidden nearby while the chief of
the tribe came for a farewell visit and received professions of friendship. But the notable fact is that this idea was recorded at all—and in
such transparent terms of bad conscience.

Good will was thus tempered by necessity. It was also conditioned
by these officers' sense of duty. They had a primary task to perform
and would not let hollow threats or passing sympathies deter them.
They stood firm when Teton Sioux seemed determined to block their
way. Lewis and Clark kept moving instead of giving in to moving
pleas from the Indians or the offer of personal favors. A more positive
way of stating the point is that they evidently kept their word. They
did not flinch from directness. They said no and meant no. They also
made promises and fulfilled them. They had a sense of ongoing purpose and direction that was evident in their behavior. It seems altogether credible, too, that they believed in the language they repeated
to Indians at conferences and councils along the Missouri. "Children," they addressed the people they met:

> Commissioned and sent by the great Chief of the Seventeen great
> nations of America, we have come to inform you, as we go also to
> inform all the nations of red men who inhabit the borders of the Mis-
> souri, that a great council was lately held between this great chief of the
> Seventeen great nations of America, and your old fathers the french and
> Spaniards; and that in this great council it was agreed that all the white
> men of Louisiana, inhabiting the waters of the Missouri and Mississippi
> should obey the commands of this great chief; he has accordingly

adopted them as his children and they now form one common family with us: your old traders are of this description; they are no longer the subjects of France or Spain, but have become the Citizens of the Seventeen great nations of america, and are bound to obey the commands of their great Chief the President who is now your only great father. (*Letters* 1:204)

This language is embarrassingly paternalistic to modern ears. But to Lewis and Clark themselves Jefferson was the great patron, if not the father. They were conditioned to see Indians as simpler beings, childlike at best and at worst.

Lewis gave the most sustained expression to doubt and distrust about Indians in the dark, dank days of the Oregon winter. After a visit from a friendly chief and twenty-five men, he wrote:

> In the evening at sunset we desired them to depart as is our custom and closed our gates. we never suffer parties of such number to remain within the fort all night; for notwithstanding their apparent friendly disposition, their great averice and hope of plunder might induce them to be treacherous. at all events we determined allways to be on our guard as much as the nature of our situation will permit us, and never place our selves at the mercy of any savages. we well know, that the treachery of the aborigenes of America and the too great confidence of our countrymen in their sincerity and friendship, has caused the distruction of many hundreds of us. so long have our men been accustomed to a friendly intercourse with the natives, that we find it difficult to impress on their minds the necessity of always being on their guard with rispect to them. this confidence on our part, we know to be the effect of a series of uninterupted friendly intercouse, but the well known treachery of the natives by no means entitle them to such confidence, and we must check it's growth in our own minds, as well as those of our men, by recollecting ourselves, and repeating to our men, that our preservation depends on never loosing sight of this trait in their character, and being always prepared to meet it in whatever shape it may present itself. (*Journals* 6:330–31)

Ronda criticizes this passage for its "phrases reminiscent of Puritan fears of the howling wilderness and savage devils." He calls it one of the low points of the expedition and tries to explain it as an isolated outburst of loneliness at this extreme distance away from home (211–12). On the other hand, Reuben Gold Thwaites notes this same passage as a sign of healthy caution. He contrasts it with the freedom that officers of the ship *Tonquin* allowed to Chinook Indians a few years later, which resulted in their deaths and the ship's destruction (4:90n).[1] But this passage contains its own peculiar balance of feelings. It bears witness to a general feeling of confidence and friendly intercourse between the party and these Indians, a mood so deeply entrenched that Lewis has to shake himself to resume a martial discipline. These words record the events of February 20, 1806—late in the winter at Fort Clatsop and just a month before the party began its return. It was not too early for Lewis to begin remembering some dangerous encounters on the way west and anticipating some steps for "recollecting ourselves" before breaking camp. As a foresighted commander, Lewis had to think this way in order to bring his party upstream again with few trade goods and again cross the plains without risking a senseless incident.

A final asset that opened genuine friendship between Lewis and Clark and many Indians was that the explorers' ultimate mission was to learn. They came bearing arms, to be sure, and goods and wonders and a message from the great chief of the seventeen nations. But they also arrived evidently needing help—needing advice for daily subsistence and counsel for further travel. And they soon became conspicuously observant and inquisitive about everything. They must have asked and asked again, if only to get the words repeated that they had to copy into their vocabulary lists. They thus came predisposed to respect the greater knowledge of the new people they met and to profit from their example. They did not come with any urge to change the Indians' customary lives or save their souls. Rather, they needed the Indians' information to make sense of where they were as well as to obtain some account of lands, rivers, plants, and animals that lay beyond their direct observation. Jefferson had sent them to explore, record new information fully and carefully, and return with it safely. This could be done only if the Indians cooperated—spoke openly, revealed their practices freely, and came along as guides.

These three qualities of the party's aims and temperament—good will, firm authority, and willingness to learn—took a little time to unfold. Before they could appear, some initial contact had to be made; some crucial first impressions had to be exchanged. There had to be a beginning point in language. Indians of the Far West, of course, spoke unknown languages and knew little or no English. So the explorers prepared beforehand and brought interpreters. These included George Drouillard, the expert hunter, who was half-Shawnee and skilled at Indian sign language; Toussaint Charbonneau, the French trader who had lived for many years among Indians of the Upper Missouri; and his wife Sacagawea, who was brought specifically to open relations with her original people, the Shoshones.

At one point, these arrangements were stretched to an almost comic extent. Clark wrote that when the party met some Salish Indians on their passage through the Rockies, "what we Said had to pass through Several languajes before it got in to theirs" (*Journals* 5 : 188). Clark later explained that he spoke English to Private François Labiche, who spoke French to Charbonneau, who spoke Hidatsa to Sacagawea, who spoke her native language to a Shoshone boy held captive by the Salish, and he in turn spoke to the Salish (*Letters* 2 : 519). But as Lewis noted a few days later, the party's Shoshone guide, Old Toby, "could not speake the language of these people but soon engaged them in conversations by signs or jesticulation, the common language of all the Aborigines of North America." Lewis goes on with a doubtful confidence: "It . . . is understood by all of them and appears to be sufficiently copious to convey with a degree of certainty the outlines of what they wish to communicate" (*Journals* 5 : 196–97). We can ponder that sentence and what it seems to say with three further considerations. It speaks of "outlines" conveyed with a vague "degree of certainty." This supposedly universal language was being carried on by Old Toby alone, with no hint of confirmation (or capacity) on the part of Drouillard. And the Salish language seemed so extremely different—in Clark's words, "a gugling kind of languaje, Spoken much thro the Throught" (5 : 188)—that Sergeant Ordway's journal notes a thorough bewilderment. There had been a longstanding legend that some far western Indians were descendants of long lost Welshmen from a time before Columbus, or even lost tribes of Israel. Ordway reported a "bur" on their tongues and says of these mountain people: "We supposed that they are the welch Indians if their is any such from the language" (Ronda 156; *Journals* 5 : 189n).[2] For all Lewis and Clark knew for certain, Old Toby and the Salish could have been exchanging sly remarks about the explorers—or tolerantly confusing one another.

In meeting the Shoshone horseman for the first time, Lewis did not even have such doubtful support. He had to make himself understood, suddenly and immediately, to a stranger who was distant, aloof, and beyond any common spoken language. To comprehend that moment of encounter we must turn to it now in detail and closely follow its gestures and their failures.

Before the lone Indian appeared on August 11, Lewis had ordered the three men with him to spread out and had arranged a signal for their communication. Drouillard was sent to the right, Shields to the left, "with orders to surch for the road which if they found they were to notify me by placing a hat on the muzzle of their gun" (5:68). In other words, these four explorers remained within sight of each other, though far enough apart that they could not be heard, or should not be heard if they hoped to make contact with the Indians. In these circumstances the Indian came into view, and Lewis approached him cautiously and tried a signal he believed was universal:

> I kept McNeal with me; after having marched in this order for about five miles I discovered an Indian on horse back about two miles distant coming down the plain toward us. with my glass I discovered from his dress that he was of a different nation from any that we had yet seen, and was satisfyed of his being a Sosone; his arms were a bow and quiver of arrows, and was mounted on an eligant horse without a saddle, and a small string which was attatched to the underjaw of the horse which answered as a bridle. I was overjoyed at the sight of this stranger and had no doubt of obtaining a friendly introduction to his nation provided I could get near enough to him to convince him of our being whitemen. I therefore proceeded towards him at my usual pace. when I had arrived within about a mile he mad a halt which I did also and unloosing my blanket from my pack, I mad him the signal of friendship known to the Indians of the Rocky mountains and those of the Missouri, which is by holding the mantle or robe in your hands at two corners and then throwing up in the air higher than the head bringing it to the earth as if in the act of spreading it, thus repeating three times. this signal of the robe has arrisen from a custom among all those nations of spreading a robe or skin for ther gests to set on when they are visited. (5:68–69)

We should note several touches in just this brief beginning. Lewis takes in details over a distance that required a telescope, and he sees a man different from any he has seen before. He approaches, he says, with excited confidence that he can make friendly contact. Yet he also sends a message of unexcited steadiness: "I therefore proceeded towards him at my usual pace." And instead of displaying somehow that he is different—friendly, as he says, because of being a white man—Lewis works to match the stranger before him. The Indian makes a halt. Lewis makes a halt. The Indian waits. Lewis takes out a blanket to make a signal in the language of Indians. And, seeking welcome himself, Lewis sends a signal that, to his understanding, means that he offers friendship and welcome to this other. The signal seems to have been accurately remembered; it is described in similar terms in two later handbooks of Indian sign language. But those later accounts explain it rather differently. To W. P. Clark, the blanket signal was a sort of question mark, and a gesture that left the blanket spread on the ground expressed the idea of "a weaker party, having had enough, and for any party of laying down hostilities"; it was a call for an armistice.[3] To another observer, it was the signal of hospitality, meaning, "Come and sit down and we'll talk things over."[4] This signal, in short, was not as obvious in its meaning as Lewis supposed. And the captain was not a practiced signaler either.

"This signal had not the desired effect," the account goes on, perhaps because a competing signal was catching the Indian's attention. "He still kept his position and seemed to view Drewyer an Shields who were now comiming in sight on either hand with an air of suspicion, I wold willingly have made them halt but they were too far distant to hear me and I feared to make any signal to them least it should increase the suspicion in the mind of the Indian of our having some unfriendly design upon him" (5:69). Lewis's account expresses a rapid reading of moods across space. Did the Indian "view Drewyer and Shields . . . with an air of suspicion?" Or did they now come in sight with an air of suspicion? The likelihood is that both sides were apprehensive, and Lewis acutely perceives the Indian's cause for alarm as he was outnumbered and being approached from three angles. Lewis does not remark that Drouillard was also attempting to signal the Indian on his part, but that is another possibility that could have increased the confusion. What the Indian might also have perceived was tension and frustration in Lewis's behavior as he restrained himself from natural communication with his own men.

Lewis had to act quickly, but his immediate gestures were again misguided and were turned awry by his companions. He tried to hold out gifts, to show himself disarmed, to display himself, and to call out that he was a white man. But every one of these moves was ineffectual and probably inept. The passage as a whole seems to show a curious, patient horseman doing his best to attend to mangled gestures and finally giving up and making a prudent retreat:

> I therefore haistened to take out of my sack some b[e]ads a looking glas and a few trinkets which I had brought with me for this purpose and leaving my gun and pouch with McNeal advanced unarmed towards him. he remained in the same stedfast poisture untill I arrived in about 200 paces of him when he turn his ho[r]se about and began to move off slowly from me; I now called to him in as loud a voice as I could command repeating the word *tab-ba-bone,* which in their language signifyes *white man.* but loking over his sholder he still kept his eye on Drewyer and Sheilds who wer still advancing neither of them haveing segacity enough to recollect the impropriety of advancing when they saw me thus in parley with the Indian. I now made a signal to these men to halt, Drewyer obeyed but Shields who afterwards told me that he did not observe the signal still kept on the Indian halted again and turned his hor[s]e about as if to wait for me, and I beleive he would have remained untill I came up whith him had it not been for Shields who still pressed forward. whe I arrived within about 150 paces I again repepeated the word tab-ba-bone and held up the trinkits in my hands and striped up my shirt sleve to give him an opportunity of seeing the colour of my skin and advanced leasure towards him but he did not remain untill I got nearer than about 100 paces when he suddonly turned his hose about, gave him the whip leaped the creek and disapeared in the willow brush in an instant. (5 : 69−70)

Were beads and trinkets a proper offering to a man "mounted on an eligant horse"? Was leaving pouch and gun behind a meaningful gesture if they were merely handed over to another marksman—and two others remained visibly armed nearby? Certainly Lewis's shouts that he was a white man did no good. The Shoshones had either had no experience with white men at all or had no particular reason to be favorably impressed. And modern conjectures about what Lewis shouted indicate that *ta ba bone* did not exactly mean that he was white. Maybe it was a meaningless phrase. Maybe it meant "stranger." Maybe it derived from a phrase meaning "one originating from the sun" or from the east (5 : 72n). John Rees, who lived among the Shoshones in the late nineteenth century, guessed that Lewis was actually shouting, "Look at the sun," which might explain why the horseman looked over his shoulder while still keeping an eye on these men.[5] Whatever these words meant, Lewis could easily have mispronounced them. And by repeating them while shaking trinkets and rolling up his sleeves, he might well have signaled something offensive or frightening or so exasperatingly absurd that the horseman could put no more trust in any communication and rode off.

In his recollections for the day Lewis expressed his exasperation mildly: "I now felt quite as much mortification and disappointment as I had pleasure and expectation at the first sight of this indian. I fet soarly chargrined at the conduct of the men particularly Sheilds to whom I principally attributed this failure in obtaining an introduction to the natives. I now called the men to me and could not forbare abraiding them a little for their want of attention and imprudence on this occasion" (5:70). We can bet that he was loud and very inelegant in what he said on the spot. For with the disappearance of this Indian went the aim of this whole day and of weeks leading up to it. "With him vanished all my hopes of obtaining horses for the preasent" (5:70). The frustration must have been extreme. Here were four men on foot, near the final, trickling headwaters of the Missouri, where canoes could no longer serve. There was a sole Indian mastering a fine horse with just a string and no saddle. And yet despite every ingenious and energetic offer, horse and horsemen were gone in an instant, leaving just a flick of tail in the face of a civilized officer and white man.

Lewis, however, does not turn any of the blame for this loss onto himself, and later in the day we find him rigging up new gestures just as futile. When he stopped to cook breakfast, he noticed nearby hills and calculated that the Indians might see their approach from a distance and run off. "During this leasure I prepared a small assortment of trinkits consisting of some mockkerson awls a few strans of several kinds of b[e]ads some paint a looking glass &c which I attatched to the end of a pole and planted it near our fire in order that should the Indians return in surch of us the[y] might from this token discover that we were friendly and white persons." And for the rest of the day he carried a signal of his own identity. "After meeting with the Indian today I fixed a small flag of the U' S. to a pole which I made McNeal carry. and planted in the ground where we halted or encamped" (5:70, 71).

The next day this party of four set out again, searched carefully, and came upon some evidence of a small Indian camp. They went on to reach the last source of the Missouri and cross over to a creek that ran toward the Columbia—but sighted no Indians at all. It was a day later, and further into the valley of what is now the Lemhi River, that they again tried and failed to make contact, this time with three people and some dogs. Lewis tried all his previous signals and invented a new one but could not succeed even with the dogs:

> We had proceeded about four miles through a wavy plain parallel to the valley or river bottom when at the distance of about a mile we saw two women, a man and some dogs on an eminence immediately before us. they appeared to vew us with attention and two of them after a few minutes set down as if to wait our arrival we continued our usual pace towards them. when we had arrived within half a mile of them I directed the party to halt and leaving my pack and rifle I took the flag which I unfurled and avanced singly towards them the women soon disappeared behind the hill, the man continued untill I arrived within a hundred yards of him and then likewise absconded. tho' I frequently repeated the word *tab-ba-bone* sufficiently loud for him to have heard it. I now haistened to the top of the hill where they had stood but could see nothing of them. the dogs were less shye than their masters they came about me pretty close   I therefore thought of tying a handkerchief about one of their necks with some beads and other trinkets and then let them loose to surch their fugitive owners thinking by this means to convince them of our pacific disposition towards them but the dogs would not suffer me to take hold of them; they also soon disappeared. I now made a signal for the men to come on, they joined me and we pursued the back tarck of these Indians which lead us along the same road which we had been traveling. (5:77)

Then suddenly, about a mile farther along this road, the party surprised three women at close range and frightened two of them into submission. This encounter is notable for two important reasons. The first is that it takes place not only between white explorers and Indians but also between a band of armed men and three frightened women. It thus recalls the abduction of Sacagawea and two other girls from this same tribe many years earlier when she was still a child or a very young teenager.

> We had not continued our rout more than a mile when we were so fortunate as to meet with three female savages. the short and steep ravines which we passed concealed us from each other untill we arrived within 30 paces. a young woman immediately took to flight, an Elderly woman and a girl of about 12 years old remained. I instantly laid by my gun and advanced towards them. they appeared much allarmed but saw that we were to near for them to escape by flight they therefore

seated themselves on the ground, holding down their heads as if reconciled to die which the expected no doubt would be their fate. (5:78)

These women signal very effectively, to Lewis's perception, though he does not take in that by their postures they also seem to conceal their faces and sexual organs—to turn themselves into expressionless objects and so retain some measure of composure or inner privacy in the event of being overmastered.

The second crucial point is that to communicate effectively Lewis has to make physical contact. He does it twice, to the hand of the older woman and to the faces of all three, before he can assure them that he recognizes their customs and means them no harm:

> I took the elderly woman by the hand and raised her up repeated the word *tab-ba-bone* and strip up my shirt sleve to sew her my skin; to prove to her the truth of the ascertion that I was a white man for my face and hads which have been constantly exposed to the sun were quite as dark as their own. they appeared instantly reconciled, and the men coming up I gave these women some beads a few mockerson awls some pewter looking-glasses and a little paint. I directed Drewyer to request the old woman to recall the young woman who had run off to some distance by this time fearing she might allarm the camp before we approached and might so exasperate the natives that they would perhaps attack us without enquiring who we were. the old woman did as she was requested and the fugitive soon returned almost out of breath. I bestoed an equvolent portion of trinket on her with the others. I now painted their tawny cheeks with some vermillion which with this nation is emblematic of peace. after they had become composed I informed them by signs that I wished them to conduct us to their camp that we wer anxious to become acquainted with the chiefs and warriors of their nation. they readily obeyed and we set out, still pursuing the road down the river. (5:78–79)

Direct touch may have been the key that mattered most. Two miles farther along that road, Lewis and his men at last meet sixty warriors on horseback and, once the women have interceded, find themselves clasped to the chests of these men. Lewis is again almost comical in his official opening gesture. "When they arrived I advanced towards them with the flag," he writes, "leaving my gun with the party about 50 paces behind me" (5:79). But the chief and his men are much more direct and forthcoming:

The chief and two others who were a little in advance of the main body spoke to the women, and they informed them who we were and exult-ingly shewed the presents which had been given them   these men then advanced and embraced me very affectionately in their way which is by puting their left arm over you wright sholder clasping your back, while they apply their left cheek to yours and frequently vociferate the word *âh-hi'-e, âh-hi'-e* that is, I am much pleased, I am much rejoiced. bothe parties now advanced and we wer all carresed and besmeared with their grease and paint till I was heartily tired of the national hug. (5:79)

Lewis is evidently embarrassed to record this messiness in a civi-lized journal. But is he thrown more off balance by the grease or by the caress? He seems to try to shrug it off here as an alien peculiarity, a wearisome "national hug." He goes on trying to offer more accus-tomed gestures. He has a pipe lit and offers a smoke. But the Indians sit down in a circle first and take off their moccasins. Lewis cannot take this as mere nakedness, trust in being at ease and leisure, or simple comfort. He has to interpose a reason for such exposure. "This is a custom among them as I afterwards learned indicative of a sacred obligation of sincerity in their profession of friendship given by the act of receiving and smoking the pipe of a stranger. or which is as much as to say that they wish they may always go bearfoot if they are not sincere; a pretty heavy penalty if they are to march through the plains of their country" (5:79).

This day's narrative goes on with an evident tension over such points. There are exchanges of gifts, speeches (in sign, presumably), and more smokes. But Lewis is evidently most comfortable when the Indians are fully on their feet again and he can hold them at the dis-tance of a symbolic gesture. "They now put on their mockersons, and the principal chief Ca-me-âh-wait made a short speach to the war-riors. I gave him the flag which I informed him was an emblem of peace among whitemen and now that it had been received by him it was to be respected as the bond of union between us" (5:79–80). Just as evidently, the Indians want relaxed, leisurely contact. On the march to their camp, they soon drop the formal order of march with which the warriors came out in fear of their enemies, and once they have their guests in a lodge and have brought out pipe and tobacco, "we were requested to take of our mockersons, the Chief having pre-viously taken off his as well as all the warriors present" (5:80). Lewis wants information, wants symbolic gestures, wants a pact of peace. Cameahwait seems to want time together, warm contact, shoes off in a lodge, without haste for anything definite to be done. This little struggle goes on through a couple of pauses for meager eating (including the first bit of salmon Lewis has seen), through the evening, past midnight. Lewis finally gives up and leaves his men dancing with the Indians "nearly all night" (5:83).

Lewis should not be faulted, I think, for keeping up his formal edge, any more than Cameahwait should be dismissed for his very different manners. Both of them are deeply conditioned to see things so very differently that it is wonderful they communicate as well as they do. Lewis, after all, is what he is: a very literate army officer. He has his daily responsibility to keep records and thus stay in touch with Jefferson and the world of science. By this time he has grown accustomed to thinking in elaborate terms and relating every experience to a larger and larger compendium of information. In effect, every day for him is another balancing act in which he advances a few more miles between the Atlantic and the Pacific while juggling unforeseen exigencies of geography, climate, diplomacy, and subsistence into entirely new patterns in the back of his mind. While making contact with these Shoshones, he is naggingly aware that he has to pick their brains for information about the way across the mountains; trade with them trustingly to obtain guides and horses without delay; and prepare them for the arrival of Clark and the main party within a few days. These considerations, in fact, may have obliterated some of what Lewis actually did and felt in the moment when he had these first encounters. His journal entries as we now have them are later recollections, carefully rewritten to make a full record.

Cameahwait, meanwhile, can more easily choose to be barefoot with his guests. He is, after all, surrounded by his own people in a valley he has known all his life. He has no journals to keep, no pressing drive to get on to the coast before winter. Instead, his hungry tribe is eager to get into the plains for buffalo but is still suffering from a recent attack by Plains Indians.

Besides, these people not only speak in a different vocabulary but think in different terms. John E. Rees claims that the Shoshone language was much more fluid, especially about personal names. He agrees with other observers that their names referred to a significant moment in the bearer's life and could change with circumstances.

The spirit which actuated the event that selected his name was propitious; to a Shoshoni, the particular designation, together with his physical body—the recipient of that name—were most secret things. To tell that name, or to have that body photographed, was to lose part of his nature which he would miss in the hereafter. When asked to give his name, he is unwilling to do so, but an Indian with him may give it; yet if there is a way of evading the matter, the Indian with him will not give the true name, but will make up a name from something that may occur to him at that particular moment. (Shoshoni place names are invented similarly on the spur of the moment.) Thus the name *Cameahwait* ["he does not walk"] was chosen to fit the occasion when Lewis was trying to get the band to accompany him back to the main expedition; Cameahwait's real name, *Too-ite-coon*, ["fires a black gun"] was concealed; and on another day and under other circumstances, Too-ite-coon might have been called almost anything else.[6]

Lewis made a similar note concerning Shoshone names after learning both of the chief's names on better acquaintance. "The people have many names in the course of their lives, particularly if they become distinguished characters. for it seems that every important event by which they happen to distinguish themselves intitles them to claim another name which is generally scelected by themselves and confirmed by the nation" (*Journals* 5 : 159). If names of people and places were so secret and sacred, subject to variation and disguise, it does not seem far-fetched to suppose that direct touch was an important way for the Shoshones to become acquainted with strangers. A seeming waste of time over pipe ceremonies, close contact around a circle, all-night dancing, and a shared antelope hunt the next day could have been a very sensible exercise in diplomacy—much more sensible than taking a flag as a "bond of union" (whatever that meant) or an "emblem of peace" from a man who seemed to want to talk all the time.

There was such a large gap in language between these two leaders that both deliberate and inadvertent misunderstandings were always possible. In fact, evasion and deception were necessary talents both would exercise when they came to crucial bargaining about crossing the mountains, making promises, and trading goods for horses. Lewis's keenness of mind for this challenge is evident in his pages. Cameahwait's emerges less obviously. But it shows up very definitely in the fact that almost immediately Lewis began to learn. He might write line after line about all that he told these Indians; about all the medals

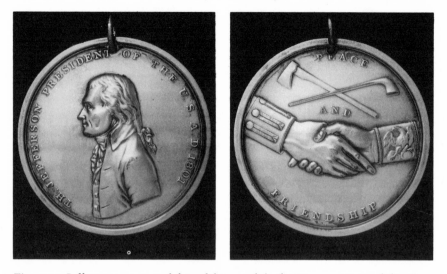

Figure 6. Jefferson peace and friendship medal of 1801, courtesy of the Oregon Historical Society (obverse: #OrHi 38091; reverse: #OrHi 38090).

he gave them, with the president's head on one side and clasped hands and peace pipes on the other (see fig. 6); and about how patiently he explained what they meant. But to communicate effectively and get what he wanted, he had to act otherwise. He had to set aside his collection of symbols and act like a Shoshone so that even he could not tell the difference any longer.

Before two days had passed, the terms of this conflict were set. Lewis wanted Indians to accompany him back to meet Clark and the main party and help carry their baggage across the Divide. But the Indians were skittish. How could they know who these four men really were? How could they be sure they were not leading the tribe's warriors and horses into a clever Plains Indians trap? The Shoshones had fine horses—"indeed many of them would make a figure on the South side of the James River or the land of fine horses" (5:92)—but otherwise they were poorly equipped, poorly fed, poorly armed. The morning for departure came, and the Indians moved slowly if at all. Cameahwait addressed them and apologized to Lewis. Lewis saw into their fear and understood it. But he tried three or four verbal maneuvers without effect. He tried shaming Cameahwait for putting so little confidence in white men. He tried the threat that such behavior would deter white men from coming to trade. He upbraided the Indians for their lack of courage. He held out the promise that Clark was coming with canoes full of food and merchandise.

To Lewis's perception, the taunt about courage was the telling blow. Cameahwait mounted his horse and "harangued" his people to come along, since he would face death himself to find out the truth. But a few lines later Lewis has his own doubts about the effect of all this rhetoric. He writes that followers came along out of the "capricious disposition of those people who never act but from the impulse of the moment" (5:97). What intervenes between balk and talk on the one hand and committed movement on the other is a chain of conspicuous gestures. Cameahwait mounts his horse, and Lewis makes his own highly visible moves of courage and preparation:

> Shortly after this harange he was joined by six or eight only and with these I smoked a pipe and directed the men to put on their packs being determined to set out with them while I had them in the humour   at half after 12 we set out, several of the old women were crying and imploring the great sperit to protect their warriors as if they were going to inevitable distruction. we had not proceeded far before our party was augmented by ten or twelve more, and before we reached the Creek which we had passed in the morning of the 13th it appeared to me that we had all the men of the village and a number of women with us. (5:96–97)

The evident courage of some attracts the imitation of others. But what sparked the first telling movement? Was it, as Lewis says, that with Cameahwait he "touched him on the right string; to doubt the bravery of a savage is at once to put him on his metal" (5:96)? Or was it Cameahwait's own judgment that after two days he had sized up these four aliens and could trust them? Was it words in the moment or something deeper? The puzzling detail is that, for all his impatience to get under way, Lewis did stop to smoke a pipe with those who were first to volunteer. It would be worth a great deal to know whether he also took off his moccasins as they would have wanted him to do.

Once under way, the Indians again became anxious. The next morning Lewis sent two hunters out in search of provisions but very clumsily asked the chief to hold back his hunters, whose "hooping and noise" might frighten the game. Of course this excited new suspicions that these white men might be sneaking ahead to betray the Indians. The Shoshone therefore sent bands after them to keep an eye on them. In a curious turn of phrase, Lewis calls these Indian bands "two parties of discovery," thus echoing the name of his own Corps of Discovery. But this was just the first of many curious touches on this August 16, touches in which the identity of one group stands sharply apart at one moment and merges indistinguishably with the other a few lines later. If the Indians seemed "capricious" to Lewis, his own vacillations have to seem striking to a later reader.

The hunters brought in three deer and an antelope. The Indians devoured the first animal raw, so hungrily and disgustingly that Lewis doubted he and they were of the same species. Yet in the same passage he has to admit that he did share this meat soon after with "a pretty keen appetite myself" and took a share of the next deer and the next and the antelope, too, when it arrived (5:103–4). And if Lewis betrayed his alienation from these famished people, he turned about soon enough to agree to their orders about stopping and then joined them immediately in swapping garments and appearances:

> Being now informed of the place at which I expected to meat Capt C. and the party they insisted on making a halt, which was complyed with. we now dismounted and the Chief with much cerimony put tippets about our necks such as they temselves woar I redily perceived that this was to disguise us and owed it's origine to the same cause already mentioned. to give them further confidence I put my cocked hat with feather on the chief and my over shirt being of the Indian form my hair deshivled and skin well browned with the sun I wanted no further addition to make me a complete Indian in appearance   the men followed my example and we were son completely metamorphosed. (5:104)

Cameahwait is obviously making a prudent effort of disguise, and Lewis is quick to catch on and cooperate. But there is also a moment of kindness here on both sides—kindness in its root sense of "kindred feeling." The chief places the tippets with great ceremony on the white men's necks, and Lewis was to prize his for a long time. He later wrote: "The tippet of the Snake Indians is the most eligant peice of Indian dress I ever saw"; and he described it in detail as a painstaking composition of dressed otter and ermine skins which reached from the neck, over the shoulders, and down to the waist. "These they esteem very highly, and give or dispose of only on important occasions" (5:127–28). When Lewis was painted by the artist Charles B. J. F. Saint-Mémin in 1807, he wore this tippet hung over his buckskins

Figure 7. Charles B. J. F. Saint-Mémin, portrait of
Meriwether Lewis in a fur tippet (1807), courtesy of
the New-York Historical Society, New York City.

to stand out in a full-length portrait as the successful explorer of the
West (see fig. 7).

The metamorphoses went deeper. The combined party moved on
to the Three Forks and found that Clark had not yet come so far.
Lewis knew immediately that he was in trouble. His promised meeting with canoes full of goods was proving hollow. But for a moment
he turned his literacy to advantage. He had left a note for Clark there

on a stake, which he now ordered Drouillard to bring to him. Thinking quickly, Lewis "now had recourse to a stratagem in which I thought myself justifyed by the occasion, but which I must confess set a little awkward" (5 : 105). He made up a story that Clark had already arrived there and left this message, asking Lewis to stop and wait for the rest of the party to come. In return, Lewis now wrote out a message for Clark "by the light of some willow brush" (5 : 105) and immediately dispatched it downstream with Drouillard and one of the young Indians. Lewis and his two remaining men stayed as voluntary hostages with Cameahwait. For the rest of the night, his mind fidgeted over what could be causing Clark's delay. He also imagined the total defeat of this expedition if the Indians who were dispersed uneasily about him suddenly fled. Yet he still had to keep up appearances of calm. "My mind was in reallity quite as gloomy all this evening as the most affrighted indian but affected cheerfullness to keep the Indians so who were about me" (5 : 106).

But Lewis had already made his most dramatic gesture when the party first came to the Three Forks. Dressed as an Indian while Cameahwait was endowed with his cocked hat, Lewis gave up his last symbol of white authority: he handed over his gun.

> When we arrived in sight at the distance of about 2 miles I discovered to my mortification that the party had not arrived, and the Indians slackened their pace. I now scarcely new what to do and feared every moment when they would halt altogether, I now determined to restore their confidence cost what it might and therefore gave the Chief my gun and told him that if his enimies were in those bushes before him that he could defend himself with that gun, that for my own part I was not affraid to die and if I deceived him he might make what uce of the gun he thought proper or in other words that he might shoot me. the men also gave their guns to other indians which seemed to inspire them with more confidence. (5 : 104–5)

Was this an act of bravery? If so, it must have touched the same "string" Lewis noted earlier and described later: "Among the Shoshones, as well as all the Indians of America, bravery is esteemed the primary virtue; nor can any one become eminent among them who has not at some period of his life given proofs of his possessing this virtue" (5 : 159).

Or was it an act of despair? Lewis writes that in his musings that night his mind dwelt "on the state of the expedition which I have ever held in equal estimation with my own existence, and the fait of which appeared at this moment to depend in a great measure on the caprice of a few savages who are ever as fickle as the wind" (5 : 106). These are dark thoughts in a season of dark thoughts in Lewis's life. Two days later, on August 18, he would turn thirty-one and pen the most gloomy self-examination of the entire journal:

> This day I completed my thirty first year, and conceived that I had in all human probability now existed about half the period which I am to remain in this Sublunary world. I reflected that I had as yet done but little, very little indeed, to further the hapiness of the human race, or to advance the information of the succeeding generation. I viewed with regret the many hours I have spent in indolence, and now soarly feel the want of that information which those hours would have given me had they been judiciously expended. but since they are past and cannot be recalled, I dash from me the gloomy thought and resolved in future, to redouble my exertions and at least indeavour to promote those two primary objects of human existence, by giving them the aid of that portion of talents which nature and fortune have bestoed on me; or in future, to live for *mankind,* as I have heretofore lived *for myself.* (5 : 118)

This from the man who had just led his party to the Divide and made confident arrangements for completing the journey to the Pacific before winter. This from someone whose energies made him anything but indolent and whose records, even to this point, would much "advance the information" of later readers. Of course, one can find devout parallels for this kind of needlessly unhappy introspection. Here, for example, is a private entry on his birthday by the famous eighteenth-century Christian moralist Samuel Johnson, who by this date (1764) had been honored with a royal pension for his single-handed production of *A Dictionary of the English Language* and had become revered by many as a poet, critic, and conversational sage:

> I have outlived many friends. I have felt many sorrows. I have made few improvements. Since my resolution formed last Easter I have made no advancement in knowledge or in Goodness; nor do I recollect that I have endeavoured it. I am dejected but not hopeless. . . .
> I have now spent fifty five years in resolving, having from the earliest time almost that I can remember been forming schemes of a better life. I have done nothing; the need of doing therefore is pressing, since the time of doing is short.[7]

But Johnson was becoming an old man by the standards of his time when he wrote these lines, and he was habitual in his gloom; he wrote such meditations at Easter, at the turn of the year, and on other regular occasions. Lewis, by contrast, is young and rarely records such a long personal meditation. A year earlier, in fact, his birthday had been the cause of celebrations in camp, with extra whiskey and dancing until late hours. The note touched here by Lewis suggests either that he was afflicted (as Johnson was) with an occasional but recurring deep inner melancholy or that something in particular had very recently weighed on his mind to make him doubt his personal worth and promise. And the most noteworthy recent experience of failure was this time alone among the Shoshones, where communication was uncertain and everything he cherished seemed to hang on the cooperation of utter strangers.

Was handing his gun to Cameahwait an act of complete trust? Surely Lewis did not expect to be shot by this chief who had embraced him, notwithstanding his later line about "savages . . . fickle as the wind" (5:106). Reflective as he was in general and quick-witted as he was throughout this encounter, he must have made a settled decision to hand over this powerful symbol of who he was—and make it explicit that he would die with these Indians, that Cameahwait might shoot him. The memorable general line he wrote later about these people resounds with respect: "They are frank, communicative, fair in dealing, generous with the little they possess, extreemly honest, and by no means beggarly" (5:119). And we catch a breath of that in Lewis's admission that it "set a little awkward" to deceive a man like Cameahwait with the stratagem about the note from Clark.

Finally, we must ask whether Lewis was not making a great inner yielding in this moment. By this gesture, he was making his metamorphosis complete. If bravery was what these people expected of men, he here conspicuously risks his life before them. If Cameahwait had honored him with his tippet, which now hung on Lewis's shoulders, the captain here gives in return not only the cocked hat of the white soldier but the last distinguishing mark, the gun. And if Rees is right about Shoshone names, Lewis made this exchange of identities absolute, though without knowing it. By refusing to go any further, Lewis became "Ca-me-ah-wait," the one who would not walk. And by giving up his gun, he submitted himself to this chief's still-secret name: "Too-et-te-con-e," or black gun (5:159).

The next day Clark and the main party finally came into view. Sacagawea arrived, rejoicing to be again among her people. She recognized Cameahwait as her "brother" (though, given the fluidity of the language, he may easily have been a cousin; experts still have their doubts[8]); and she began to interpret spoken exchanges. The Shoshones were impressed and astonished at the trade goods, the people, and almost every novelty they saw. Clark's ways with these Indians were immediately winning. He came much better advertised than Lewis had been, but his effect is still wonderful to read. "The Three Chiefs with Capt. Lewis met me with great cordialliaty embraced and took a Seat on a white robe, the Main Chief imedeately tied to my hair Six Small pieces of Shells resembling *perl* which is highly Valued by those people and is prcured from the nations resideing near the *Sea Coast.* we then smoked in their fassion without Shoes and without much cerimoney and form" (5:114). By the end of his first entry Clark has learned both of the chief's names and has received one in return: Kan-me-ah-wah—either the chief's own name given in a friendly exchange or a close equivalent, "come and smoke," an invitation to join the barefoot band (5:115).

But with this arrival there was also an evident loss. Now trade and gifts, speeches and smoking, even sexual encounters, went on between one people and another. But Lewis reverted, as he had to, to being Captain Lewis, at an observant, responsible distance from both his men and these Indians. The time alone with first one Indian, then three, then a few, then a tense band traveling to an uncertain rendezvous—that was over. So was the revealing necessity of communicating by gestures instead of words and of risking life in an exchange of identities.

Elsewhere on this long expedition, Lewis recorded hundreds of acute observations about many Indians. Elsewhere he profited from the display of immediately favorable signs. The sight of Sacagawea in his party was itself an immediate signal of good will among people along the Columbia, "as no woman ever accompanies a war party of Indians in this quarter" (5:306). Elsewhere he could amass comparative information about tribes and record variations, as though Indians were a completely different order of beings, like the plants, animals, birds, and fish he was also observing and recording. But nowhere else did Lewis have such an opportunity and inducement for direct intimacy with another unique person among the Indians. Cameahwait clasped him close, pushed off his shoes, traded his precious clothing, accepted his gun.

The reader may well be puzzled about what these actions meant. Were Lewis and Cameahwait bonded beyond severance? Not at all. Within days the chief tried a stratagem of his own—to slip away with his people before the white men had gained all they wanted, and before the good hunting was over on the plains (5:166). A year later, when Clark's party retraced this route they found their caches still untouched but no fresh sign of Indians (Thwaites 5:124). The Shoshones had gone on, vanished. Few in the party returned to the Rockies; perhaps no one saw them again. Yet if this was a passing encounter, it was not casual. In its details it revealed two complex leaders to each other and to themselves. Was Lewis courageous, inventive, forthright, and honorable? Yes, but he also had to admit to being depressed, at a loss, wary, and deceptive. He was seen, he was touched, both outwardly and within. Above all he was puzzled at how another chief was reading him and was to be read. The best we can do is pore over these pages ourselves, seeking a balanced understanding of confusing signals.

Chapter 7   Reading the Birds

Lewis and Clark observed and described hundreds of plants and animals, and much of their popular fame derives from their accomplishments as naturalists as well as geographers. They looked closely, recorded copiously, and took time and care to preserve and transmit specimens. Many living wonders of the Far West first came to the attention of science because of their efforts. A few still bear the names they invented for them. Two species of birds bear the captains' own names—Lewis's woodpecker and Clark's nutcracker. Fittingly, they are scarce birds with rather anomalous features, still flying in western forests, still propagating there, still to be seen—with effort—by keen-eyed observers in the wilderness.

In observing and recording the forms and ways of animals, Lewis and Clark were repeating a human activity of ancient standing. What distinguishes us from other animals? This question evidently troubled our forebears from a time earlier than civilization, literacy, or even contrived forms of shelter. The famous cave paintings of France and Spain, dating from twenty-thousand years in the past, show vivid bison, horses, cattle, and deer. No one can know how exactly these paintings were made or what function they served among people who left no writing or other symbols. But it is evident that to execute these images at all, human beings had to define themselves differently. To make such recognizable, even brilliantly effective figures, they had to develop coordination, memory, and communicative skills that no other animal has. Perhaps they envied and revered the beasts they hunted and drew them in an effort to compensate for or magically control their larger, swifter bodies and keener senses. What is certain is that they had to observe these animals closely and repeatedly, bear them in memory, and internalize them into their tactile ways with their fingers' ends. They had to become artists as well as hunters, mastering and digesting other animals with their minds. There was no other way they could have carried them underground, into narrow passageways, and projected them again by flickering firelight in lively form on inanimate stone. Art seems to begin here; perhaps so does humanity, in the work of recording animals and refiguring them in the mind's eye.

Of all the types of animals, fish, flesh, and fowl, the birds of the air have continued to exert a special fascination on us. Their bodily form, with rounded heads, upright bodies, and two feet, resembles our own. Plato does not actually define man as a "featherless biped," but the joke is as old as Diogenes the Cynic—and it has its point. The one figure of a human in the cave paintings at Lascaux has the head of a bird.[1]

Birds also build artificial dwellings; they often mate and care for their young monogamously; they migrate and adapt to far-flung regions. And, above all, they fly. They seem to do in space what human beings do in mind, abstracting themselves from the limitations of mundane existence and looking down with a fine insouciance from their lofty gliding. What is an angel in our usual imagining but a human form with wings?

Before there were such angels there were eagles to bear signs from heaven to the upward gaze of mortals. There are eagles from Zeus in Homer, and Zeus himself came to Leda as a swan. Noah sent out his raven and dove from the Ark. The Greeks and more famously the Romans had official augurs who prophesied by observing the flights of certain birds. Mediterranean historians also credited the phoenix of Egypt or Arabia, the immortal bird that perished in fire after a long life cycle, only to have a successor arise from its ashes. These examples will do to recall the mysterious ideas long associated with birds in literature and art. They could seem gods themselves or at least living symbols or messengers of divine powers.

Some of the feelings as well as the reasonings behind these attitudes toward birds remain with us in the common experience of hunters and bird watchers. There is the thrill of suddenly coming upon or detecting another seemingly autonomous being, surviving and even singing in the wilderness—or sustaining its wild life in some odd nook of our familiar, developed landscape. There is another elation at being able to enter and pass through an alien domain without alarming its watchful, high-perched sentinel. And at last there is a moment of determinative contact. For earlier people, there had to be highly developed skill or inventiveness to overmatch the power of flight and secure a dinner. For us there is still the necessity of intense concentration along gun sights or through a camera lens, even a moment of suspended breath, to fix a game bird on the wing or a sharply focused warbler in its full setting.

At the time of Lewis and Clark, however, the age-old reverence and wonder over wild birds had undergone a recent and confusing development. To the explorers' contemporaries, the Romantic poets in England, the bird as an awe-inspiring figure of high intelligence and divinity reached a new zenith. Blake, Wordsworth, Coleridge, Keats, and Shelley all celebrated birds in poems that remain among their most famous, finding images of themselves and poetry embodied in "light wingèd Dryads of the trees." But for over a century there had been a very different movement in European science, a pressure to rid the observer's mind of legendary, mythical, literary associations and reduce birds to terse configurations of directly observed beak, iris, coloring, size, wingspan, and foot shape. These separate movements were not entirely antithetical, for ornithology as well as poetry urged its practitioners to look intently for the *rara avis*. But they were to look with very different eyes. Without fully knowing it, Lewis and Clark looked with a discipline derived from both modern science and centuries of bird lore. Not surprisingly, their journals mainly record matters acceptable and directly useful to science, but they also betray stirrings of another kind.

The development of scientific ornithology in early America has been expertly surveyed by Kevin R. McNamara.[2] His reading of explorers' books, travelers' accounts, local histories, and explicit works of ornithology shows that a disciplined observation of birds was hard to achieve before 1800. A century and more after the work of John Ray and decades after the death of Linnaeus, observers still retailed old legends, repeated biblical symbols, accepted tales of prodigious creatures, and looked on plump fowl with an eye of appetite rather than disinterested analysis. But a new scientific attitude was emerging nevertheless.

The word *ornithology* and the idea of looking only for characteristic marks came into English thought with John Ray's publication of *The Ornithology of Francis Willughby* (1678). As McNamara notes:

"Ray's *Ornithology* disregards all *literaria* and seeks only to 'describe each *Species*, and to reduce all to their proper *Classes* or *Genera*.' Ray and Willughby 'wholly omitted what [they] find in other Authors concerning *Homonymous* and *Synonymous* words, or the diverse names of Birds, *Hieroglyphs, Emblems, Morals, Fables, Presages,* or ought else appertaining to *Divinity, Ethics, Grammar,* or any sort of Humane learning: And present [the reader] only with what properly relates to Natural History.' "[3]

Systematic works of the eighteenth century stressed this same explicit exclusion of literary, ethical, and legendary considerations in favor of direct observation and comparison. The Englishman Mark Catesby published an illustrated two-volume work along these lines: *The Natural History of Carolina, Florida, and the Bahama Islands . . .* (1731, 1743).[4]

Catesby's work was superseded in the even stricter system of Carl von Linné, known to later history by his Latin name Carolus Linnaeus. Linnaeus not only eliminated extraneous matter but enforced an extreme impersonal terseness. Here is his description of the bald eagle, for example:

> Cere and legs yellow; legs somewhat downy; body brown; head and tail white.
>
> Inhabits woods of *Europe* and *America;* 3 feet 3 inches long; feeds on hogs, lamb, and fish, which it takes from other birds, nest large, eggs 2.
>
> *Bill* yellow; *head, neck, irids* and *tail* white; *toes* yellow; *claws* black; rest of body chocolate.[5]

McNamara points out that the eagle, the "king of birds," was a traditional opener in earlier collections of bird lore.[6] Here it is merely another species, outlined by the most distinctive characteristic marks that anyone might see.

Not many observers, however, could be so rigorous. Old habits and strong preoccupations were still guiding their pens. As clergymen-naturalists left off stressing birds as God's creatures, promoters of new regions noted wondrous birds that were worth traveling to see or that promised easy living to new settlers. John Filson in 1784 thus reported an ivory-billed woodpecker in Kentucky, and Jonathan Carver in 1781 mentioned powerful ospreys in the Far West that could draw fish to the surface.[7] As late as the close of the century Timothy Dwight was composing his *Travels in New England and New York* (published in 1821–22), in which he aestheticized and moralized about the birds he encountered, and William Bartram's *Travels through North and South Carolina, Georgia, East and West Florida* (1791) combined very accurate descriptions with personal reflections and a need to see not only birds alone but also their interconnections with their settings.

It was from mixed materials like these that Lewis and Clark's masters drew their information and instruction. Thomas Jefferson's *Notes on the State of Virginia* lists ninety-three birds, along with their Latin names assigned by Linnaeus and Catesby; he adds the common names of thirty-two more.[8]

Benjamin Smith Barton, the Philadelphia naturalist whose *Elements of Botany* Lewis carried across the continent, used many of William Bartram's observations in compiling his *Fragments of the Natural History of Pennsylvania* (1799). He also included many miscellaneous comments about birds apart from sheer descriptions.[9] There were lingering eccentricities, which persist in every science, where single observers and authors set down what they found worthy of record. But the clear direction of collective science by 1800 was to pare away everything extraneous to a short list of distinctive appearances, habits, and sounds.

This direction of science was perhaps most manifest and palpable in the work of Charles Willson Peale. Peale's great museum of natural science in Philadelphia displayed thousands of animal specimens, including over seven hundred birds. These were carefully mounted in naturalistic painted settings and arranged very precisely in Linnaean categories. After 1802, when part of the museum was moved into the upper chambers of Independence Hall, the bird collection was its dominant feature. It covered the wall of the Long Room, one hundred feet long and twelve feet high. There, under busts and portraits of scientists and national heroes, stood 140 glass cases, "the insides of which are painted to represent appropriate scenery, Mountains, Plains or Waters, the birds being placed on branches or artificial rocks, &c," according to a printed *Guide* of 1806 (see fig. 8).[10]

Not all of these birds were American, for Peale happily acquired specimens from sea captains and correspondents abroad. But here for Meriwether Lewis to see and study were scores upon scores of birds, all arranged by categories and common features for easy comparison.

Figure 8. Titian R. Peale, "The Long Room, Interior of Front Room in Peale's Museum," courtesy of the Detroit Institute of Arts.

Although there is no direct proof that Lewis saw the museum or conferred with Peale before he headed west, it is hard to believe that he did not. He was in Philadelphia in 1803 specifically to learn from Jefferson's scientific colleagues, and Peale was certainly one of them. At just this time Peale had worked up a series of forty lectures on his zoological collection. And the museum in any case was a center of attraction for visitors and natural scientists. It displayed the newly excavated and reassembled skeleton of the mammoth, an American buffalo, many Indian artifacts, and other wonders. Later, Peale's museum was the obvious place for Jefferson to send on the specimens that he received from Lewis and Clark, and there they were displayed, conserved, and copied, and so transmitted to others' knowledge during the decades when the scientific portions of the journals lay unedited and unpublished. Peale was especially attentive about birds, and he mounted and painted many specimens he received from the expedition. Alexander Wilson later compiled his great *American Ornithology* (1808–13) by relying heavily on Peale's collections. It is hard not to think that from the Long Room Lewis set out, to the Long Room he returned, and the Long Room—that full, orderly, proud, scientific chamber superimposed upon the shrine of American independence—remained vividly impressed in his mind as he collected birds across the continent. (When he returned to Philadelphia, Lewis not only sat for a portrait by Peale but also submitted to the making of a life mask and donated his prized ermine-skin tippet, the gift of Cameahwait, to the museum. The result was a wax figure of Lewis in full regalia, with a card expressing high ideals of brotherhood and peace.)[11]

But if truth to nature was coming to mean truth to an orderly Linnaean system for ornithologists and explorers, it was figuring very differently in many poems of this period. The work of Ray, Catesby, Jefferson, and Peale aims at identifying each bird and placing each species in its place in a table. The effect is to reduce every particular animal encountered to a mere instance or exemplary specimen, a mere "it." Wordsworth and many others directly address many single birds much more reverently, as "thou"—even a godlike, self-sufficient "thou":

> Thou, ranging up and down the bowers
>   Art sole in thy employment;
> A Life, a Presence like the Air,
> Scattering thy gladness without care,
> Too bless'd with any one to pair,
>   Thyself thy own enjoyment.[12]

These lines are from "The Green Linnet," composed in 1802 or 1803 and published in 1807, a poem Coleridge singled out for quotation as a fine example of Wordsworth's "perfect truth of nature in his images and descriptions." Coleridge compares this quality in Wordsworth to a reflection from a natural mirror, such as a perfectly calm lake or the moistened or polished surface of a pebble. "What," he asks, "can be more accurate yet more lovely than the two concluding stanzas?"[13]

Yet if we turn to these stanzas they say nothing at all about distinguishing marks that a naturalist would recognize or find useful in any way:

> Upon yon tuft of hazel trees,
> That twinkle to the gusty breeze,
> Behold him perch'd in ecstasies,
>   Yet seeming still to hover;

There! where the flutter of his wings
Upon his back and body flings
Shadows and sunny glimmerings,
    That cover him all over.

While thus before my eyes he gleams,
A Brother of the Leaves he seems;
When in a moment forth he teems
    His little song in gushes:
As if it pleased him to disdain
And mock the Form which he did feign,
While he was dancing with the train
    Of Leaves among the bushes.[14]

The first of these stanzas reveals not a distinctive bird at all but an extraneous setting of hazel trees behind an "ecstatic" flutter of confusing shadows and glimmerings. The second suggests a sudden burst of song that coincides with the emergence of a "form" now visible outside its camouflage of leaves. Yet if we reread with a Wordsworthian patience, the indistinct imagery here is precisely the effect of a small bird barely visible as it flutters in a distant tree. For the poet, what matters is his own kinship with nature, realized through his close attention to this fluttering and song. "A Brother of the Leaves he seems." Is the green linnet perceived as a twin of the *leaves* in which he gleams, or is he a brother, a fellow being, of the *poet*? The answer is complex. "Brother" is finally a name for a feeling of human kinship; it is not a proper term for taxonomy. Neither birds nor leaves have brothers as we know them. So to "seem" a brother, this linnet seems for a moment human-hearted, either dancing among its fellow leaves or gleaming for the eye of its fellow observer. It is a living intermediary between the bright but expressionless leaves and the person who cannot see into them. Yet as the linnet emerges in its "little song" it becomes both more nearly human and more definitely an animal in nature: he sings *as if* he could have a mind to see himself as the poet saw him a moment earlier. The poem ends with a suspension that suggests an important transcendence. The linnet almost outgrows itself to take on a new mental life along with a definite form outside the leaves. And the poet definitely outgrows the illusion that bird and leaves are the same blur or that the bird is, even in song, a serious rival.

To a modern bird-watcher these verses may seem highly overwrought without making the green linnet a whit more understandable. But they are typical of Wordsworth's poetry and of his devotion to seeing deep into the heart of things in nature. They are also repeated and refigured in a number of other Romantic poems in which a solitary observer finds human, poetic, even godlike powers in the flight and song of particular birds. The green linnet may remain an obscure species despite Wordsworth's lines here, but the nightingale is forever bound to the odes of John Keats; the skylark is a vivid figure of Percy Bysshe Shelley; the albatross has never been the same after Coleridge and his Ancient Mariner. These poeticized birds were becoming as legendary as the owl of Minerva, the eagles of Rome, or the ancient phoenix in the same years that our explorers were crossing America and publishing their reports.

Where do Lewis and Clark fit into this complicated background of schematic science and intense poetry? One level of their response to birds is a simple compromise. They drew them. They did not draw many, and their sketches would not win prizes, but they record significant features unmistakably, such as the double upper beak or "elevated orning [awning]" of the northern fulmar (*Journals* 6:386). These figures show the hand of the explorer attentively copying nature, as primitively and directly as any cave dweller's.

But the explorers' much more extensive records place them firmly on the side of the scientists. Lewis and Clark recorded appearances and paid little attention to the charm or mythic possibilities of birds or any other animals. At least they tried to do things that way.

An outstanding example of their procedures can be found in their records of the black-billed magpie. This was one of the first new species they spotted, and their descriptions are typical in form of later entries about many other birds. Yet this species, like every other, has its own peculiarities. The explorers' observations and reports over a period of months reveal how they came to get a deeper feeling for magpies yet still missed some features that now seem obvious to anyone who has lived around these birds for a time.

Clark's opening record is brief but perceptive: "17th of Septr. Monday 1804   above White river   Dried all those articles which had got wet by the last rain, a fine day   Capt Lewis went hunting with a vew to see the Countrey & its productions, he was out all Day   Killed a Buffalow & a remarkable bird of the Spicies of Corvus, long tail of a Greenish Purple, Varigated   a Beck like a

143

Crow   white round its neck comeing to a point on its back, its belley white   feet like a Hawk   abt. the size of a large Pigeon" (*Journals* 3 : 82). Short as it is, this entry correctly notes the species and the outstanding features of coloring, tail and body size, and beak and foot shape. Its only word of emotion or judgment is "remarkable."

This sighting occurred as the party was just entering the High Plains, in what is now South Dakota, and daily meeting new animals worth noticing. In this same entry, Clark also makes the first mention of a coyote and notes the features of what the party would name the mule deer: "a Curious kind of Deer, a Darker grey than Common   the hair longer & finer, the ears verry large & long   a small resepitical under its eye   its tail round and white to near the end which is black & like a Cow   in every other respect like a Deer, except it runs like a goat.   large" (3 : 82). On this same date, Lewis noted prairie dogs and skunks and spent himself trying to pursue some wary antelopes, thus learning that they "are watchfull and extreemly quick of sight and their sense of smelling very accute it is almost impossible to approach them within gunshot." And when they ran: "I beheld the rapidity of their flight along the ridge before me   it appeared reather the rappid flight of birds than the motion of quadrupeds. I think I can safely venture the asscertion that the speed of this anamal is equal if not superior to that of the finest blooded courser" (3 : 81–82). In the midst of so many new animals—and so many intriguing large animals—the magpies must have stood out as "remarkable" to be noted at all. In recopying his notes, Clark added three more words: "a butifull thing" (3 : 83).

Just how strangely beautiful it was comes out in Lewis's much longer entry. At first sight, this description may seem brutally factual and anatomical, with cold measurements of every dimension and a ruthless plucking and counting of feathers. One has to feel relief that Wordsworth never saw such an avian autopsy report: it surely would have made him despair over American sensibilities. Yet this page still deserves to be read in full, and reread, too; for its length and probing bespeak a deep curiosity about mysteries of living color:

> one of the hunters killed a bird of the *Corvus genus* and order of the pica & about the size of a jack-daw with a remarkable long tale. beautifully variagated. it note is not disagreeable though loud—it is twait twait twait, twait; twait, twait twait, twait.

	F	I
from tip to tip of wing	1	10
Do. beak to extremity of tale	1	8 1/2
of which the tale occupys		11
from extremity of middle to toe to hip		5 1/2

it's head, beak, and neck are large for a bird of it's size; the beak is black, and of a convex and cultrated figure, the chops nearly equal, and it's base large and beset with hairs— the eyes are black encircled with a narrow ring of yellowish black it's head, neck, brest & back within one inch of the tale are of a fine glossey black, as are also the short fathers of the under part of the wing, the thies and those about the root of the tale. the belly is of a beatifull white which passes above and arround the but of the wing, where the feathers being long reach to a small white spot on the rump one inch in width— the wings have nineteen feathers, of which the ten first have the longer side of their plumage white in the midde of the feather and occupying unequal lengths of the same from one to three inches, and forming when the wing is spead a kind [of] triangle the upper and lower part of these party coloured feathers on the under side of the wing being of dark colour but not jut or shining black. the under side of the remaining feathers of the wing are darker. the upper side of the wing, as well as the short side of the plumage of the party coloured feathers is of a dark blackis or bluish green sonetimes presenting as light orange yellow or bluish tint as it happens to be presented to different exposures of ligt— the plumage of the tale consits of 12 feathers of equal lengths by pai[r]s, those in the center are the longest, and the others on each side deminishing about an inch each pair— the underside of the feathers is a pale black, the upper side is a dark blueish green which like the outer part of the wings is changable as it reflects different portions of light. towards the the extremety of these feathers they become of an orrange green, then shaded pass to a redish indigo blue, and again at the extremity assume the predominant colour of changeable green— the tints of these feathers are very similar and equally as beautiful and rich as the tints of blue and green of the peacock— it is a most beatifull bird.— the legs and toes are black and imbricated. it has four long toes, three in front and one in rear, each terminated with a black sharp tallon from 3/8ths to 1/2 an inch in length.— these birds are seldom found in parties of more than three or four and most usually at this season single as the halks and other birds of prey usually are— it's usual food is flesh— this bird dose not spread it's tail when it flys and the motion of it's wings when flying is much like that of a Jay-bird. (3:83–85)

A modern handbook confirms that these passages record the dimensions and markings recognizably. "Blackbilled Magpie, *Pica pica*, 17 1/2–22" (44–56 cm). Large black and white bird with long tail and dark bill. Bill, head, breast, and underparts black, with green iridescence on wings and tail. White belly, shoulders and outermost flight feathers, which are conspicuous as white wing patches in flight. Call a rapid, nasal *mag? mag? mag?* or *yak yak yak*."[15]

But of course Lewis and Clark's descriptions note much more. They accurately place the magpie as a *corvus* and a *pica*—a rare instance of Latinate classification in these journals. And on October 6 Clark first referred to these birds as "magpyes," which is also accurate; the American bird has a very close counterpart in Europe.[16]

Both writers take orderly notes, demonstrating a strict modern training. But Lewis goes on and on. He lacks a vocabulary for the striking impression this bird obviously made. Like Clark, he can only repeat and vary the words "remarkable" and "beautiful." But with persistent, patient hands and eyes he works to unfold and itemize, until color after primary color glows in its turn: "a dark blackis or bluish green sonetimes presenting as light orange yellow or bluish tint," "these feathers . . . become of an orrange green . . . pass to a redish indigo blue, and again at the extremity assume the predominant colour of changeable green." The bird before us is dead, "killed by a hunter," but its colors will not stay still, nor can Lewis's language for it, as that wonderfully sinuous last clause shows.

This earnest attention continues in the journals. The following April 14, Lewis found color again in reporting the birds' nests and eggs: "Their nests are built in trees and composed of small sticks leaves and grass, open at top, and much in the stile of the large blackbird comm to the U' States. the egg is of a bluish brown colour, freckled with redish brown spots" (*Journals* 4:36). A few days later Clark enlarged this observation: "I observe that the Magpie Goose duck & Eagle all have their nests in the Same neighbourhood, and it is not uncommon for the Magpie to build in a few rods of the Eagle, the nests of this bird is built verry Strong with Sticks Covered verry thickly with one or more places through which they enter or escape"

(4:75). And by June 15 those nests had served their purpose: "The deer now begin to bring forth their young the young Magpies begin to fly. The Brown or grizzly bear begin to coppolate" (4:348).

Meanwhile, the party had not only observed these birds but had also managed to capture a few of them alive. As winter ended at Fort Mandan, four were packed in cages, along with a living prairie dog and a grouse, and shipped down the river to reach President Jefferson. Only the prairie dog and one magpie survived. But these specimens traveled thousands of miles by way of St. Louis, New Orleans, Baltimore, and Washington before they finally found a home at Peale's museum. There the magpie survived the winter and was later mounted to serve as a model for Alexander Wilson. Paul Russell Cutright traces these travels in detail and sums up the distinction of these two prairie creatures: "Not before or since have any other animals been privileged to reside in both the President's Mansion and Independence Hall and, in travels about the country, have passed through the solicitous hands of such a distinguished group of men as Captains Meriwether Lewis and William Clark; William Claiborne, Governor of Orleans; Henry Dearborn, Secretary of War; Thomas Jefferson, third President of the United States; Charles Willson Peale, eminent painter and Curator of the Philadelphia Museum; Alexander Wilson, outstanding artist-naturalist; and Alexander Lawson, foremost engraver" (*LCPN* 382–83).

This special treatment for the magpie, atypical of the expedition's observations and methods, is only an extreme case of a constant practice. Long descriptions, especially in Lewis's hand, are supplemented by later remarks for dozens of species. If the magpie alone was shipped alive to Philadelphia, that may be because the magpie alone was easy enough to catch and hardy enough to survive the long voyage in a cage. Other specimens were skinned and preserved; Jefferson once wrote out his method and Peale was justly proud of his (in comparison to specimens he received from abroad, his mountings lasted for decades). Lewis reports that he "killed and preserved" specimens, including the birds now known as Clark's nutcracker and Lewis's woodpecker. (The skin of the latter may now be an item still surviving at the Museum of Comparative Zoology at Harvard.)[17]

Lewis's curiosity remains astonishing. At one point his relentless probing took him right to the verge of a significant discovery about hibernation. The incident occurred just a few weeks after the first sightings of magpies. Lewis's entry is dated October 16, 1804, but evidently it was written after observations on subsequent days:

> This day took a small bird alive of the order of the [*blank*] or goat suckers. it appeared to be passing into the dormant state. on the morning of the 18th the murcury was at 30 a[bove] o. the bird could scarcely move.— I run my penknife into it's body under the wing and completely distroyed it's lungs and heart— yet it lived upwards of two hours   this fanominon I could not account for unless it proceeded from the want of circulation of the bl[o]od.— the recarees [Arikara Indians] call this bird to' -na   it's note is at-tah-to'-nah'; at-tah'to'-nah'; to-nah, a nocturnal bird, sings only in the night as does the whipperwill.— it's weight—1 oz 17 Grains Troy. (3:178)

This entry reports significant details and correctly relates this bird to the whippoorwill. But it remained unpublished for a century, while Audubon came upon the species by himself and named it, and naturalists went on doubting torpidity in birds. It was another poor-will observation, conducted over a period of eighty-five days in 1947–48, that provided scientific proof of this "fanominon." [18]

Later, Lewis recorded another observation or two that nicely support the enduring fame of his name. Mention Clark's nutcracker and Lewis's woodpecker to a watcher who has seen them and you may well hear that the first is a crow that flies like a woodpecker and the other a woodpecker that flies like a crow. Cutright explains that the latter does not follow the usual undulating flight path of woodpeckers and is a strange bird in other ways, too (*LCPN* 173). Clark's nutcracker, by contrast, is a corvid that undulates. But Lewis observed this woodpecker's flight himself: "It is a distinct species of woodpecker," he wrote; "it has a long tail and flys a good deel like the jay bird." In fact, his first sighting was of a bird "as black as a crow" (*Journals* 4:407). When he captured and preserved specimens a year later, he saw through that blackness to another rich variety of colors (Thwaites 5:70–71).

Why did Lewis give so much attention to obscure details about living things? Neither his instructions nor the standards of natural history required it, and his other duties could have kept him fully occupied. Jefferson's letter of instructions listed only "other objects worthy of notice," including "the animals of the country generally, &

especially those not known in the U.S." (*Letters* 1:63). This is a very subordinate directive, well below the main tasks of surviving, tracing a direct link across the continent from the Mississippi to the Pacific, and opening new understandings with the Indians of this vast region. Jefferson may have urged Lewis privately or even tacitly to be very observant about natural phenomena, but certainly these other demanding tasks had to come first. And as we can see from the entries on the magpie, brief but accurate notes like Clark's would have sufficed to claim a new species for science. Yet the records of the journals are often lavish. Virginia C. Holmgren lists 134 bird species seen and recorded by Lewis and Clark, including 34 that might count as discoveries new to science.[19] Cutright lists 51 discoveries by including species (such as the white-fronted goose, the ruffled grouse, and the magpie) that had not been reported in America, along with some others (*LCPN* 429–38).

This is a long list of birds for this era, if one considers the carefully compiled list of 125 American birds in Jefferson's *Notes on Virginia*, similar numbers from other contemporary lists,[20] and Cutright's remark that fewer than a score of these had been fully described before Lewis and Clark returned from the Pacific (*LCPN* 386). The eyes and mind of Meriwether Lewis were simply extraordinary. For long stretches of time his journal entries are occasional or nonexistent, but when he does take up his pen, the records return to life. In crossing the rough, mountainous terrain of northern Idaho, for example, he made entries for five days. As Cutright remarks, during that period "he contributed more faunal and floral information than all the other journalists combined during the entire Bitterroot transit" (*LCPN* 210).

During the winter months at Fort Clatsop these observations and many others were consolidated and set in order. Lewis began with a catalog of fir trees on February 4, 1806; proceeded through other plants in subsequent entries; took up "quadrupeds" on February 15; then sea animals, fish, and smaller mammals. On March 1 he began on the birds west of the Rockies, which "for convenience I shall divide into two classes, which I shal designate from the habits of the birds, *Terrestrial* and *Aquatic*" (*Journals* 6:366). He then went on to reptiles and some more fish—with interruptions to record the golden eagle and white-fronted goose. The zoological recording seems to have come to an end only because the time had come to break up camp and begin the homeward journey—and Lewis always kept an eye for new species on that route, too.

Even the diligence, curiosity, and care of a Lewis could not do everything or avoid some naïve mistakes. As Holmgren notes, he could not always succeed in gaining a specimen for close study. Sometimes he could not get close or see a bird at all. The first bird named on the way up the Missouri was a "nightingale," which the party only heard singing after dark. There are no nightingales in North America, but Clark states they named a creek for this one.[21] The party also ate many "pheasants," which must have been grouse. Sometimes Lewis had to make do with inference: "I beleive the Callamet Eagle is sometimes found on this side of the rocky mountains," he wrote at Fort Clatsop, "from the information of Indians in whose possession I have seen their plumage" (6:406).

The common, beautiful, and available magpie provides a good instance of what Lewis and Clark missed as well as what they noted. The long and perceptive descriptions, based on observation, capture, dissection, and preservation, still leave out some leading characteristics of this bird. As ranchers, campers, and hunters have come to know, it can be as pesky and intrusive to others as Lewis and Clark were to it. Like people, but not many other birds, magpies can change to other foods when their usual sources become scarce. In particular, they will peck at living flesh as well as insects or carrion. This behavior was noted as their outstanding characteristic by Pierre-Antoine Tabeau, who traded on the Upper Missouri in 1803–4, met Lewis and Clark there, and later looked after the prairie dog they sent down the river to Jefferson. Tabeau's discussion of birds of this region describes only the magpie and the golden eagle. Here, in full, is the magpie:

> The magpie, the most beautiful bird of the country, is here the plague of the savages' horses. These barbarians are so clumsy and so careless with their wooden saddles that often the horse's skin and flesh from the neck to the rump are torn away. The voracious bird at the sight of this raw and living flesh buries its claws in it and tears the poor sentient animal. The horse kicks, prances, runs about with all its might, but in vain. The bird, fixed on the sores, loosens its hold only when the horse throws itself upon his back to roll. Yet scarcely does he rise up once more than the enemy seizes again its opportunity. It is observable that

among a large number of galled horses, the magpie always chooses the one that it has once tasted, so that the beast finally succumbs, if it be not rescued. Some owners, more through interest than through pity, cover the sores with a piece of leather or with a buffalo paunch sprinkled with ashes.[22]

It is hard to believe that Lewis and Clark did not observe this noteworthy and annoying behavior. But apart from one passing reference to numbers of magpies attacking the meat of freshly killed game, I can find no mention of it in their journals.[23]

Many people have also noted the magpie's traits of intelligence and vocal mimicry. Lewis records that the bird has a large head for a bird of its size; like other members of the crow family, it has a large cranial capacity. It is curious. It learns to respond to human signals. It can steal and hide food and other small items. It can deftly elude trained falcons and torment other predators competing over carrion. Birds captured young are favorite pets, and many have been trained to repeat whistles and words.[24]

The close similarity of American and European magpies, along with some fossil evidence, may indicate that this species has been around on widely separate continents for a very long time, perhaps millions of years. If so, then Lewis and Clark's intrusion into magpie territory was a disturbance in a very well settled habitat. These men looked closely at a few specimens, but a greater number of these birds were looking back at a few odd mammalian bipeds in buckskin, profiting from their leavings of carrion, maybe even taking in and clucking a few repetitions of their noises.

How can we know, from what we catch by glimpses or merely capture and dissect, what the intelligence of animals—singly or in herds or flocks—may be making of our world? The question faintly occurred to Lewis and Clark when wild animals like buffalo and antelope appeared tame and came close or gently followed to look at these travelers. In a famous entry written near the mouth of the Yellowstone, Lewis noted that game animals covered the whole face of the country, but "the buffaloe Elk and Antelope are so gentle that we pass near them while feeding, without apearing to excite any alarm among them, and when we attract their attention, they frequently approach us more nearly to discover what we are, and in some instances pursue us a considerable distance apparently with that view" (*Journals* 4:67).

The idea had been put more forcefully by William Blake in the 1790s. This poet and self-proclaimed prophet declared that "if the doors of perception were cleansed everything would appear to man as it is, infinite." In a famous line, he asked readers to open their sight, hearing, taste, touch, and smell to infinite possibilities: "How do you know but ev'ry Bird that cuts the airy way, / Is an immense world of delight, clos'd by your senses five?"[25]

The reader of Romantic poetry may regret that Lewis could not know or would not heed Blake or Wordsworth, just as modern naturalists may regret that he could not find time to study new species with greater leisure and write up discoveries for earlier and more systematic publication. But the journals show a man observing about as much as he conceivably could have done under the conditions he met and the preconditions he had willingly accepted. Lewis bore the discipline of Jeffersonian scientific training and accepted the limitations of space in his miscellaneous daily logs. He made the most of his opportunities and went on noticing anyhow.

The necessity of looking occasionally, randomly, with full preparation but without rigorous direction, may even have been a boon. Perhaps it enabled Lewis to see better. Without tight preconceptions of what he should or must find, he was free to notice the new and the oddly connected—to take in, for example, a coyote, an antelope, a mule deer, and a magpie all in one day. Without feeling any embarrassment that he was not expert enough to do justice to any of them, he wrote them up on his terms.

If Lewis lacked the deeper sensitivity that the Romantic poets cultivated, he escaped their consistent distortions of vision, too. Scratch Keats's nightingale, Shelley's skylark, or Wordsworth's linnet and it bleeds human blood, or the ichor of an idealized poetic spirit:

> Hail to thee, blithe Spirit!
> Bird thou never wert,
> That from Heaven, or near it,
> Pourest thy full heart
> In profuse strains of unpremeditated art.[26]

So Shelley begins "To a Skylark." Lewis will never write like that, much less Clark. The birds they see are not metaphoric presences or brothers of the leaves but wholly distinct, living beings. Their steady curiosity about them as strange, colorful, elusive, and sometimes tasty things of flesh and feathers is a sharp corrective to Romanticism at its most romantic.

Most important, Lewis and Clark failed to stop and look the magpie deeply in the eye for the very good reason that they were developing a wider perspective than the eagle's. Step by step they were composing an overview of the continent. That was their assigned mission and also their chosen quest. The task required all kinds of observations, almost all the time, to go into a complex cumulative record of a distinctly human migration. When they were done they could hold volumes of handwritten lore about the ways of thousands of leaves and needles, fins, paws, hooves, and wings. They could also make a map of it all and so hover as no mortal yet had done, high over the Cordilleras and the watercourses flowing north, west, east, and south to the sea.

Chapter 8 Finding Words

THE PAGES OF the Lewis and Clark journals can be puzzling, amusing, or exasperating because of the many mistakes and hasty slips the writers have made in composing plain English prose. Clark's inventive spelling is notorious; he seems to have sounded out many words and made do with whatever letters approximated the sounds. Lewis frequently had trouble with spelling too. And in the haste and strain of keeping up daily entries both writers left out letters or entire words or got confused in sentences that begin with one structure and somehow leap into another. For many readers, Clark's evident struggles with the language make him seem a charming primitive. Lewis, by contrast, had a much larger vocabulary and an often impressive mastery of technical terms in natural science. But Lewis, too, has left readers guessing at times, especially when he reached after elegance and created stilted phrases and words no dictionary has ever known.

At Fort Clatsop in 1806, for example, Lewis recorded that the local Clatsop and Chinook Indians were fond of tobacco; they smoked it slowly and seemed to inhale the smoke, swallow it, and hold it for a long time. "I have no doubt the smoke of the tobacco in this manner becomes much more intoxicating and that they do possess themselves of all it's virtues in their fullest extent" (*Journals* 6:179). So far, so good; Lewis here sums up in a long but perceptive sentence. But as he goes on to explain how the smoke eventually gets discharged he has to invent a unique term whose meaning is by no means clear. "They freequently give us sounding proofs of it's creating a dismorallity of order in the abdomen, nor are those light matters thought indelicate in either sex, but all take the liberty of obeying the dictates of nature without reserve." Apart from obvious misspellings, the troublesome word is "dismorallity." Other words here reinforce the idea that the

Indians were doing something Lewis thought embarrassing—making "sounding proofs" with indelicate handling of "dictates of nature." But what were the Indians actually doing: farting, belching, gurgling, competing with each other in making loud abdominal rumblings? The language here obscures this point. Lewis is apparently caught in a dilemma of trying to report something too indelicate for him to mention outright, and he leaves us forever guessing.

His words create another problem, too. "Dismorallity" is found in no dictionary except the Lewis and Clark lexicon compiled in 1940 by Elijah H. Criswell—which cites only this sentence.[1] Criswell lists this word as a "humorous coinage." But is it? How can we tell that Lewis is amused here rather than embarrassed? Or perhaps he is ingeniously devising a neutral term for the conflicting moralities of the explorers and the easygoing Indians, high on nicotine. "Dismoral" is not the same as "immoral" or even "amoral"—and after all these are "light matters," if that phrase means what it seems to, not outrageous but silly or playful. It is finally impossible to determine the tone controlling this passage. Its meaning seems locked into just what Lewis wrote, and the key term belongs to him alone.

The passage remains vexing for another reason: it reports a discovery, a practice with tobacco Lewis has not seen before, which obviously deserves to go into his journals and reach other readers. The journals of these explorers report hundreds of new sights and experiences, and for many of them they borrowed, bent, or coined new terms. Criswell compared the vocabulary of the Thwaites edition of the journals with the entries of the *Oxford English Dictionary* and counted over a thousand "new words first appearing in the Journals, including unrecorded terms and earliest uses."[2] These words include names for newly discovered plants and animals as well as terms used as occasion demanded—like "dismorallity." By introducing so many new terms into these journals, what kind of language did Lewis and Clark create for themselves? Is it still English? Is it a new variety of American English, an amalgam of many dialects, or an odd patchwork of new contents straining in old structures? Above all, how can this language be read? What clues can a reader use to decipher entirely new terms for entirely new discoveries—or can that be done?

Unfortunately there are no great shining principles and few rules of thumb for such language as this. New terms and rare terms are sometimes completely inscrutable and keep whole passages locked tight.

About others we can only make informed speculation, through inferences based on context and usage elsewhere. I have done so earlier, for example, in looking at Lewis's rare uses of the terms *sublime, picturesque,* and *evil genius.* Some pages yield a little to educated guesses; others are so obvious that needed synonyms and emendations spring readily to mind and rightly appear in brackets in the Moulton edition. If we cannot resolve all linguistic puzzles, however, we can point out where problems lie. Many of Lewis and Clark's troubles arise from general limitations we should be aware of in language itself and in these authors' evident nervousness about it.

One of the primary difficulties of language is that it encodes even spatial, simultaneous, and disparate experiences in very rigorous serial sequences. From time to time everybody loses control of the sequences we call spelling, word order, and sentence or paragraph coherence. The human mind seems to rebel against marshaling ideas so artificially and repeating them perfectly. This problem was well understood in the late eighteenth century, according to Michel Foucault, who quotes and cites several French philosophers on the subject:

> What distinguishes language from all other signs and enables it to play a decisive role in representation is . . . that it analyses representation according to a necessarily successive order: the sounds, in fact, can be articulated only one by one; language cannot represent thought, instantly, in its totality; it is bound to arrange it, part by part, in a linear order. Now, such an order is foreign to representation. It is true that thoughts succeed one another in time, but each one forms a unity, whether one agrees with Condillac that all the elements of a representation are given in an instant and that only reflection is able to unroll them one by one, or whether one agrees with Destutt de Tracy that they succeed one another with a rapidity so great that it is not practically possible to observe or to retain their order. It is these representations, pressed in on one another in this way, that must be sorted out into linear propositions: to my gaze "the brightness is within the rose"; in my discourse, I cannot avoid it coming either before or after it. If the mind had the power to express ideas "as it perceives them," there can be no doubt that "it would express them all at the same time." But that is precisely what is not possible, for, though "thought is a simple operation," "its expression is a successive operation." [3]

The order of letters in spelling, of words in grammar, of sentences in paragraph structure, of paragraphs or discrete topics in whole compositions—keeping them all straight is a taxing, delicate balancing act. It sometimes drives students to despair, and it defeats the vigilant efforts of very practiced scholars and copy editors. We all make slips, surprise ourselves with solecisms and unintended implications that become jokes or embarrassments, land in deep misunderstandings because of ambiguous meanings when even a few letters get out of order. If groups of highly educated readers differ sharply, they most likely argue over what linear orders of symbols best represent ideas that are not necessarily linear at all. If they avoid violence, it is probably by exchanging reams of linear arguments.

These problems are commonplace, though we often take it for granted that speech and writing are natural rather than artificial, since most people get by and make themselves understood somehow from an early age. A more startling consideration is that no one can hope to be ultimately authoritative about a complete language. The orders we rely on often derive from arbitrary conventions—in other words from rules made by one group or another of speakers or writers. It is entirely arbitrary that a word is usually spelled *color* instead of *colour,* that the comma regularly goes inside instead of outside quotation marks, and that readers instantly recognize a difference between cattle and priests but not between llamas and lamas.

The standard of good English may be thought to reside in the deliberate, careful writings of expert authors. But who are they? Shakespeare left most of his plays to the hazards of time and later editors; Milton was blind and could not read proof; and both lived long before there were established national reference works like dictionaries to give them any guidance or support. When James A. H. Murray worked at editing examples of usage for the *Oxford English Dictionary* in the 1880s, he learned through frustrating inquiries that great authors could be very misleading. George Eliot wrote to explain that she used "adust" instead of "dusty" because it suited the rhythm of her prose; Robert Louis Stevenson answered that "brean" in one of his works was a misprint for "ocean." Murray commented harshly to his son about one of the great poets of the age: "Browning constantly used words without regard for their proper meaning. He has added greatly to the difficulties of the Dictionary." [4] But even that magisterial lexicographer found himself baffled in trying to decide what words should and should not be included as standard diction in a modern language. An advisor urged him to exclude *appendicitis* as mere medical jargon. Murray had seen into this problem already and pondered the risk that medical or scientific terms might "any day . . . burst on the world as famous poisons, disinfectants, anaesthesians, or cholera prophylacts, & so be in every body's mouths."[5] He consulted the Regius Professor of Medicine at Oxford, took his advice, and cut out *appendicitis;* then 1902 rolled around and Edward VII became a celebrated victim of appendicitis just before his coronation.

Nonetheless, to make writing work we do rely on some very elaborate, authoritarian rules. By the time of Lewis and Clark there were well-known dictionaries to be reckoned with, along with common printing house conventions about spelling and punctuation. Some famous writers still had their peculiarities and indifferences to these constraints, but there was a well-understood difference—and long had been—between halting literacy and easy, cultivated prose. The distinction was evident enough to embarrass and intimidate both our explorers when they looked ahead to publication.

Perhaps self-defensively, Clark once wrote: "Learning does not consist in the knowledge of languages, but in the knowledge of things to which language gives names. Science and Philosophy."[6] Jerome Steffan uses this line to defend Clark, insisting that his actual perceptions in science and diplomacy put him on a par with Meriwether Lewis, even though his erratic spelling and grammar make him appear far less intellectual.[7] But to Clark himself language remained a sore point. After Lewis's death, he was asked to write up the journals for full publication, but he refused. In the words of Charles Willson Peale: "I would rather Clark had undertaken to have wrote the whole himself and then have put it into the hands of some person of talents to brush it up, but I found that the General was too diffident of his abilities" (*Letters* 2:493). Clark's reasons for diffidence show up glaringly in his own plea a few days later. He applied for the help of Nicholas Biddle, a wealthy young Philadelphia attorney, editor, and former diplomatic secretary. But in addressing Biddle very formally, he still could not help making glaring slips in the crucial words of important sentences: "As I have been disappointed in hereing from you on this subject feel my self much at a loss to adress you. . . . Cant you Come to this place where I have my Books & memorandoms and stay with me a week or two; read over & make yourself thirily acquainted with every thing which may not be explained in the Journals? If you will come it will enable me to give you a more full view of those parts which may not be thirily explained and enable you to proceed without dificuelty" (*Letters* 2:494). Biddle came to visit Clark a few weeks later, in 1810, stayed three weeks, and took extensive notes from conversations about the journals. Later they exchanged letters on further questions of detail, and Clark sent George Shannon to visit Biddle and give further oral advice.[8]

Robert B. Betts has traced three different attitudes readers might take to this confessed weakness in Clark's learning. A robust, no-nonsense approach may see language as a mere medium for more important things. "The man who helps make an empire may spell as he chooses," wrote Seymour Dunbar.[9] A more sentimental view, once expressed by Bernard DeVoto, is that misspellings add a unique "charm" to the original journals.[10] Betts himself claims to "salute" Clark's ingenious ways of handling language by listing many entertaining contortions of spelling and his "magnificent verbal slips." We might add a fourth attitude of compassion for Clark's diligent struggles to keep accurate records by hand with a pen that would not flow smoothly for him. The man who stood on Tillamook Head and gazed at the ocean evidently felt a powerful sense of wonder. But all he could write was: "From this point I beheld the grandest and most pleasing prospects which my eyes ever surveyed. . . . the nitches and points of high land which forms this Corse for a long ways aded to the inoumerable rocks of emence Sise out at a great distance from the Shore and against which the Seas brak with great force gives this Coast a most romantic appearance" (*Journals* 6:182). Vocabulary is strained here; every other word seems forced in a futile effort to see everything and somehow jot it down. Yet the labor of reinventing every hard word seems to leave no leisure for reflection of the kind Lewis could sometimes manage; Clark's lines build to a predicate of vague cliché. Perhaps there is something democratically clumsy in such lines: this is American Everyman's first postcard from the Pacific, achieved with touching earnestness. But from what we have just seen of Clark's negotiations with Biddle, this explorer deserves respect and not condescension. Clark understood that he could not write effectively and later took every sensible step to compensate. He pleaded to talk instead of writing, to let out the wealth of what he knew in a way that came much more easily to him. By this means he showed a real depth of self-knowledge and ingenuity. And he managed to provide Biddle, and us, with about fifty pages of helpful clarification.

Lewis's pages show a different combination of difficulties. Like Clark he often suffered from troubles in spelling. But he also carried and applied a technical vocabulary for description that makes many of his botanical and zoological paragraphs especially hard for the general reader. And he seems to have betrayed his own shyness about the journals when their exposure to others became imminent. He wrote the first long account for the press, immediately after the party's return, but then had Clark recopy it, sign it, and send it home (*Letters* 1:325–35). To be sure, Clark's home on the Ohio was much closer to St. Louis than Lewis's in Virginia; Clark was the less capable writer; and what was needed in that moment was an accurate, brief report that would circulate as soon as possible. On this occasion Lewis may simply have been acting kindly toward Clark and sensibly as the excursion's commander. But on other similar occasions, Lewis also receded from view. When the first shipment of specimens and records was sent down the Missouri from Fort Mandan in the spring of 1805, Lewis penned a letter to Jefferson but had Clark recopy it and sign it for them both. In its original draft form, this letter begins with apologetic words: "As Capt. Lewis has not Leasure to Send a correct Coppy journal of our proceedings &c. . . ." As it was finally worked out, this letter still contained apologies about journals that were being sent in their original state "with many parts incorrect" (*Letters* 1:226). Donald Jackson surmised that Lewis was embarrassed at this point, that he did not have lengthy journals of his own to show Jefferson; but he was also patently embarrassed at the raw appearance of these records, whether Clark's or his own, as they went out to the eye of a cultivated reader. Could he have touched them up? After the expedition finished, Lewis found it impossible to set his hand to revising. The journals were still in his possession, apparently without a line of further development, when he died. And he had been scolded by Jefferson for failing to keep up their correspondence (*Letters* 2:444, 469, 555).

Even a practiced writer and editor would have difficulties facing a reading public with these journals. Nicholas Biddle admitted his severe problems, too, in trying to match what the explorers had found with what readers could or would understand. The narrative passed through his hands to become a "history" of the expedition, while scientific descriptions were passed on to Benjamin Smith Barton. Barton never did complete his portion, and Biddle found the labor "excessively troublesome"; it took him months of "a most persevering & undivided attention," working eight hours and more a day (*Letters* 2:550, 555n). He had to smooth the narrative and in places he edited severely to avoid giving offense. When he came to the buffalo-calling dance on the plains, which involved sexual intercourse between young hunters' wives and older men and white visitors, he put the entire passage into Latin. Perhaps he was flustered, or maybe he had language difficulties himself or a clumsy printer—but he also made blunders in his Latin.[11] Biddle finally withheld his name from the title page of the *History* when it appeared in 1814 and let his assistant Paul Allen take that credit. Like Lewis, he sought the safety of anonymity—though Biddle was also governed by the code that a gentleman does not write for publication.

Diffidence on the part of Lewis, Clark, and even Biddle thus combined with the inherent difficulties of keeping any language in good order. And together these problems complicated the work of the expedition in three important areas. One was the attempt to understand and record the very different languages of the Indians. Another was the effort to see beyond the limits of commonplace experience and language when exploring a new world. Combined with that was the task of explaining wholly new discoveries to one's own people, who had no adequate expressions for them.

When Lewis and Clark met with new groups of Indians, they were instructed to take down their vocabularies as part of Jefferson's ongoing project in comparative philology. Jefferson had forms printed with a basic vocabulary in English and blank spaces for writing out the equivalent Indian expressions. His own collection of these sheets was pillaged and all but destroyed during his move from the White House to Monticello in 1809, but its remnants were given to the American Philosophical Society. The vocabularies collected by Lewis and Clark apparently went to Benjamin Smith Barton but were never published and have never come to light. But it is certain that many were collected; and twenty-three were among Lewis's effects at the time of his death.[12] Jefferson later wrote that Lewis "was very attentive to this instruction, never missing an opportunity of taking a vocabulary" (*Letters* 2:611). Yet in both design and execution this effort had some glaring liabilities.

The terms printed in Jefferson's vocabulary forms are simple, mainly monosyllables: *fire, water, earth, air, sky, sun, moon,* and nouns related to weather, time, and the seasons; *man, woman,* and nouns for family relations and parts of the body; *life, death,* and nouns for foods, animals, features of the landscape and trees; *joy, sorrow,* and numbers; adjectives including terms for colors and sizes; pronouns (not including *it*); twenty-six verbs (but not *go, do, have, put,* or *be*); *yes* and *no.*[13] One may be tempted to see a wonderfully simplified universe in this list. "Jefferson's list is a thoughtful one," Kim Stafford writes: "it speaks for elemental life on earth. It names the essences and relations of creature, time, generation, event. 'To kill' and 'to dance' are adjacent not by alphabetical coincidence or legal code or logical necessity. They are adjacent because life requires it. 'Yesterday/today/tomorrow' is the configuration of both casual conversation and sacred myth. 'Yes' and 'no' are two sides of one door."[14] But in fact this list seems to be a random selection of words, designed mainly for Jefferson's own ends: to compare language forms and try to trace origins and developments of major world languages. He used comparative vocabularies in his *Notes on the State of Virginia,* in the section on "Aborigines," to make the wild conjecture that America had been populated before Asia.[15]

Clark later told Nicholas Biddle: "In taking vocabularies [the] great object was to make every letter sound" (*Letters* 2:503). This seems to echo a Jeffersonian stress on the structure of language rather than particular meaning. But how was that "great object" to be accomplished by Clark's hand? The English language is notorious for having many sounds for some of its letters. And Clark stumbles in trying to write even simple words. Betts has counted twenty-seven different ways he spells "Sioux."[16] That word, of course, is a French transliteration of a contracted word in the Ojibwa language—but all these complications illustrate the point. In the early nineteenth century there was no standard system of symbols for recording what we now call phonemes, no alphabet that gave one sign, one unique notation, to every speech sound. French had one loose system, English another, in the same alphabet.

When Melville Bell devised his system of Visible Speech in the 1860s, he took a great innovative step toward true intercultural understanding, for each sound was represented by a symbol that indicated how the lips, tongue, and throat should be coordinated. The inventor and his son, the famous Alexander Graham Bell, promoted this system for improving elocution, training the deaf to speak, and transmitting speech variations by telegraph. As a young man in North America, Alexander Graham Bell took down Indian pronunciations by this same method, with noteworthy success. A large photograph of Bell in full Mohawk regalia is on display at the Bell Museum in Nova Scotia; it records his initiation into the tribe for having mastered its language.[17] Without such a system, Lewis and Clark were simply at a loss. Irresolvable disagreements persist about how to pronounce the name they most consistently write as "Sacagawea," which language it came from, and what it means. Since we cannot directly hear the word as they heard it, we cannot know; we cannot even be sure they heard it right, since they were listening through their peculiar sense of alphabetical English. Another telling example is the name of the river now called Big Nemaha in Nebraska. When they came upon it in July 1804, Ordway recorded it as the "Grow Mahan"; Clark as "Ne Ma haw," "Ne Ma har," or "Ne Ma how"; Floyd as "Granma mohug"; Whitehouse as "Grande-mo-haugh"; and Gass as "Moha."[18]

It is obvious, too, that the explorers did not dwell long enough, or bend their attention, to learn more than shreds and patches of any Indian language. One way or another they simply did not have time. They had to keep moving, and when they stopped they had plenty of other work to keep them busy. As a result they never could extend or amend Jefferson's word lists, let alone perceive deep differences of grammar as well as vocabulary. And walled out of Indian language in this way, they were walled out of Indian experience. The party coexisted with the Mandans and the Clatsops, ate with them, smoked, danced, traded, even had sexual intercourse. But they lived in the illusion that they were communicating much by speaking English or using signs. There were abrupt limits to how well they grasped the ways Indians knew their regions and their resources; their systems of verbal symbols barely touched one another.

Another way of putting it is that Lewis and Clark lived walled in, not only by their stockades but also by their own daily habits of speech. Anyone who has gone abroad on a group tour will catch the analogy immediately. One may roam apart in the ancient castles or ruins, taste the local delicacies, join in the street fairs, and haggle in the markets. But there is always a reassuring social web to return to: a regular place on the bus or the boat, someone who has binoculars to share, another who has a first aid kit or a fund of jokes when it rains, and always a group that easily speaks the same language and constantly assimilates the strange into the same familiar terms.

Traces of this situation show up even in these journals, which are devoted to noticing new things far afield. Whatever her original name may have been, the woman who traveled with the Corps of Discovery took on an Anglicized nickname. She was "Janey" at least twice in these records (*Journals* 6:84; *Letters* 1:315). And Ronda's study of the captains' relations with Indians shows that again and again they misunderstood very alien customs and diplomacy and projected psychological or economic reasons based on their own folkways.

When the explorers finally reached the West Coast, they came upon people who regularly traded with English-speaking sea captains. We can only wonder who got the better of these encounters. The Indians had learned to get the most for the goods they offered, and they may well have known how to tease. Lewis writes very seriously: "The persons who usually visit the entrance to the river for the purpose of traffic or hunting I believe are either English or Americans; the Indians inform us that they speak the same language with ourselves and give us many proofs of their veracity by repeating many words of English." But then come the proofs—spelled here just as Lewis wrote them—to both confirm and explode the idea of the "same language" on one coast and another: "musquit, powder, shot, nife, file, damned rascal, sun of a bitch &c." (*Journals* 6:186–87). Readers also must laugh at the thought of Clark sounding out the names of Chinook chiefs for one page of his journal and the Chinook versions of sea captains' names for another. They came in "vestles," he tells us, like "skooners" and "slupes" (6:154–56).

By now the point has been made that, as Lewis and Clark handled it, the English language was a medium that could obscure or bemuddle what they saw, as well as clarify and preserve it. But it should also be clear that they both recognized this constant problem and took decisive steps to get around it. Instead of relying entirely on written records, they preserved samples, packed them carefully, and sent them or carried them back down the Missouri. They sent a few living animals. They drew sketches and made maps. It may be helpful to note that these same methods were being used many decades later when the pioneer photographer F. Jay Haynes helped the Northern Pacific Railway fit up a special exhibition railway car. To lure illiterate or non-English-speaking people to take the train and come west to buy or settle land, it contained a display of large panoramic photographs along with stuffed deer, antelopes, birds, and samples of plants and minerals.[19]

In their journal keeping the explorers could also try to avoid some difficulties by recording very unambiguous data. Whether accurately or not, they tried to find themselves on a grid of longitude and latitude by means of frequent astronomical sightings. They measured the miles they covered and kept track of compass bearings. They roughly categorized the plants and animals they saw, trying to fit them into orderly patterns. But they went on to write and write and write nevertheless—well over a million words before they were done.[20] And to incorporate new things and experiences they had to stretch such language as they had and make it new, too. English was their basic medium, the language they knew from childhood and trusted their readers to understand. But to do their work fully they had to mine their memories for odd words and expressions, pick up new ones, and even create some on the spot.

Elijah Criswell has outlined four broad categories of new terms to describe the contents of his Lewis and Clark lexicon. One of these categories may seem absurd: "failures to name," including such items as "animal that inhabits a shell," "duck not seen before," and "singular plant."[21] Where a single term failed them, however, the captains often provided longer descriptions that proved fully adequate for identifying a species. In one notable case, the incapacity to name had a long-lasting result.

The wild bears of the West have coats of many colors. The fiercest were at first called white bears, or sometimes yellow bears. But as the bears were killed and examined, the party found that their fur was gray tipped. Clark used the term "grisley" on May 5, 1805, and the party eventually adopted it for lack of anything better. The name "grisly," or horrible, bear had actually been used before by Alexander Mackenzie in his journal of 1793. And it was being repeated on a broadside in Philadelphia in 1803 while the Corps of Discovery was moving west. A French trader had captured one such bear and displayed it at Peale's museum until it grew too wild and had to be killed. Peale's handbills quoted Mackenzie and claimed that this was "the most formidable wild beast on the continent of America." But the first book in America to discuss the "grizly bear" was Patrick Gass's 1807 account of the Corps of Discovery.[22]

Moreover, the struggle to pin down the coloring of bears eventually led Lewis to make a penetrating assertion that the bears "of the speceis common to the upper parts of the missouri . . . may be called white black grzly brown or red bear for they are found of all those colours. perhaps it would not be unappropriate to designate them the variagated bear" (*Journals* 7:256). This was on the return trip, on May 14, 1806. The next day Lewis worked out further reasoning on this point: "It is not common to find two bear here of this speceis precisely of the same colour, and if we were to attempt to distinguish them by their collours and denominate each colour a distinct speceis we should soon find at least twenty" (7:260). Since color was not the best discriminator, he went on to describe other bodily features in detail. Two weeks later he brought out several bear skins for the Nez Perces to discriminate. "The white, the deep and plale red grizzle, the dark bron grizzle, and all those which had the hair of a white or frosty colour without regard to the colour of the ground of the poil, they designated Hoh-host and assured us that they were the same with the white bear" (7:313).

Thus Lewis and others made a deeper discovery by failing to assert a definite name, or rather by suspending their name for a season. By closely examining details over a period of many months, writing out many descriptions, keeping specimens, and consulting local hunters, they came to synthesize much knowledge about grizzlies and about black and cinnamon bears as well. The name they evolved may have endured because they took so long to fix it upon a definite species.

When the party named things more readily, they usually applied terms that were already current in English or another language. Criswell calls this naming *adaptation* if the term was already used in American English of the Atlantic coast, or *adoption* if it was picked up from the languages of the French traders and boatmen, the Indian peoples, the early hunters of the West, or Latinate scientific terminology.

Criswell defined adaptation as "the extension of the meaning of a term to cover a new thing."[23] The risk in such naming is that it may blur important distinctions and even result in wild errors—such as calling a lily a kind of violet. The advantage is that it makes the object named immediately understandable to readers back home. An ant, a catfish, a hickory tree, a pigeon, a snail, a tick, or a whale would have been familiar to Lewis and Clark and their people before they embarked, and by using these terms with explanations of slight differences or newly noticed details they could be clear, concise, and effective in their reporting.

In using old terms for new things, of course, the explorers were inevitably blurring important distinctions. They were also implicitly asserting American dominion over the features of the West. They were taking them over in their own language, uniting the western wren to the eastern wren, the trees rooted on the Pacific slopes of the Rockies to those rooted in Virginia or Kentucky. And since the language of the United States was English, they were also enlarging and reinforcing strong bonds of identity between Europe and this continent. This sort of linguistic colonization had been going on for a long time before Lewis and Clark, and its consequences make some of their adaptations a kind of second-generation effort. As we saw in the previous chapter, when the explorers came upon black and white birds on the plains, they had the term *magpie* available even though there had never been any sightings of magpies east of the Mississippi. The term was familiar from books in English and probably from folklore carried across the Atlantic by earlier immigrants.

Two of the most distinctive plains animals have enduring names that depend on this kind of transmission and the oblivion that goes with time and great distance. No matter how emphatically a taxonomical purist may insist that the American bison is a *bison,* it had become familiar to Americans as a *buffalo* long before 1800. Why not? No one who spent all of life in America was going to see any other kind of buffalo, nor would anyone in Britain know buffalo except by report from Asia, Africa, and southern Europe. Similarly, the light-springing, tawny and white, horned mammals of the prairies persist as *antelope* rather than *pronghorn* for much the same reason. There are no "true" antelopes in America, and the term had been used for centuries in Europe to name a legendary ancient horned beast from the banks of the Euphrates. Lewis and Clark used *buffalo* freely and wavered between *antelopes* and *cabras* or *cabrie* (from Spanish or French).

Adoptions of words from other languages still present problems to readers of the journals. These terms usually meant nothing by themselves to the Americans of this time; Lewis and Clark had trouble spelling them, or spelling them consistently; and since they did not know the original languages, these writers had no particular feeling for them. Still, some of these expressions became indispensable and commonplace in these records: Indian words for foodstuffs (*camas, wappato*); French words or translated French phrases (*calumet, bois roulé, Nez Perce, big horn, Yellowstone*); hunters' names for animals (*beaver-eater, ermine, fisher*).

After listing these terms, Criswell goes on to mention terms adopted from science, such as *argali, civet, mungo,* and *ibex.*[24] But there is surely an important difference. The latter carry on and deepen the appropriation of new things into an established American or European language—in fact into an artificial system of international nomenclature. The other adoptions indicate a breakdown in other languages, forcing the writers to pick up terms where they find them, coincidentally with their picking up specimens or experiences of the things to which they refer.

Finally, the Corps of Discovery moved into regions where they found neither Indians nor earlier European explorations to guide their language. They had to make up terms by combining an animal or plant to its locale or use, or by noting another outstanding feature. Criswell calls this *invention,* and his lists include terms that have stayed with us ever since: *mule deer* (named for their large ears), *black-tailed deer, prairie dog* (though Lewis also used *barking squirrel*), *mountain ram* and *mountain sheep, calumet eagle, mat lodge.*

These linguistic innovations make the journals sometimes richer, sometimes more obscure. Criswell's long inventories are a help, and his lexicon is sometimes a necessary reference work. But it has its limitations, too. It was compiled from the Thwaites edition of the original Lewis and Clark journals, a reprint of Gass's journal, and the Quaife edition of Ordway's journal—the best primary sources Criswell could consult in the 1930s. But it leaves out much Lewis and Clark material that has come to light since then and been painstakingly edited—so that every surviving quirk of spelling and linguistic borrowing has now been double checked, studied, and preserved in print. Criswell also suggests, if only by his title, that Lewis and Clark were influential coiners of new terms, or "linguistic pioneers." A few of their words have had a long life. But in fact the main source of information about their expedition until the end of the nineteenth century was Biddle's *History,* which severely edited and recast their language and omitted their extensive descriptions and discussions as naturalists. Their direct influence on the language was very small.

Finding Words

Lewis and Clark were not sophisticated linguists but diligent writers making the best of confusing circumstances. Behind them was a world of American English, itself a developing language whose formalities sometimes embarrassed them. In their luggage were works of European science, which they occasionally consulted for taxonomic and descriptive terms. Alongside them were French-speaking boatmen and guides and young soldiers brought up in dialects of the eastern woodlands. On the shores of the rivers they piloted were Indians and traders who had entirely different vocabularies for novelties of the West. And ahead of them were surprises that no writing or speech seemed to have taken in before. Day after day, these writers had to keep journals. As they made their entries, they had to make compromises.

It may well be that their writings have become more rather than less intelligible with time. Lewis and Clark covered so much distance, into such varied regions, that it would have been very hard for a reader of 1810 or even 1860 to follow or imagine their narratives, even if they had been amply and sensitively annotated rather than condensed. What they meant by *grizzly bear, antelope, prairie dog,* or *mat lodge* has become much more understandable because of later exploration and settlement. Hundreds of later writers have familiarized these terms and others. Explorers have opened paths and then roads for travelers and tourists; a few sketches have been supplanted by many canvases, then by thousands of photographs and hundreds of nature films in color and with sound. It is still true that the sense of many pages of these journals can be appreciated only by someone who has looked around the horizon in Montana, been hungry in the wilds of Idaho, and lived through a damp winter month along the Pacific. But a young, cloistered, urban, English-reading bookworm—as far removed as Moscow or Malaysia—may now recognize much in the language of the explorers that would have seemed strange in the Philadelphia of 1806.

Finally, finding words was only a preliminary task for Lewis or Clark as he sat with pen in hand. Combining words to say something memorable or exact was a different labor, which we have already seen both these men could perform astonishingly well. For all their problems with words by themselves, they still put out effort and talent to compose long, descriptive, and reflective passages that remain worthy of study. Within them one can see intelligent minds weighing new words, patiently linking them to sights, sounds, shapes, textures, and circumstances that someone far away might recognize. The journals do not quite satisfy their ostensible purpose—to hold the West of 1804–6 in a language meaningful for both science and common readers. They never passed through authorial revision and publication to that end. But in their surviving raw state, the daily entries still have an important place in American literature, for they bring fresh vision and fresh speech to the West, which soon enough after they were written did become well known—in fact, became tabled, mapped, surveyed, settled, domesticated, and thus obliterated within little more than a century. These pages catch wild things, as it were, on the wing. If readers must pause and wipe their lenses, try to sound out the puzzling spelling, supply the missing or suppress the unnecessary letters, recall the variant mentioned five entries earlier—so much the better. This is not English, nor American English, but the peculiar stuff of Lewis and Clark, in which the words, too, may emerge with the freshness of surprise. This is the language of discovery. And to know western America from its beginnings in English, one has to notice it coming into focus just as these writers did, at the tips of their pens.

Chapter 9 The Rhythms of Rivers

DURING THEIR long excursion into the Far West, the Corps of Discovery stayed in almost constant contact with running water. Their instructions from President Jefferson had directed them to trace the Missouri to its source, find the most direct connection to the Columbia River system, and then follow the Columbia to the Pacific Ocean. As good subordinate army officers, that is precisely what Lewis and Clark did. In fact, they were on water or very close to it from the time Lewis cast off from Pittsburgh in his keelboat in late August 1803 until their return to St. Louis over three years later. They came to know the Ohio, the Mississippi, the Missouri, the Yellowstone, and the Columbia intimately.

Behind Jefferson's instructions lay the president's understanding of how important rivers were and would be to the development of the continent. As we have already seen in part, rivers had long been the main access routes into the interior and the main trade routes out. French and British traders had penetrated far into the West by sailing from Europe into the St. Lawrence River or Hudson's Bay and then moving by canoes and over light portages across the Great Lakes and into other river systems, including the Missouri-Mississippi. LaSalle had canoed down to the mouth of the Mississippi in 1682 and named its region Louisiana. For a century afterward, explorations, trade routes, and military outposts had been developed along the Ohio, on the Great Lakes, and ever farther west. The discovery of the Columbia River by an American seafarer in 1792 opened a new passageway into the country beyond the Rockies. It also stimulated Jefferson's eagerness to find and claim a water route all across the continent.

Meanwhile, control over the mouth of the Mississippi had become a chafing issue for the newly formed United States. The settlement, prosperity, and allegiance of western territories depended on who held New Orleans and what trading rights that power allowed or refused. When Jefferson learned that France had regained Louisiana from Spain, it was an abrupt jolt to his sense of international relations. "There is on the globe, one single spot, the possessor of which is our natural and habitual enemy," he wrote in 1802. "It is New Orleans, through which the produce of three-eighths of our territory must pass to market, and from its fertility it will ere long yield more than half our total produce and contain more than half our inhabitants." Napoleonic France, Jefferson predicted, would use possession of New Orleans for new and energetic expansion in America, a drive to empire that would completely reverse "all the political relations of the U.S. and . . . form a new epoch in our political course." To keep America safe would mean relying on protection from a power Jefferson had consistently opposed. "The day that France takes possession of N. Orleans . . . seals the union of two nations who in conjunction can maintain exclusive possession of the ocean. From that moment we must marry ourselves to the British fleet and nation."[1] Significantly, these strong words were written to Robert R. Livingston, the American minister to France—and a man who was already deeply involved in exploiting American rivers, as we shall see. A year later Livingston had negotiated the purchase of New Orleans for the United States along with all of Louisiana beyond the Mississippi.

The importance of rivers was more than a large-scale political and economic matter to Jefferson and his contemporaries. It was a palpable reality that had touched their lives from birth. Jefferson's estates, family relations, social and political connections—all were maintained and fostered by the waters of the James River and its tributaries in Virginia. As a young man he had initiated a project for improving navigation on the Rivanna River so that produce from his farms could get to market. He once listed this as the first act he ever did to make an improvement in the world, and his biographer concurs that "it was his first piece of constructive public service."[2] Later, Jefferson and many others worked to develop rivers and waterways as advantageous links to the western country beyond the Alleghenies. The *Notes on Virginia* contains a long second section on American rivers, concluding with a comparison of the Hudson, Potomac, and Mississippi as "principal connections with the Atlantic." Jefferson does some special pleading there in favor of the Potomac, and he went on to promote that particular water link to the Ohio country for the rest of his life. Even George Washington, his fellow Virginian and promoter of western development, could not credit some of the wild calculations Jefferson used to favor this link. Jefferson corrected his numbers a little but still exaggerated disadvantages elsewhere.[3]

While Jefferson reasoned and argued, Lewis and Clark carried out the hard work of tracing water routes from sea to sea. The Ohio, Missouri, and Columbia rivers stretched hundreds of miles along their route. Each of them was interrupted by at least one major natural barrier or great falls system that the party had to go around with great labor or pass through at great risk. In the long trek through the un-mapped West beyond Fort Mandan, they also repeated a pattern of struggle and relief: weeks of hard towing, poling, or rowing against the current, followed by weeks of gentler passage downstream on the other side of the Continental Divide.

The river supplied water, fish, and game birds and animals for food. It also swirled with hazards and sudden upheavals that forced delays, repairs, and new beginnings on the spot with improvised rafts and canoes. As the days grew short and winter came on, the Missouri became impassable ice; the Columbia, a tract of gray water under sodden gray mists and drizzles. With spring, the waters were high and hard to resist; in summer, they could vanish from baked creek beds. Either way, the rivers could distort the landscape and leave explorers puzzled about where their main course lay. As solid ice or snow, liquid clear or turbid, or vaporous fog or mist, the river remained constant against the sides of the small vessels of the party and within view of almost every camp. Other scenery changed dramatically. But water was water, elementary, constant, and yet always demanding vigilant attention.[4] It is an old commonplace of mammalian biology that our warm blood is an inner river that replicates the nutritious fluids of ancient seas. The Corps of Discovery traversed the veins, arteries, and many capillaries of the continent—and mingled their own blood in these flowing streams.

Of course the rivers became a part of them too. In American history and literature, the outstanding figure from the Ohio-Missouri-Mississippi basin is Mark Twain, who idealized American childhood as a river town, river raft, riverboat experience. But long before Twain was born, Lewis and Clark had mapped his way, and felt it too.

The name that Samuel Clemens took as an author sings of the river: "by the mark twain" was the cry of the leadsman on the bow for a sounding of two fathoms of water. And Tom Sawyer's name is almost as nautical. According to the *Dictionary of American English,* a sawyer is "a log or tree caught in a river so that it or its branches 'saw' back and forth with the waves." The term is used in that sense for a river hazard in Twain's books, as it had been in the Lewis and Clark journals. It may seem that Twain, who was born in 1835 and wrote his Mississippi River classics long after the Civil War, belongs to a completely different era from Lewis and Clark, and in many ways that is true. But in some of his central themes and ways of perceiving American geography, he remains locked in an outlook that those earlier men shared. Their journals show them handling a complex, integrated view of the Missouri that Twain later struggled to attain in writing about his river.

The first part of Twain's *Life on the Mississippi* was published serially in 1875 as *Old Times on the Mississippi.* That was before *Tom Sawyer* had appeared or *Huckleberry Finn* had taken shape. The *Old Times* chapters comprise Twain's autobiography as a riverboat pilot between 1857 and 1861, the story of how he learned the river by memorizing every feature of it between St. Louis and New Orleans as an apprentice to some stern master pilots. As Twain tells it, the education was grueling and even violent at times. But as a result he became forever bound to the river and saw into new aspects of its beauty. A long passage at the end of chapter 9 describes this change in his outlook:

> The face of the water, in time, became a wonderful book—a book that was a dead language to the uneducated passenger, but which told its mind to me without reserve, delivering its most cherished secrets as clearly as if it uttered them with a voice. And it was not a book to be read once and thrown aside, for it had a new story to tell every day. Throughout the long twelve hundred miles there was never a page that was void of interest, never one that you could leave unread without loss, never one that you would want to skip, thinking you could find higher enjoyment in some other thing. There never was so wonderful a book written by man; never one whose interest was so absorbing, so unflagging, so sparklingly renewed with every re-perusal. The passenger who could not read it was charmed with a peculiar sort of faint dimple on its surface (on the rare occasions when he did not overlook it altogether); but to the pilot that was an *italicized* passage; indeed, it was more than that, it was a legend of the largest capitals, with a string of

shouting exclamation points at the end of it; for it meant a wreck or a rock was buried there that could tear the life out of the strongest vessel that ever floated. It is the faintest and simplest expression the water ever makes, and the most hideous to a pilot's eye. In truth, the passenger who could not read this book saw nothing but all manner of pretty pictures in it, painted by the sun and shaded by the clouds, whereas to the trained eye these were not pictures at all, but the grimmest and most dead-earnest of reading-matter.[5]

Twain goes on to complain that in gaining mastery over the river he felt a sense of permanent loss. The passenger could always have a naïve sense of wonder that the expert boatman could never afford: "All the grace, the beauty, the poetry had gone out of the majestic river!" (284). He develops this point by making a luscious description of a river sunset from the passenger's point of view and then deflating it with a pilot's hard-mouthed version of the same scene. Twain's feelings are evidently torn here between exultation and regret over his learning as a pilot. He makes a sharp dichotomy between the pilot and the passenger and so grasps explicitly for a moment a strain that would enliven his most famous books, in which naïve expertise is happily reborn in the adventurous competence of Tom and Huck. But in the passage quoted above he joins both visions in an adult synthesis that he shares with the sophisticated reader: "Throughout the long twelve hundred miles there was never a page that was void of interest, never one that you would want to skip, thinking you could find higher enjoyment in some other thing. There was never so wonderful a book written by man." Coming to see into the river with alert learning, in other words, was the most satisfying experience of his life.

There is no such pondering of different ways of seeing in the Lewis and Clark journals, no retrospective comment quite like this one. But both the naïve wonder and the expert insight can be found there. Sometimes they are closely bound to one another, especially in Clark's records of ascending the Missouri in 1804.

Clark's language in two of these entries breathes with the fresh wonder of being in an entirely new landscape. On the Fourth of July, he found and named Independence Creek in what is now Kansas and camped for the night in a plain "open & butifully diversified with hills & vallies all presenting themselves to the river covered with grass and a few scattering trees" (*Journals* 2:346). With a practical eye he noted "a good Situation for a fort" on a nearby hill. But on a separate sheet of paper he combined matters practical and romantic. On one side he listed the names of his French engagés and totaled "46 men 4 horses & a Dog" as the members of the party at that point. On the other side, he expatiated on the lush and sensuous scenery:

> The Plains of this countrey are covered with a Leek Green Grass, well calculated for the sweetest and most norushing hay—interspersed with Cops [copses] of trees, Spreding ther lofty branchs over Pools Springs or Brooks of fine water. Groops of Shrubs covered with the most delicious froot is to be seen in every direction, and nature appears to have exerted herself to butify the Senery by the variety of flours Delicately and highly flavered raised above the Grass, which Strikes & profumes the Sensation, and amuses the mind throws it into Conjecterng the cause of So magnificent a Senerey in a Country thus Situated far removed from the Sivilized world to be enjoyed by nothing but the Buffalo Elk Deer & Bear in which it abounds & Savage Indians. (2:346–47)

Clark has a practical sense of beauty: the plains seem rich with nourishing hay and fruit. But he also gives a rare outburst here about the scenery while its perfumes overcome him and drive him to wondering conjectures. At this time Clark had yet to meet a "savage Indian" or see a buffalo; he may well be crudely exaggerating and heightening this scene for the benefit of later "sivilised" readers. But what is one to make of his entry for July 19, when he walked after elk into boundless, level prairies?

> After assending and passing thro a narrow Strip of wood Land, Came Suddenly into an open and bound less Prarie, I Say bound less because I could not See the extent of the plain in any Derection, the timber appeared to be confined to the River Creeks & Small branches, this Prarie was Covered with grass about 18 Inches or 2 feat high and contained little of any thing else, except as before mentioned on the River Creeks &c, This prospect was So Sudden & entertaining that I forgot the object of my prosute and turned my attention to the Variety which presented themselves to my view. (2:394)

This scenery is astonishing, even if it emerges in prose so flat and matter-of-fact that the reader could easily skip over it—so astonishing that it stops the explorer in his tracks. For a moment, he confesses, he forgets what he is pursuing and just looks and looks. Surely this is the casual, surprised wonder at a scene that Twain regretted losing by becoming a pilot and had to labor to reconstruct as a genteel author.

Yet if Clark was making these incidental notes on landscape he was also keeping a trained and wary eye on the river, hour after hour. The same Clark who may seem hopeless with the English language was a man to be trusted in command of boats on risky waters. Here he was maneuvering handily around snags and sandbars and against heavy currents that bore dangerous driftwood and snapped the tow ropes. Later he would plan portages around racing waterfalls and guide new-built canoes through foaming narrows. Twain may complain about the burden of a pilot's acquired learning; Clark would certainly have valued any more he could have got. The journals show him making the best of rough intelligence against a river no one had really piloted before.

"The water we Drink," Clark notes, "or the Common water of the missourie at this time, contains half a Comn Wine Glass of ooze or mud to every pint" (2:312). Mark Twain could work up such a fact into three paragraphs of river folklore in the third chapter of *Life on the Mississippi*. But for Clark the measurement of mud is a scientific note jotted next to the mileage and compass bearings for June 21. The full entry for that day, not a particularly noteworthy date, shows that Clark may well have been noticing something important—not a curious fact about drinking water, but a rough measure of how thick and hence forceful these waters could be: "The river rose 3 Inches last night   after the Bows man Peter Crousat viewed The water on each Side of the Island which presented a most unfavourable prospect of Swift water over roleing Sands which rored like an immence falls, we Concluded to assend on the Right Side, and with much dificuilty, with the assistance of a long Cord or Tow rope, & the *anchor* we got the Boat up without any further dang. [damage] than Bracking a Cabin window & loseing Some *oars* which were Swong under the windows" (2:313). Yet for all his careful recording of fact, this page, too, records one of Clark's occasional yieldings to sheer awe. "At Sun Set the atmespier presented every appearance of wind," he writes dutifully, but then goes on: "Blue and white Streeks Centering at the Sun as She disappeared and the Clouds Situated to the S.W, Guilded in the most butifull manner" (2:313).

By looking attentively at the Missouri, Clark even managed to make very perceptive scientific observations. The geographer John Logan Allen calls one of his entries an almost exact "modern portrayal of the riverine environment of the Great Plains."[6] Allen has even higher praise for a process of reasoning Clark records in assessing the changing course of the great river. On August 6, Clark had been able to walk across a narrow neck of land and so cut off many miles of a meandering loop in the course of the river. He went on to notice the process by which waters flowing through such a bend built the land up again and eventually forced a new channel to break through:

> I walked on Shore this evening S. S.   in Pursueing Some Turkeys I [s]truck the river twelve miles below within 370 yards, the high water passes thro this Peninsulia; and agreeable to the Customary Changes of the river I Concld. that in two years the main Current of the river will pass through. In every bend the banks are falling in from the Current being thrown against those bends by the Sand points which inlarges and the Soil I believe from unquestionable appearns. of the entire bottom from one hill to the other being the mud or ooze of the River at Some former Period mixed with Sand and Clay easily melts and Slips into the River, and the mud mixes with the water & the Sand is washed down and lodges on the points. (2:448)

Allen comments: "More than a half century before John Wesley Powell would lay the foundations for scientific topographical analysis of river valleys, Clark set down a word picture of fluvial processes that was remarkable for its clarity and prophetic in its content."[7]

Clark thus seems to surpass even Mark Twain in his powers of seeing and feeling for a great river. He came fresh to the natural landscape and was overwhelmed by its beauty. And he came untutored to the navigation of challenging waterways and excelled at analyzing and overcoming their difficulties. What in Twain's writings often seems a forced yoking of points of view is in Clark's an easy shift of focus between insight and appreciation.

Twain's understanding of the river, however, has another dimension that Lewis and Clark could not anticipate—at least not directly. For the river pilot of the 1850s, navigation had become a much more complex, hazardous matter than adventuring with sails, paddles, and tow ropes hauled by a few dozen companions. The Mississippi pilot stood on a high and fancy deck, looking down on river towns that depended on him for their commerce. His vessel was large enough to carry a valuable cargo and dozens of important passengers. And it was pushed along by a mighty, fiery, mechanical power that was as likely as any snag or sandbar to end its career with disaster. Fires, explosions, engine failures, and collisions were the common destroyers of old-time paddle wheelers. As Twain well knew, they moved with a new speed, even against the stream, and could hurl a hull suddenly upon fatality unless the pilot was quick as well as ever-watchful. The pilot was riding another monster besides the river itself and breathing another steam besides the mist that sunlight boiled up from its surface.

Twain's *Old Times* chapters conclude, in fact, by underscoring the dangers of mechanical power and the bewildering fickleness of that power in the course of its development through time. Chapter 20 describes a sudden boiler explosion and fire that sank a boat Twain had just missed taking. He caught up with the survivors in Memphis and watched his younger brother die slowly from scalds and other injuries. The chapter ends with the mournful words, "We bore him to the death room, poor boy" (359). From what we have already seen of Twain's changed awareness of the river on becoming a pilot, these words also carry the weight of his own lost innocence. The boy died, the man emerged, and the river was never the same.

But as the next, very brief chapter goes on to explain, the agency of change, the steamboat, also suffered a mysterious transfiguration: "In due course I got my license. I was a pilot now, full fledged. I dropped into casual employments; no misfortune resulting, intermittent work gave place to steady and protracted engagements. Time drifted smoothly and prosperously on, and I supposed—and hoped—that I was going to follow the river the rest of my days, and die at the wheel when my mission was ended. But by and by the war came, commerce was suspended, my occupation was gone" (360). In an earlier chapter, Twain had explained this historical change a little more fully: "First, the new railroad stretching up through Mississippi, Tennessee, and Kentucky, to Northern railway centres, began to divert passenger travel from the steamers; next the war came and almost entirely annihilated the steamboating industry during several years; . . . and finally, the railroads intruding everywhere, there was little for the steamers to do, when the war was over, but carry freights," and that could be done as it is to this day, with barges and "a vulgar little tugboat" (329). After all the costs of learning and loss, Twain became a successful pilot only to see that calling completely disappear.

The merging of a boy's death and a career's end remains brief and awkward at the end of the *Old Times* chapters, like an unhealed wound. Other writers have dwelled on the mystery of outgrowing early aspirations and even made poetry out of the passing of young rivals or companions. Milton's *Lycidas,* Gray's "Elegy Written in a Country Church-Yard," Wordsworth's "Tintern Abbey," and Arnold's "Thyrsis" are famous examples in the English tradition; in each one the poet recalls an idealized youth in a natural scene, a scene that time and change have forever destroyed or overshadowed. The burden on the survivor is to find a way, like Milton's shepherd swain, to go on to "fresh woods, and pastures new" or, like the mature Wordsworth, to explain the "abundant recompense" he has found in an adult life far from his boyhood immersion in streams and woods. Twain's narrative follows this same contour but ends with a brief, raw paragraph that leads nowhere. For Twain, the confrontation with lost youth is complicated by an awareness of baffling historic change. The same steam power that created wondrous riverboats also seared one's flesh and blood and then, worse yet, swept away to abandon the river for rail lines farther west. America the beautiful and natural had been overturned by speed, by industrial power in the form of continental business enterprises, and by the recent upheaval of a mechanized Civil War. Twain here knows all that violent history and knows his own implications in it. To recapture his own innocent aspirations he must confess that he was trying to master both the unending river below the keel of his boat and the strange new power that was throbbing within it. And that power has gone on to perplex and betray many thoughtful writers long after Mark Twain.[8]

The Industrial Revolution was evidently far removed from men who were straining their backs and cutting their feet while hauling on elk-skin tow ropes along the Missouri in 1804. But if they were far away in space, Lewis and Clark were not really cut off in time from the power that would soon overturn everyone's understanding of American landscape and distance. In its timing, aims, sponsorship, and outcome, the Corps of Discovery was closely allied to new forms of locomotion. Their expedition expressed the same urge for discovery that was soon to put steamboats on American inland waterways. The party's canoes came back downstream to St. Louis in September 1806; that was just months before Robert Fulton launched his successful experiment on the Hudson. And Fulton's work derived very obviously from twenty years and more of American tinkering, false starts, and limited successes at placing awkward contraptions in wooden hulls. Steam technology and steam navigation had been advancing together in the eastern states as in no other part of the world. Early inventors had opened visionary schemes of exploiting western rivers. They dreamed of starting upstream from New Orleans. And with such plans they had forced their way into the public chambers, private parlors, and secret meditations of George Washington, Benjamin Franklin, Thomas Jefferson, and many other early statesmen. So it was not merely coincidence that while Lewis and Clark were recording currents and compass bearings in the West, Fulton was in the last stages of exploiting technology, politics, and financial opportunities in Europe and the eastern states. Both these lines of pursuit would converge during Jefferson's second term as president to spell the final subjugation of American rivers.

The American invention and development of the steamboat involved far too many intricacies and technicalities to be fully repeated here. As James Thomas Flexner tells the story in *Steamboats Come True,* it also reflects the drive and peculiarities of three or four striking personalities.[9] But even in summary, this historical development connects directly and very obviously with the expansionist energies and ideals of Jeffersonian America.

John Fitch was the first inventor to run a crude steamboat on American waters, but before he did that, he too had been an adventurous frontiersman. As a surveyor and land speculator in the Ohio region, he had been captured by Indians in 1782, nearly scalped, passed along to the British at Detroit, and eventually exchanged home by way of Quebec. He later drew and published his own map of the Old Northwest. His plans for building a steam-powered vessel arose in 1785 and bedeviled him for the rest of his life. He had no training as an engineer, no prior experience with steam engines, no access to another trained mechanic, no financial backing. He was also a neurotic, lonely individualist who had abandoned his wife, child, and religion in Connecticut. But he drew up plans, submitted them to Congress, approached the Spanish ambassador with his ideas for inland navigation "particularly adapted for the Mississippi River," talked to Benjamin Franklin, and even made his way to Mount Vernon to solicit the patronage of Washington. He pressed on, found a skilled collaborator (a German watchmaker who eventually became master of the United States mint), drew in some financial backers, and by 1787 had a workable scheme in progress.

By August of that year he had a boat perfected and ready to demonstrate. It was propelled by a framework of parallel oars or paddles, and it could go only about three miles an hour. But in Flexner's words it was "not only the first steamboat to move consistently on American waters, but the most efficient steamboat that had ever been built." [10] It also appeared at a wonderfully opportune moment, for it ran on the Delaware River at Philadelphia just at the time of the Constitutional Convention. Most of the delegates came out to see it; so did many leading Philadelphia scientists.

Fitch went on to develop larger schemes, and in 1790 he had a regular steamboat running between Philadelphia and Trenton, New Jersey. It could go up to eight miles an hour, propelled by large paddles that pushed out from the stern. Despite some breakdowns it stayed in continuous operation for the summer months, covering a total of over 2,000 miles. The drawback was that it did not make a profit. The following winter Fitch saw his further schemes collapse for a lack of capital and credit. He again turned to lobbying politicians and financiers with interests in western expansion and Mississippi navigation; he even obtained a Spanish permit to take a new boat into the river through New Orleans. But in the meantime he lost his collaborator and all hopes of further development in Philadelphia. One last burst of hope carried him to France in 1793 to build steamboats—but he arrived just as the government in power was overthrown. The British blockade left him stranded in England, where he had gone to purchase an engine. Over the next few years he made his way back to America, impoverished and frustrated by the failure of other schemes and inventions. By 1797 he had returned to the West, where he made a legal bond with a tavern keeper in Bardstown, Kentucky—trading the promise of some of his remaining western acres for enough daily whiskey to hurry him into his grave.

As soon as he began to work on steamboats, Fitch found himself in direct competition with another adventurous American, James Rumsey. Flexner characterizes Rumsey as a sharp, smooth, sociable gambler in comparison to the crude, lonely, conscience-ridden Fitch. But both men had begun life as poor artisans and both were driven by ambitions that would give them no rest. One day in 1784 Rumsey, who was then an innkeeper at Bath in western Virginia, welcomed George Washington under his roof. Rumsey made himself agreeable, took Washington into his confidence, and soon showed him a model he had made of a mechanical boat that could "walk" upstream by means of poles attached to an inner paddle wheel. Washington must have felt a serendipitous glow, for his diary records that he was traveling specifically "to obtain information of the nearest and best communication between the eastern and western waters, and to facilitate, as much as in me lay, the inland navigation of the Potomac."[11] He gave Rumsey a certificate praising this invention, and along with other Virginia leaders he began finding ways to promote this man's work. Rumsey's original model had no steam engine involved, but a few months later the inventor was writing Washington about boats with greater power that might move upstream on the Mississippi or the Ohio. In July 1785, Rumsey was appointed chief engineer of the Potomac Company, where he was to further Washington's plans to make the Potomac navigable far inland and connect it by a short portage with the Ohio.

Rumsey thus set to work on the Potomac while Fitch was experimenting on the Delaware. He also took over an idea Benjamin Franklin had been considering, to propel boats by a stream of water pumped from the stern—a rudimentary form of jet propulsion. Both his original pole boat and his first attempted steamboat had some brief success in early trials. By December 1787 he was ready to make two public demonstrations, in which an improved steam vessel moved against the current at an estimated three miles an hour with a load of two or three tons.

Before the Constitution was ratified, in other words, two steamboat inventors had carried their ideas into tangible form and proved them before others, including leading statesmen. Thereafter they both kept busy by attacking each other, securing monopoly rights from state legislatures, and patching up leaking hulls and shaky financial arrangements.

While Fitch was working on his larger boat, Rumsey sailed for Europe to obtain a sophisticated engine directly from Boulton and Watt. Negotiations for a partnership with these renowned engineers fell through, but in London Rumsey met Thomas Jefferson, and he saw him again in Paris. Jefferson was impressed. After describing Rumsey's steamboat plans and improvements in a letter, Jefferson pronounced the inventor "the most original and greatest mechanical genius I have ever seen."[12]

Jefferson's favor was to prove valuable within a few years, for at the instigation of competing inventors, specifically steamboat inventors, Congress set up the first patent commission in 1790. Its members were the attorney general, the secretary of war, and the secretary of state. By this time Jefferson had returned to America and become the first secretary of state. As a leading scientist as well as public official he took on major responsibility for reviewing the patent applications.[13] The hearings on steamboat patents produced a muddled decision on August 26, 1792—granting Fitch, Rumsey, and another claimant overlapping rights by repeating the exact words of each man's application. But Jefferson's favor for Rumsey was well known and at least it gave him a psychological advantage while the claims were pending. Rumsey meanwhile had remained in England, dodging bailiffs one month and riding high with new backers another. By the end of 1792 he was preparing another boat to demonstrate for the Royal Society. The boat sailed a short distance in 1793, but by then Rumsey had died of a sudden stroke while eagerly explaining another mechanical device.

By the 1790s the competition between Fitch and Rumsey had produced results but no lasting success. It also reflected the peculiar American drive to conquer space and time, along with the peculiar American social structure that allowed humble, untrained dreamers to force their way into the notice of the great and secure their direct encouragement. Most significant, the union of steam power with river navigation became a matter of intense competition in America because of the pressing need to connect the eastern states with the rich interior country. Flexner explains:

> Never before in the history of the world had the time and place been equally ripe for a mechanical boat. The oceans had not created the need; sailboats crossed them so effectively and cheaply that they were not to be supplanted by steam until generations after it was used for inland trade. In Europe, those countries that possessed long, wild, turbulent rivers had been denied the blessings of the industrial revolution; a steamboat could not have been built on the Danube or the Volga because the necessary skills were unknown, and in any case the static medieval society had no great need to move men and goods in bulk. On the other hand, countries like England and France were small, and their rivers were little and flat; the old methods of transportation sufficed. The same had been true of the American Colonies as long as they did

not penetrate beyond the Atlantic plateau; it was the settling of the West that called imperiously for a steamboat.[14]

Yet in the 1780s and 1790s no well-coordinated effort proved possible in America. Fitch, Rumsey, and others remained parochial tinkerers, jealous of each other and cut off from techniques and improvements that were commonplace in England and France. Their separate states were likewise half-hearted in their encouragement—offering conditional monopolies but no hard investments; stimulating westward expansion but fearful of western development to the point of rivalry or secession. The federal government, just getting established under the Constitution, had many other preoccupations. And in the agricultural, small-trade society of the late eighteenth century, steam power was so newfangled anyhow that there was no way to accommodate it even into farsighted public policy. Benjamin H. Latrobe prepared a report on behalf of the American Philosophical Society in 1803, listing many weighty reasons why steamboats had failed and seemed destined to prove chimerical. He also listed the total of five steam engines then in operation in America—not one was being used to move a boat or other vehicle.[15]

Sometimes these provincial conditions could work to the advantage of inventors. Because they did not know Watt's engines or principles, Fitch and Rumsey had to start from scratch. They therefore made improvements as they rediscovered them and became intimate with the peculiar requirements of mechanics afloat. Another inventor, Samuel Morey of New Hampshire, tried completely different methods in the 1790s. He later claimed to have used twin paddle wheels instead of Fitch's cumbersome paddles. And he obtained a patent for an internal combustion engine with a carburetor. David Bushnell and John Stevens, working independently, made use of a screw propeller.

But it still took until 1807 before regular, profitable steamboats could be established on American waterways. It also took a new and much more sophisticated outlook than Fitch's or Rumsey's. Robert Fulton was another rags-to-riches American dreamer. But he came to the Hudson River after twenty years in Europe, and he came to steamboats after exhausting his grand schemes for developing European transportation networks and creating an ultimate weapon to end all wars. Fitch, Rumsey, and Jefferson were all born in the same year, 1743. Fulton (1765–1815) was a closer contemporary of William

Clark (1770–1838). But if these two men shared an interest in American rivers, westward expansion, and military operations, they came to those subjects with outlooks so different they might well have lived in different centuries. While Clark was going west armed with muskets and rifles and improvising navigation by sail, paddle, and pole, Fulton was presenting plans for networks of elaborate canals to European empire builders and making promises and threats about destroying entire navies.

Fulton may once have seen the loveliness of the American landscape with a fresh and appreciative eye, for he grew up in rural Pennsylvania, learned miniature painting as an apprentice to a Philadelphia jeweler, and left for London in 1787 to study in the studios of Benjamin West. But in Europe his painting career came to nothing after a short time. From scratchy miniatures he turned to industrial designs on a grand scale; as a civil engineer he promoted many successful inventions, including the steamboat, canal systems, and submarine warfare. Fulton borrowed others' ideas unashamedly in putting together his plans, and he careened wildly in his moral outlook. He sometimes stood out as an idealist, promoting a weapon so dreadful it would open the seas to freedom of commerce. At other times he bargained nakedly in England and France—countries then at war with each other—holding out for the highest rewards while threatening to go over to the other side. But his wily opportunism was combined with real engineering talent. In the end, his international daring and experience prepared him very well for finding and exploiting American opportunities.

The submarine was Fulton's chief project for many years, and in promoting it he resembled no one quite so much as Swift's hero in the opening books of *Gulliver's Travels*. The mercurial Captain Gulliver seems tiny in one land, enormous in another, and finally returns home having lost all sense of proportion. At one moment he is pompous and righteous; at another he trips over a snail shell or betrays his own nasty nakedness through tattered clothing. Yet somehow he always gets to the center of power in foreign countries, has secret discussions with the king or his highest ministers, and proves himself indispensable in war and peace. He steals away a whole navy for the Lilliputians, and to the King of Brobdingnag he makes an offer that only a blockhead could refuse: an invention (gunpowder) "into an heap of which the smallest spark of fire falling, would kindle the whole in a moment, although it were as big as a mountain, and make it all fly up in the air together, with a noise and agitation greater than thunder." With such power he promises to blow up armies, cities, and navies; he describes the results in vivid detail. "This I humbly offered to his Majesty as a small tribute of acknowledgment in return of so many marks that I had received of his royal favour and protection."[16]

So, a century after Swift, Fulton laid out plans to carry mines by submarine, attach them to the hulls of men-of-war or anchor them in harbors, and blow up entire navies in a single attack. The French finally agreed to let him try out his working submarine in 1800—though the two British brigs he approached had been warned and slipped away. The British later arranged trials too and authorized two attacks with mines against the French fleet at Boulogne in 1804 and 1805. In his negotiations over these plans Fulton directly addressed Napoleon and met with the younger William Pitt. He wrote glorious manifestos about weapons so unthinkable they would rid the seas of all despotic powers. Then he wrote threatening letters, demanding costs, royalties, and prize money for his unique contribution to invincible naval superiority. Finally, when each side set him down or shunted him aside, he exclaimed in confused outrage—just as Gulliver did—against the short views and narrow principles of stubborn political leaders.

The limited success of his work in naval warfare served Fulton's long-range purposes nevertheless. In traveling and negotiating as he did, he also happened to assemble exactly the means necessary to establish steamboats in America. He signed a contract in Paris in 1802 to join forces with Robert R. Livingston, make a trial vessel with an English steam engine, and so develop a boat for service on the Hudson River. By this agreement Fulton gained many advantages at once. Livingston was a wealthy American as well as a powerful political figure in the state of New York. He was in Paris at this time as Jefferson's minister to France—as we have seen, he was sent with explicit instructions to keep Napoleon from tyrannizing New Orleans, and within the year he helped negotiate the Louisiana Purchase. As it happened, Livingston had already been busy in steamboat experiments in America. Along with his brother-in-law, the inventor John Stevens, he had gained monopoly rights for steam vessels in New York. For a time Livingston and Fulton would join forces in rivalry against Stevens and rearrange the family connection when Fulton married Livingston's sister Harriet. By planning a new boat for the Hudson River these new partners were also exploiting the best natural waterway into the American interior. Despite Jefferson's propaganda in favor of the Potomac, Washington and Rumsey's efforts to improve it, and Fitch's efforts on the Delaware, the Hudson remained the shortest, most open link between the eastern states and the West. Finally, by agreeing to design a boat using a Boulton and Watt engine, these partners were adopting the best expertise available in the world for steam power design and manufacture.

Fulton brought his own talents and advantages to this contract, too. He knew exactly what to order from Boulton and Watt. While he was on the spot in England, he badgered American and British officials to get an export permit so that he could take this equipment overseas. He seems to have studied the work of his predecessors very closely; he experimented with models and made theoretical modifications; and he had learned from his own direct experience in handling surface and underwater vessels. For his first Hudson boat he designed a light, narrow hull with paddle wheels. Later he modified the design to make an attractive, comfortable, even ornate passenger vessel. In effect, he created the prototypes of those floating palaces whose approach would excite many river towns in coming decades. A modern professor of naval architecture claims that Fulton was not just a borrower but a very brilliant, original designer:

> Fulton's many detractors, who loudly proclaim he did not invent the paddle wheel, or the steam engine, or the combination of both, should note that he was the first designer of ships to regularly use the results of published model tests to power his vessels. No other designer dared to try this during the first half of the nineteenth century. Although a modern hydrodynamist might object to almost every step in the process, as explained by Fulton, it must be remembered that he was ultimately successful. His vessels, after his Paris experiments, all exceeded the speeds he predicted for them. And at least one of his assumptions, that his paddle wheels had an efficiency of fifty per cent, is quite reasonable in the light of experiments performed over a century later. Furthermore, the subdivision of ship resistance into pressure and frictional terms is still a basic assumption of the present-day naval architect. . . . Fulton [also] showed great engineering judgment in tailoring his early hulls to meet the heavy, inefficient engines of low power that were available to him. He saved weight where he could, and, wherever weight is saved, horsepower and fuel-consumption values are lowered.[17]

In addition to designing boats, Fulton worked out elaborate schemes for canals. And as he worked through experiments in France and on the Hudson he kept an eye fixed, like Fitch and Rumsey before him, on eventually developing western rivers. The boat that made him famous set sail from New York to Albany on August 17, 1807, and steam-powered boats remained in constant, profitable service thereafter.[18] By 1811 Fulton and Livingston had secured monopoly rights from the Louisiana territorial legislature. That same year they had a boat built at Pittsburgh under the direction of Nicholas Roosevelt, an engineer who had worked with Livingston earlier. The *New Orleans* cast off in September and, despite floods and earthquakes, made it all the way downstream to begin regular service between the Gulf and Natchez. Flexner records that a competitor, Henry M. Shreve, soon designed better boats—with flatter hulls and high decks—to meet the requirements of western rivers; the first of these made it from New Orleans to Louisville as early as 1817. In 1830 the fur trading companies of John Jacob Astor had a vessel built in Louisville to navigate up the Missouri, and in 1832 the *Yellow Stone* made it from St. Louis to the mouth of the Yellowstone River.[19]

Thus the rivers that were powerful, daunting forces to the Corps of Discovery were becoming easy channels of commerce within decades after their return. Although it had taken them months of hard labor to ascend a thousand miles, with steam it could be done in a matter of days. Rivers did not change, but ordinary Americans' perceptions of them did. And the same steam power that could carry a flat hull against the current was soon being mounted on carriages that ran on iron rails. When Patrick Gass, the last survivor of the Lewis and Clark company, died in 1870 at the age of ninety-eight, railroad lines had been laid all across the continent. The final link, Thomas Eads's iron bridge across the Mississippi, was under construction at St. Louis.

In the midst of his plans and experiments, steam must have seemed a strange stuff to Robert Fulton. Was it a vapor, a mere will-o'-the-wisp, as it had been to most observers for centuries? Or was it a great but controllable force, already harnessed by Watt to drive heavy metal pistons and thus rearrange time and space? To prove it was the latter, Fulton had to let go of the earth, travel widely, even sink beneath the sea and coldly calculate the comparative destructive powers of two great empires. He had to return to America prepared to take hold of the Hudson and then the Mississippi—and hurry to do that before his company's monopoly rights ran out. Was he a hardened, grasping thief of others' ideas, boldly and brilliantly reforging them to conquer water with fire? Or was he, like them, just another unwitting servant of a force of science and empire that would make its way onto ships and railroads and reshape every continent on earth—if not in 1790, then in 1807 or 1820, but in any case very soon?

Questions like these did not burden Fulton, for he died in 1815. But we have seen them haunting Mark Twain. And they have continued to puzzle American historians. To Henry Adams in the 1890s, the date of Fulton's first success on the Hudson marked a radical division between an old world and a new: "The problem of steam navigation, so far as it applied to rivers and harbors was settled, and for the first time America could consider herself mistress of her vast resources. Compared to such a step in her progress, the mediaeval barbarisms of Napoleon . . . signified little more to her than the doings of Achilles and Agamemnon."[20] In the final volume of his *History* of this period, Adams repeated the point. The people of the United States at the end of Madison's term as president in 1817 had not only "escaped from dangers, they had also found the means of supplying their chief needs. Besides clearing away every obstacle to the occupation and development of their continent as far as the Mississippi River, they created the steamboat, the most efficient instrument yet conceived for developing such a country. The continent lay before them, like an uncovered ore-bed."[21] But what would such new power, combined with vast territory and rich resources, make of human character or democratic institutions? That question was a burden to Adams to the end of his life.

For Lewis and Clark, the steamboats of Fulton were not a threat but rather a distant, subsequent development that heightened their achievement. These explorers crossed the continent by wind, river current, and animal power—and it turned out that they did it during the last years when those ancient methods of transportation remained unrivaled. They moved at their pace, too, slowly enough to blend with the rhythms of nature. Nevertheless, their deeds were another expression of new science and power over space and time. Theirs was the stamp on the other side of Mr. Jefferson's thick coin. As inventors encouraged by this president were overcoming the rivers of the East, Jefferson's explorers were mapping the rivers of the West. If Natty Bumppo, Huckleberry Finn, or the Nick Adams of Hemingway's early stories would later flee the harsh scream of the steam whistle and hurry west, he could still find dense forests and open plains, free-running rivers, and abundant game. But he would also move into territory already charted and surveyed, see animals already named and described, fish in waters already navigated and surmounted by these predecessors.

Chapter 10   Themes for
a Wilderness Epic

THE TERM *epic* has often been used
to describe the Lewis and Clark expedition. In its loose, modern usage, the word is an adjective that means grand, colossal, larger than
life; it has been beaten to death in advertising blurbs for novels, films,
and television spectacles. But as a noun, *epic* still has some meaning
left as the name for a particular kind of story. An epic tells of extraordinary deeds—wars, travels, and feasts on a scale far beyond our
own, even direct encounters with gods and monsters. The heroes of
epics meet superhuman adversaries as well as the most threatening or
imposing human counterparts, and their heroic actions disclose the
full measure of human power, intelligence, and worth.

The Lewis and Clark story seems to fit this pattern very naturally,
to be a tale of genuine heroism in early America, for in tracing the
Missouri to its source, crossing the Rockies, and encountering new
peoples who had long held the West, the Corps of Discovery was
challenging great and unforeseen powers. They were testing their own
characters against vastness, wilderness, and alien human cultures. Because they survived and succeeded, Lewis, Clark, Sacagawea, and
many others in the party have remained visible public heroes in many
states—memorialized in statues, parks, monuments, roadside markers, and the names of many schools, towns, counties, festivals, and
natural features such as mountains and rivers. The signers of the Declaration of Independence and the delegates who shaped the Constitution are celebrated in the eastern states; the Corps of Discovery is
memorialized along the Missouri and in the Pacific Northwest. Clad
in rougher clothing, engaged outdoors in gathering food and pressing
through plains and forests, they are a far cry from the proud gentlemen who sat deliberating together in Independence Hall. But like

their eastern counterparts, these western explorers are remembered as founders of the great American nation.

Frank Bergon stresses the epic qualities of the Lewis and Clark story in the introduction to his popular edition of the journals; in fact, his essay is organized around the idea of epic deeds and epic features in the explorers' writings. "Of course," he admits, "it is only from the hindsight of 180 years that it might be suggested that these journals, with their daily logs of temperature, astronomical observations, tabulations of longitude and latitude, technical descriptions of flora and fauna, anthropological data, misspellings, and neologisms, might serve as an appropriate American epic." Nonetheless, he goes on to praise the journals in well-considered epic terms:

> They tell a heroic story of a people's struggles through a wilderness and the return home. Better than more artfully constructed poems or novels or plays, they embody with the colloquial directness and power of an oral epic the mythic history of a nation. Like ancient epics, they tell the story of the tribe, in this case the story of a people moving west. It is not the story of an individual frontiersman but of a pluralistic, fluctuating community of thirty-five to forty-five people, including soldiers, woodsmen, blacksmiths, carpenters, cooks, French *engagés,* a black slave, a Lemhi Shoshone woman, and a newborn baby of mixed race, all heading west. In retrospect, that story portrays the fall of one civilization and the rise of another. It dramatizes the relationship of a people to the natural world and the design of a nation committed to the belief that—as William Gilpin expressed it seventy years later—"the *untransacted* destiny of the American people is to subdue the continent." [1]

Here in six sentences are six overlapping stories or themes: an adventure in the wilderness, the origin of a nation, a tribe moving west, a success story of a pluralistic society, a change of civilizations, the rise of a new creed in the midst of nature. Perhaps all six should be further refined and interrelated to bring out *the* central story of America. But certainly all are themes at the heart of American history; all are also central to the story of the Corps of Discovery; and as Bergon is well aware, all are well-worn themes of the epic poems that would have been familiar to educated readers of the early nineteenth century.

Bergon's suggestion calls for a few lines of criticism and several pages of further development. The journals, as we have seen, were never finished for publication to the satisfaction of their authors.

"The colloquial directness and power of an oral epic" that Bergon describes is an illusion that only a literary imagination can project back onto these pages. Clark's embarrassment with language forced him to struggle—and now forces the reader to follow him—through many indirect spellings and structures; Lewis has his solecisms, too, and his elaborate passages that are anything but colloquial or direct.

Another strong objection should be raised about pluralism as a guiding principle in this expedition. It is true that the company was made up of many people, mainly enlisted soldiers and common workers, who came to depend on each other for survival. But it was also a strict military company in which the officers were conspicuously privileged over the others. Offenses were severely punished with the lash. And while there were a black man, a Shoshone woman, and many of "mixed race" in the company, there is no evidence that these differences were acknowledged with respect. York, Clark's "servant," was a slave. He sometimes carried a gun and sometimes had a vote in company decisions. But he was also put on display as a kind of woolly black curiosity among the Indians, and when he returned from the West he was again forced into hardships as a slave.[2] Sacagawea rode in the captains' pirogue and shared their quarters along with Charbonneau and their baby; but she, too, could be put down suddenly and have her belt of blue beads snatched from her when it was thought necessary to conclude a good bargain (*Journals* 6:73). Members of the company danced with each other often and joined Indians in their dances, and shared their embraces too. But it is hard to tease an abiding sense of fellowship from the surviving records. When the company had achieved its purposes at any location, it moved on, leaving the Indians there forever. When the expedition was over, its members dispersed. There were few reunions even of individuals. Lewis made a final roll of his men in a report to the secretary of war, in which he held them together by order of rank and with a sharp sense of differences in worth. Some he commended particularly; most are listed just by name and rank over a general commendation for "a just reward in an ample remuneration on the part of our Government"; two are noted as of "no peculiar merit"; two are commended despite short or unsatisfactory service (*Letters* 1:364–69).

Bergon's sense of idealistic pluralism is not the most fitting theme, but there is still much more than coincidence to the three patterns he superimposes: expedition history, American history, and classic epic form. To hold the many, repetitious, and scattered journal records together, a reader has to find some pattern of coherence. An epic pattern is a useful, revealing framework for them. It cannot be fully sustained or fleshed out, but as Bergon explains it, the idea of epic points to some good questions about these writings. It was an idea and an ideal still revered by poets and readers in their time. But its values do not fit comfortably with new ideals of American democratic pluralism, and that discrepancy opens some crucial problems. What kind of hero was Lewis or Clark, or the entire corps that they led? If not pluralism, what was the central theme or principle of their shared experience? And how should readers now attempt to grasp what they wrote: if it resembles an epic, what are its ideal proportions; if it diverges, how should one resist its epic appeal?

In the time of Lewis and Clark, epic poetry was still a cherished, even revered, ideal of literary excellence and patriotic pride. "By the general consent of critics," Samuel Johnson wrote in his *Life of Milton* (1779), "the first praise of genius is due to the writer of an epic poem." Johnson goes on to explain: "Epic poetry undertakes to teach the most important truths by the most pleasing precepts, and therefore relates some great event in the most affecting manner."[3] The epic poet had to be a master of universal knowledge, capable of seeing into the depths of moral truth and presenting them in a composition of dramatic power and exquisite language. Such accomplishments were rare in the history of the world. But it was a point of national pride that in Milton's *Paradise Lost* England had attained a poem that rivaled and, according to some, surpassed the *Iliad* and *Odyssey* of Homer and the *Aeneid* of Virgil. John Dryden, who was himself poet laureate, composed an epigraph to go under Milton's portrait in a new edition of the poem in 1688:

> Three poets, in three distant ages born,
> Greece, Italy, and England did adorn.
> The first in loftiness of thought surpass'd,
> The next in majesty, in both the last:
> The force of Nature could no farther go;
> To make a third, she join'd the former two.[4]

Milton's Christian vision had superseded the pagan morality of the ancients, and his English blank verse attained greater majesty than Virgil's carefully polished Latin. Throughout the eighteenth century, ambitious English poets aspired to write epic poetry and yet despaired of surpassing Milton's achievement. Dryden and Pope gained money and fame by producing elegant translations of Virgil and Homer. They played with epic conventions in mock-epic satires: *Mac Flecknoe, The Rape of the Lock, The Dunciad.* Both poets became revered public figures; both were widely imitated. Yet neither could summon the muse, find the inspiration, or sustain the faith to sing a full epic of his own.

By 1800 there had been a century and more of epic versifying, editing, criticism, and memorizing, which made Homer, Virgil, Milton, Dryden, and Pope the familiar classics of educated readers in England and America. And there was still a felt challenge to create a more adequate epic to express a fuller vision of the universe. In England, Wordsworth was already drafting passages of a long autobiographical poem; its subject was transcendent visions revealed in meetings between the mind and nature. In America a half-dozen poets now forgotten had labored to celebrate the rise of a new nation on a new continent, dedicated to new principles of democracy and freedom.[5]

At the heart of every well-known epic there was a well-defined mythic action, concisely stated in the opening lines. As Bergon indicates, these were great stories about nations as well as heroes. One way of defining *epic* is as the story of a hero, a single person on whom the fate of a race or nation depends. The *Iliad* is about the Trojan War, but the outcome of that conflict depends on Achilles. When he fights among the Greeks they win their battles; when he withdraws, they lose; when he returns, he kills the Trojan leader Hektor and so ensures the complete downfall of Troy. Odysseus and Penelope in the *Odyssey* live out a story of extraordinary marital fidelity. Although Odysseus is alone on a desert island with an enchantress who wants him, he yearns for his own wife and family and labors past monstrous obstacles to return to them. The restoration of this marriage completes the healing of the Trojan War, which originally carried him away—a war that began over the abduction of Helen, entailed the anger of Achilles over a woman stolen from him, and led to the murder of Agamemnon by his wife (and Helen's sister) Clytemnestra. Aeneas in the *Aeneid* carries his father on his shoulders to escape Troy as it falls, resists the temptations of an alliance with Dido in Africa, and overpowers adversaries in Italy to settle his people there. His piety as well as his courage and steadfastness go into the new Roman nation that derives from him. In *Paradise Lost,* the epic story involves all people who ever lived—who fell with Adam and Eve to gain the promise of redemption through Christ. In these poems the heroes represent a kind of national character, a great founder, defender, or savior. Later poets still were teased by thoughts of global changes achieved by single men. Pope at one point thought of rewriting the legend of Brutus, the grandson of Aeneas who voyaged through the straits of Gibraltar to found a new nation in Britain. The American Joel Barlow published the *Columbiad* in 1807, a poem on the deeds and visions of Christopher Columbus.

These are the particular stories that loom behind some of Bergon's phrases: "mythic history of a nation," "heroic story of a people's struggles through a wilderness [to] return home," "a people moving west," "the fall of one civilization and the rise of another." Lewis and Clark do not consciously enlarge this pattern, but they certainly re-enact it in their expedition. And their times seemed to call for just such a deed, another westering, another empire founding, another vision of people creating a new order in the universe.

Yet by 1800 the idea of epic had also lost its value for many writers and critics. The ideal of a single, aristocratic, military hero like Homer's or Virgil's did not fit very well with current ideals of British freedom or American democracy. Besides, epic poems were addressed to the ear and the common memory of a people; they were meant to be heard and learned by heart. But in the eighteenth century the audience for English literature was no longer to be found in a central city with a common culture. It was increasingly a reading public, a widely dispersed, even multinational society of individuals who chose their own books and took them in with different tastes, in privacy and solitude. In short, the same pluralism that Bergon traces as the theme of the journals was a force undermining the unity of any epic poem. The high ambitious days of Dryden and Pope were yielding to the era of Defoe, Fielding, Scott, and Austen—writers who composed the world not once and magisterially but often and in prose accessible to multitudes.

In America, moreover, the act of nation founding had been united with the act of composing lofty and memorable language not in epic poems but in great public documents. If there was no American Milton or Pope, there had still been a Jefferson, a Hamilton, and a Madison. The Declaration of Independence and the Constitution made up what could be called the common poetry of Americans, the carefully deliberated phrases that everyone knew then and that many of us still recite from memory. And if one needed heroic deeds, the War of Independence had left its indelible marks in the minds of the people and on the familiar scenes of all the eastern states. While the achievements of the Revolution endured, however, the fame of individual leaders became mired in political controversies. Washington, Jefferson, Adams, Franklin, and Hamilton had all been spattered with the thick ink of partisan journalism by the end of the century. On the one hand, American heroism was palpable in the achievement of new freedoms and institutions, but on the other hand, not even Washington could seem fully convincing as a hero in immortal verse.

For all these reasons the Lewis and Clark expedition must remain an unsung act of heroism. It came too late for epic. It survives in its own prosaic records. It extended but could not overturn the more comprehensive founding of America.

Yet the expedition journals do touch two or three abiding epic strains—strains that do not quite match Bergon's description but underlie his far-reaching suggestions. These patterns are inescapable, I believe, and must be acknowledged by anyone who becomes caught up in reading the journals and settles down to reread and savor them as exciting texts in American literature.

First of all, the journals record extraordinary feats of physical strength and ready intelligence. Lewis and Clark achieved a transcontinental crossing such as no one had made before and few would make after them for many years. Stage by stage they conquered obstacles worthy of an Odysseus. Anyone who has paddled against the stream on the Columbia or the Missouri, looked straight on at the Great Falls or an approaching bear, endured days of hunger and nights of mosquitoes far from home, been sick and wet through during a week of cold drizzle, picked a wearying path over miles of fallen timber or numbing snow, negotiated nervously for the good of a whole company while surrounded by distrusting foreigners—whoever has done just one of these things can find an action to respect in the pages of this story. Lewis and Clark did them all. Sometimes they did two or three on the same day, then moved on over the horizon to meet another array of challenges in a different climate. By their actions they showed that these things could be done, could even be accomplished by a rather ordinary troop of foot soldiers. By being the first to do them in their long journey, they also transformed the world through which they passed. "His legs bestrid the ocean," Cleopatra says of a heroic Mark Antony in Shakespeare's play; "His reared arm crested the world. . . . Realms and islands were as plates dropped from his pocket."[6] Cannot almost the same be said of these captains? Their legs strode over the continent, including its highest mountains, and with lordly command they named the creeks and rivers they found for each other, for their companions, for their friends, for the people they admired, even for their dog.

The classicist Eric Havelock has argued that exemplary doing is the essential action of the Homeric poems. In a time before widespread reading and writing, oral poetry preserved the ways things were done. By memorizing the ways of feasting, greeting a guest, making sacrifice to the gods, taunting an enemy—as these doings were recited in the *Iliad*—the young learned the ways of their elders, and those elders held on to a standard of excellent behavior. In fact, Havelock argues, it was to break down a powerful tradition of such wisdom, rote-learned through poetry, that Plato wrote his dialogues. They presented a new kind of literate, critical thinking, and yet they enacted that newer behavior too through oral exchanges with an exemplary character named Socrates.[7]

A second dimension of the journals, therefore, is that their great deeds are told with literate sophistication. These heroes are their own best historians. They not only do wonderful things but also sit down daily to collect and comprehend what they are doing. Sometimes their actions occur in the course of their writing these pages, as they weigh, recount, and reshape their experiences and so find their way mentally through the snares and distractions that bewildered their active hours.

A third epic strain derives from their achievement in the history of world geography. The westering movement we have seen in a sequence of epics here comes to its end. The Homeric Greeks defined themselves against the world of the East. They gathered a great army and navy, sent them across the Aegean Sea, reduced an enemy city to ashes, then turned their backs on that annihilated threat. The sea lanes of Odysseus and Aeneas led westward toward recovered or new-found homes. In the familiar lines of his poem "Ulysses," Tennyson recaptured that westering urge derived from Odysseus:

> All experience is an arch wherethrough
> Gleams that untraveled world whose margin fades
> Forever and forever when I move. . . .
>   Come, my friends,
> 'Tis not too late to seek a newer world.
> Push off, and sitting well in order smite
> The sounding furrows; for my purpose holds
> To sail beyond the sunset, and the baths
> Of all the western stars, until I die.[8]
>   (lines 19–21, 56–61)

It might almost seem that the core story of the most famous epics was a constant westward movement in pursuit of the sun. Milton, too, understood that his constant theme of fall and redemption refigured the daily miracles of sunrise and sunset, that our days and lives follow the sun to the west. The shepherd in *Lycidas* drowns but rises to a new life in heaven with the sun's glorious ease and certainty:

> So sinks the day-star in the ocean bed
> And yet anon repairs his drooping head
> And tricks his beams, and with new-spangled ore,
> Flames in the forehead of the morning sky:
> So Lycidas sunk low, but mounted high,
> Through the dear might of him that walked the waves.[9]
>   (*Lycidas*, lines 168–73)

With Lewis and Clark the course of the sun came full circle. The passage to India sought by Columbus was at last complete. The party made it to the Pacific coast and found unmistakable evidence there of merchants who were carrying furs to China and then sailing on to the Atlantic.

The party could not recognize the full import of the new links they had made. Intercultural equality was not their conscious aim, as we have seen. Along with learned men like Jefferson, they often had very mistaken, even deeply prejudiced notions about the settlement of continents and the aptitudes of other people. But sometimes deliberately, sometimes casually, Lewis and Clark took step after step to integrate the peoples of Asia, Europe, and Africa on North American soil. Among Indians derived from Asian explorers of the Ice Age they brought Europeans speaking English and French and a black man descended from Africans. They carried a baby, half Shoshone and half French Canadian. They were often guided by Drouillard, the son of a French Canadian father and a Shawnee mother. Their survival frequently depended on making exchanges and learning the ways of indigenous hunters and settlers; in return, they shared their medicines with people in pain. The sexual adventures of their party introduced different genes among the people of the West. Their medals, certificates, and promises were attempts to introduce different political understandings. They tried to hear and record Indian languages. They carried back samples of Indian handiwork and tools. They even induced some chiefs to travel back with them to see and be seen in eastern cities.

So in 1806 a decisive link was forged between East and West. Although their hands were bloodstained once or twice, although extension of empire was their central purpose, and although their arrival spelled eventual doom for many western species and peoples, Lewis and Clark came not at all as Agamemnon and his hosts had come against Troy. They came not to destroy and deny but to learn.

Beyond the old world of epic beckoned the new world of science. And it was this world that they entered too, as much as the western American landscape—entered, inhabited, and enlarged. For this reason the numbers and jottings on their pages that Bergon sees as an intrusion or distraction in the the epic narrative—"their daily logs of temperature, astronomical observations, tabulations of longitude and latitude"—rather beat a steady rhythm of progress. They mark a disciplined effort—crudely done, perhaps on mistaken principles, but nonetheless far-seeing—to hold the entire planet together, to fit even unknown America into a new unity, a globe of knowledge all literate people might share.

The Lewis and Clark journals therefore resemble an epic poem in odd, paradoxical ways. For good and indisputable reasons they do not fit this genre at all, or any literary genre whatever. They are scientific notebooks, and sometimes very sketchy ones at that. Yet in the story they tell, the achievements they record, and even the minute details of their composition they repeat epic impulses toward grandeur and integrative comprehension. They present a completely new universe in a complex language that draws the reader toward a new power of universal understanding.

This ambiguity of form and formlessness may put a beginning reader off or overwhelm anyone who begins (as most probably do) by seeking just an incident of local history, some episodes of adventure, or a few bright records of natural description. Since 1806 the explorers themselves and many an editor after them have wondered how to shape these materials so as to display their riches and eliminate meaningless repetitions and details. But always the solution has been some form of narrative, either rambling or artificially compacted. It has always been a roughly implied epic of discovery. The range, depth, and significance of discovery has varied from the all-inclusive to the monographic. But book after set of books has, ineluctably, recounted a story of great deeds leading on to wonder and to a knowledge beyond wonder.

Perhaps the serious reader should be encouraged to avoid such patterning by becoming immersed in the full confusion of the complete journals, as many a book and article recommends. But anyone who begins that task had better have stamina, patience, and a large library—and a vivid imagination too. The full journals fill many thick volumes. The entries for any day are likely to be repetitious and confusing. Lewis, Clark, and their sergeants kept different sets of records in different ways. Each captain recopied his own field notes; at times each borrowed and rewrote entries from the other. But one cannot easily skip these copied versions, because there is no way to know in advance which version may contain some further lively detail or comment. During the long winters, the journals grew to include summary records and inventories of specimens collected so far. Daily logs of travels and actions overlap with scientific descriptions and observations. One also needs another set of volumes of correspondence about the expedition, and another of maps. To make sense of these pages, the reader will be grateful, too, for the labors of several skilled editors and annotators. But the result of all their apparatus is that an evening in the armchair may well conclude with a half-dozen volumes opened, bookmarked, and scattered on every nearby surface. A patient eye and mind can thus take in the full journey in close detail, and for many the process has proved rewarding. But a reader with a sense of humor will want to cover the mirrors to keep from seeing Don Quixote looking back. Who can pore so assiduously over these books without longing to follow their heroes back onto the trail—if only to get fresh air?

To reach the many readers they deserve, the journals require severe but sensitive editing. But that means some severe deleting and reshaping into a new design. From the work of Nicholas Biddle to the present, the main editorial practice has been the same: tell a coherent story by weaving together the highlights of single entries; make steady chronological progress across the continent and back; relegate technical observations to occasional notes or appendixes. In short, make a narrative—and by implication decide on a central story line, something very suspiciously akin to an epic theme.

Two popular editions of selections illustrate this point. Bernard DeVoto's *Journals of Lewis and Clark*, first published in 1953, emphasizes political geography. DeVoto even substitutes a long section from his own book, *The Course of Empire,* to keep the narrative smooth and compact over Clark's return trip along the Yellowstone River. Frank Bergon's more recent volume of the same name (1989) explicitly claims to correct DeVoto's work by including "much of the natural-history material omitted in earlier edited versions" and reprinting only passages from either Lewis or Clark, not eclectic excerpts from the captains, Biddle, and four other party members.[10] For DeVoto the guiding theme is Jeffersonian westward expansion; for Bergon it is epic visions of, by, and for the people, in the midst of natural wonders.

At least four other fine scholarly books have followed the same design. A recounting of consecutive events along the trail forms the backbone of *Lewis and Clark: Pioneering Naturalists* by Paul Russell Cutright (1969); *Passage through the Garden: Lewis and Clark and the Image of the American Northwest* by John Logan Allen (1975); *Thomas Jefferson and the Stony Mountains: Exploring the West from Monticello* by Donald Jackson (1981); and *Lewis and Clark among the Indians* by James P. Ronda (1984). Each of these books makes generous quotations from the journals and other sources to bring out a different story. Allen and Jackson re-create a tale mainly about geography and politics, as DeVoto did before them. Cutright retraces an excursion into wonders of botany and zoology. Ronda fills out a story of encounters between cultures. These are four separate studies, each with its own integrity. Yet each one is also a complete and satisfying narrative of the entire expedition. Whoever studies just one of these books can rightly claim to have accompanied the Corps of Discovery and taken a fair sampling of what all the other books stress.

The list of attempts to edit or reorganize the journals extends much further. It includes biographies of the main members of the party, focused on their heroic or not-so-heroic characters; novels and romances about their adventures; guide books for western travelers; picture books of art works collected or created on the trail; museum rooms and suites of rooms, from St. Louis to Fort Canby, Washington, that match displays with passages from the journals in chronological sequence; and special projects such as videotapes of sites on the trail and portfolios of modern large-scale maps.

All these works tell a story; in fact they all purport to tell the same story. Yet they differ widely in what they select, exclude, and embellish. Some make modest claims to supplement the journals themselves. Some make an ambitious bid to supplant those tedious volumes with a more popular or exciting version. Taken together, the collection of books, pamphlets, tapes, brochures, pictures, and off-prints about Lewis and Clark has its own epic dimensions. It is enough to fill a room, as it does in some college and museum libraries. Yet does any single work get to *the* theme of this epic? Or do they all compete and proliferate because this story intrinsically has no single center—or can reveal none in the pluralistic world in which we now live?

The travel narrative, however presented, has its boring stretches, too, despite the explorers' best efforts to record something worth noting every day. And strict, even chronology creates a further problem. It forces any teller into an awkward corner with this particular story. The way west is full of excitement. Every day is a day of suspense and new things unfolding, and the tension builds as winter closes in around remote Indian villages, then unimagined tracts of buffalo country appear, then high mountains loom up to block further passage. But this great story reaches its climaxes when the corps crosses the Continental Divide and successfully paddles down to reach the Pacific before winter. The exclamations are right there in the journals. "The road took us to the most distant fountain of the waters of the mighty Missouri," Lewis wrote on August 12, 1805, "in surch of which we have spent so many toilsome days and wristless nights. thus far I had accomplished one of those great objects on which my mind had been unalterably fixed for many years, judge then of the pleasure I felt in allying my thirst with this pure and ice cold water. . . . two miles below McNeal had exultingly stood with a foot on each side of this little rivulet and thanked his god that he had lived to bestride the mighty & heretofore deemed endless Missouri" (*Journals* 5:74). On November 7, Clark put the next great elation in few words: "*Ocian in view! O! the joy*" (6:58).

Thereafter follows a winter of wet, sick, hungry, tedious discontent, then a demoralizing climb into unconquerable barriers of snow, and at last swift passage back down the Missouri. The thousands of miles covered on the return trip resemble the thousands already seen, but the return is not all anticlimax. There are new adventures and new landmarks worth recording. But many of these have a dark under-side—Lewis's gunfight resulting in Indians slain near the Marias River; Lewis himself being shot by another hunter; the long, mean-dering, still uncompleted course of translating all the journals into print; the fading away of most of the corpsmen into unmarked graves; and the sudden, mysterious death by violence of Meriwether Lewis while he was still beating a trail in pursuit of fair fame and due reward.

No matter how the journals are edited or recounted in strict chro-nology, they do not come to a rounded, satisfying close. Every ending point one can find or impose for the history of the Corps of Discovery is raw-edged, lame, or forced—whereas the art of epic is to blend bloody strife and dislocation into the harmonies of highly civilized poetry.

By this point the reader must have discerned that this present book, too, is shaped by epic considerations. So I may as well step forward and candidly confess it. My powers do not permit me to celebrate the Corps of Discovery in anything but academic prose, but I have come to believe that their writings most consistently and variously turn on a different central theme from what others have put forward. I take them at their word, literally the main word of their name, and see their controlling action as the act of discovery—of seeing America new and transforming all subsequent seeing by summoning new lan-guages to describe the vast West. Discovery seems to irradiate all the kinds of seeing they did and every kind of jotting they made, however rough. It relates them to our time as much as to the limited science and lore of centuries past. And it is an act or series of acts that need not be traced strictly chronologically. It is an ever-new beginning; the story of Lewis and Clark is a living invitation to return to an ongoing American trail and make one's own new perceptions. That can still happen in Missouri or Montana, in botany, zoology, or mineralogy, in intercultural relations or national and international politics—whatever scenes or fields one chooses to project around the inquiring American mind. It can also occur in a later chapter here as well as an early one, on the exciting way out or the richly laden return.

A canny reader will also notice that these chapters are now moving toward an attempt at harmony. That may be because an epic shape is the unavoidable medium for this material, or it may be because I have been a student and teacher of literature for thirty years. As scientists and poets both know, discoveries worth reporting always emerge through the peculiar quirks of their inventors' minds; in that respect my designs here are no doubt as eccentric as William Wordsworth's, William Clark's, or Robert Fulton's. In any event, it should be obvious to anyone who has had a proper college humanities course that the preceding chapters loosely follow the familiar conventions of epic. The opening states and develops the theme immediately. Then the heroes are plunged *in medias res* to confront well-defended ramparts, encounter monsters, and interpret omens. They follow paths blazed for them by their elders, feast hugely on rare delicacies, exchange elaborate gifts and ceremonious speeches, learn to respect the most alien adversaries, take note of signs in the sky, and wrestle with rivers and oceans. They tour the whole world before they are through and then point onward toward home.

What remains to be told is a balance of visions: a descent to the underworld and a climb to the heights. That is the entire plot of *Paradise Lost,* as a matter of fact, and of the *Divine Comedy* of Dante. Odysseus and Aeneas also visit mysterious regions to meet the dead or to recognize the past as past beyond recovery. And there is a long tradition of rising to high promontories to look into the future. Moses stands on Mount Nebo to see the Promised Land. Milton sets Adam high in Eden in his final books to peer into the future with an angel as his guide. At the time of Lewis and Clark, Wordsworth was climbing Mount Snowdon on a walking tour and transfiguring his experiences there in the closing books of the *Prelude.* And Joel Barlow was creating visions of a free America by placing Christopher Columbus high on the Mount of Vision.

Our explorers, too, saw into the American past and future. Literally and intellectually Lewis and Clark met the outcasts of the new nation, left their own shadows behind them, and climbed to heights of vision previously unattained. To these scenes of discovery we now turn.

Chapter 11　Ghosts on the Trail

The newly recruited Lewis and Clark party built Camp Dubois in December 1803 on the Illinois banks of the Mississippi River a few miles above St. Louis. Here they would winter, gather information and supplies, and plan their excursion into the Missouri the following spring. For most of this period Captain Lewis was free to go into St. Louis, where he made valuable contacts with the merchants, traders, and other citizens who knew something of the country that lay ahead. But the rest of his company was not so welcome. Technically, Louisiana had not yet become an American possession; the flags were to change the following March. Spanish officials still governed the territory to the west, and they firmly prohibited an early intrusion by United States soldiers. Thus the party was at the frontier of the United States, looking into the mouth of the Missouri, but it was held back from further movement by the seasonal constraints of winter, the prudent need to gather supplies and information, and the political barrier of changing world empires.

In this novel geographical situation, Clark's pages record, very briefly and incidentally, three odd encounters with legendary figures from the past: Matthew Lyon, Simon Girty, and Daniel Boone. All three had fought in the American Revolution, crossed new frontiers, and faced hardships and violence with an outstanding display of courage. Now they appeared again here, at the meeting ground between the far edge of Revolutionary America and the promising eastern frontier of Louisiana. And all three turned up not so much by choice as by force of circumstance. To the young men of the Corps of Discovery they turned the lined faces of fighters past their prime. Together they cast gloomy shadows across the American path to the West.

Clark's only entry on Lyon is a simple business record, made on May 18, 1804, as the party was gathering its final stores of supplies near St. Charles, Missouri: "recved of Mr. Lyon 136 lb. Tobacco on act. of Mr. Choteau" (*Journals* 2:237). Army records of this period explain that Matthew Lyon of Eddyville, Kentucky, had been the contractor for army rations from October 1802 to October 1803; René Auguste and Jean Pierre Choteau were leading merchants of St. Louis (*Journals* 2:238n; *Letters* 1:168, 2:420). Perhaps that is all that Clark understood in this transaction. But if Lewis reviewed this entry with attention he should have recognized much more. For Lewis had been private secretary to President Jefferson, specifically selected for his keen sense of political loyalties in the army. And Matthew Lyon was a Jeffersonian Republican of outstanding fame—or notoriety. As a congressman voting to resolve the deadlocked presidential election of 1800, Lyon had furnished these men with something much more valuable than tobacco: he had delivered a decisive vote for Jefferson, which enabled the president to sponsor this expedition.

Matthew Lyon was an Irish immigrant who had earned his passage in 1765 by three years' service in Connecticut. He then moved to Vermont and did well. He had military commissions in the Revolutionary War, set up some prosperous businesses, and married a daughter of the governor. He could claim that before he entered national politics, "I had wealth, high political standing, an established character and powerful connections attached to me by long riveted confidence, as well as matrimonial affinity, to throw in the scale."[1]

But once he entered Congress in 1797 he put all these advantages at risk. He was a lone Republican from Vermont, a state of Federalist New England, and he was an outspoken politician in the dangerous final years of the Adams administration.

Lyon become a center of controversy in January 1798 when he spat into the face of another congressman while they were standing on the floor of the House. Two weeks later Roger Griswold of Connecticut returned the insult by caning Lyon in his chair. The original provocation had been an insult to Lyon's courage in battle during the Revolution, made while Lyon was privately talking about bribery in Connecticut. But hard words had turned into physical offenses unforgivable on both sides, and Lyon took the worst of it. Griswold was a Federalist leader, and he unleashed a long train of persecutions. The House voted to expel Lyon but failed of the two-thirds required.

Meanwhile, the press attacked him as a vile ruffian, "the Spitting Lyon" of Vermont, or "ragged Mat, the Democrat," and he was loudly hissed when he traveled back to Vermont after Congress adjourned. At home he ran into deeper troubles. The Sedition Act was now in place, prohibiting any inflammatory remark about the government in power or defamation of the president or federal officials. *Lyon's Republican Magazine* appeared in October and soon carried enough tinder to ignite a federal case. The result was immediate imprisonment for four months and a fine of a thousand dollars.[2]

Of course Lyon made the most of this martyrdom for freedom of the press. He wrote letters from prison, which were reprinted in many Republican newspapers. Without exaggerating he could claim to be a congressman thrown into a cold and stinking prison for speaking out against the policies of the administration. With so much publicity before the December runoff election, he regained his seat in the House by a large margin. And two years later he tasted sweet victory. The election of 1800 resulted in a tie of electoral votes between Jefferson and Aaron Burr. The election thus went to the House, where the deadlock persisted through thirty-five ballots. On the thirty-sixth the Federalists withdrew in Vermont and Maryland, and Lyon could stand as the lone Republican from New England to name Jefferson as president.[3]

Lyon would go on as a vigorous debater in Congress, but he also paid a price: he was finished as a politician in Vermont. He had even been under risk of prosecution for sedition under the state laws there, and he rode directly from prison to the halls of Congress, claiming constitutional immunity from arrest. Along with family and associates he moved on to Kentucky and later to Arkansas, a state and a territory from which he gained new seats in Congress. Thus the vigorous rough-and-tumble of political life in the time of Washington and Jefferson drove this incorrigible democrat out of New England and into active new pursuits farther and farther west. As Lyon put it in a satirical open letter to John Adams: "I am going to retire of my own accord, to the extreme western parts of the United States, where I had fixed myself an asylum from the persecutions of a party, the most base, cruel, assuming and faithless, that ever disgraced the councils of any nation."[4]

Simon Girty spent most of his life outside the borders of polite society, and spitting into the face of an enemy would have been light treatment from him. To thousands of Americans Girty was the "white savage" of the Revolution, the infamous traitor who had gone over to the British side and led merciless Indian raids against settlements in the Ohio Valley. Accounts of his insults and complicity in tortures and atrocities made him a good candidate for most hated man of his era. This would have been not only a public reputation but a well-known item of oral history in the family of William Clark, for along with Daniel Boone, George Rogers Clark had fought back against Girty's raids and had known many comrades who were killed or abused by him. William Clark's journal entry about Girty is again brief, but it carries a touch of poignancy. On March 26, Clark went to visit some Indian camps near Camp Dubois: "In one Camp found 3 Squars & 3 young ones, another 1 girl & a boy   in a 3rd Simon Girtey & two other familey—   Girtey has the Rhumertism verry bad" (*Journals* 2:181).

A full account of Girty's life may make his career more respectable to modern judgments. Both his father and stepfather had been killed by Indians on the frontier; he and his mother and two brothers had been taken captive; and he spent three teenage years among the Senecas. He spoke the Indian languages and was an interpreter at Fort Pitt and a friend of other known Loyalists there. In 1778 he fled with five others and joined the British Indian Department in Detroit. Thereafter he took part in Indian raids on American settlements, but he was not unique; his actions were directed by the British army, and he was rewarded and honored in Canada for the rest of his life. He also had reasons to ally himself with Indians whose lands were being invaded and whose own villages were being wiped out by punitive raids. Some witnesses credit him with gaining leniency for white captives; it is certain that he married one in 1784. They had two sons and a daughter, and after leaving him because of his drunkenness and cruelty his wife returned and stood by him until he died a blind and crippled veteran in 1818. The *Dictionary of Canadian Biography* sums up:

> Girty was a man of great ability in working with native leaders, but his manners were rough, his disposition temperamental, and his capacity for drink legendary. . . . Behind [his behavior] lurked a type of grim humour, born of the harsh conditions in which he had spent his life. His behaviour gave just enough substance to the old propaganda for some to take seriously the stories of his viciousness. These tales were

spread by people who could not see that hostilities between the western tribes and the new republic were caused, not by the behaviour of men like Girty, but by the white settlers' insatiable hunger for land and their government's failure to honour its agreements with Indians.[5]

It may seem odd that William Clark wrote only a line about such a remarkable and well-known western character. But a brief entry will often suffice for an experience that is already well impressed on the memory. Clark was not likely to forget having found Simon Girty in pain and among "squars" and "young ones" in a frontier camp. At this time Girty held a grant of land near Amherstburg in Canada, south of Detroit, but he dared not return into the Ohio country. One can only puzzle at his traveling cautiously to the edge of United States territory, despite evident illness.[6]

The scene is enough to recall Samuel Johnson's lines about other military conquerors (Hannibal and Charles XII of Sweden) in *The Vanity of Human Wishes* (lines 211–14, 221–22):

> The vanquished hero leaves his broken bands
> And shows his miseries in distant lands;
> Condemned a needy supplicant to wait,
> While ladies interpose, and slaves debate. . . .
> He left the name, at which the world grew pale,
> To point a moral, or adorn a tale.[7]

And to William Clark's eyes there should have been another dimension to this discovery. Just a few months earlier, he had been at the Falls of the Ohio caring for his brother, another broken, forgotten, hard-drinking veteran of the same wars.

Daniel Boone, of course, was as well known as Lyon or Girty or any other frontiersman of the late eighteenth century. Born in 1734, he was a contemporary of George Washington, and he shared Washington's renown as a type of all that was noble in the American character. He was not exactly the trailblazer, first pioneer, first settler, foremost Indian fighter, sharpshooter, and backwoods philosopher that legends still persist in making him. But in contrast to Girty, many of his actions do stand out as brilliantly heroic in the annals of early American patriotism. He too had been taken captive for many months by the Indians. He too had been brought to the British headquarters in Detroit and tempted with the offer of a British ransom. But he had remained a loyal revolutionary, had escaped to warn his fellow settlers of an approaching Indian attack, had risked his life in many battles, outwitted enemies, and taken a leading part in the settlement and defense of early Kentucky. John Filson's *Discovery, Settlement, and Present State of Kentucky* (1784) included a section that purported to be Boone's memoir. This was reprinted in London in 1793 as part of George Imlay's *Topographical Description of the Western Territory of North America*. Thereafter Boone was world famous. His kinsman Daniel Bryan composed a heroic poem about him, *The Mountain Muse* (1813); and Lord Byron made him immortal a decade later in *Don Juan:* "Of the great names which in our faces stare / The General Boon, back-woodsman of Kentucky, / Was happiest amongst mortals anywhere" (8:61).[8] It seems very likely that Clark knew Filson's book and that Lewis and Jefferson were deeply interested in Imlay's.

But Clark almost seems to have avoided direct contact with Daniel Boone. The party's boats arrived at St. Charles on the Missouri River on May 16. Boone's family had settled nearby in the late 1790s, along the Femme Osage River. Clark says nothing of these people. On May 23 he notes meeting the settlers but records no trace of their name: "We Set out early   ran on a Log and detained one hour, proceeded the Course of Last night 2 Miles to the mouth of a Creek on the Stbd. Side Called Osage Womans R, about 30 yds. wide, opposit a large Island and a Settlement. (on this Creek 30 or 40 famlys are Settled,[)] Crossed to the Settlement. and took in R & Jo: Fields who had been sent to purchase Corn & Butter &c.   many people Came to See us" (*Journals* 2:248). A notation in the journal of Joseph Whitehouse for this same date confirms that this was the right place: "passed Some Inhabitants called boons Settlement" (Thwaites 7:31). And Clark's words make it clear that the party stopped, traded, and engaged with "many people." Why no mention, then, that here was the final country of Daniel Boone?

Was Clark embarrassed, perhaps, that this renowned American had by this time abandoned the United States, or that his native land had proved ungrateful to him? The precise motives for Boone's westward migration are beyond recovery. But they were mixed. He may have felt hemmed in by developing farms and settlements in Kentucky. Timothy Flint, in his popular *Biographical Memoir of Daniel Boone* (1833), claims that Boone had been the model for James Fenimore Cooper's character named Leatherstocking or Natty Bumppo. Once he saw the land about him changing before axe and plow, "he sighed for new fields of adventure, and the excitement of a hunter's life" and moved on.[9]

But it was also true that by the late 1790s all the land claims Boone had made in the West had been upset by legal processes as much as by farm tools. He had lost them all to new laws, land speculation, and political changes over which he had no control. He might have spilled his blood and toiled through anxiety and hardship to settle and defend Kentucky, but after the age of sixty he had to give up his acres there. When he moved further west and put the Mississippi River behind him he knowingly crossed over into Spanish territory. He accepted Spanish land grants and the office of magistrate under Spanish authorities. And then those were called in question when the United States purchased Louisiana and Lewis and Clark came up the river to survey new American holdings.

In fact the legend of Daniel Boone is complicated by contradictory images. Boone the heroic fighter was a single man of cunning and cold nerve who could survive on his own in a wilderness, lend himself to long adoption among the Indians while preserving his own steadfast identity, or face down a panther in the dark. Boone the heroic settler was not such a lone titan but a family man and a deeply sociable being. It was his proud boast in the Filson memoir that "my wife and daughter [were] the first white women that ever stood on the banks of the Kentucky River."[10]

Bringing women west meant passing from hunting and adventure in the wilderness to permanent settlement. The Boones reared and defended their children and tried to provide for them by acquiring title to more and more land. In effect, the life of Daniel Boone was a patent attempt to fulfill Jefferson's idealism about opening western lands to settlement. In the *Notes on Virginia* Jefferson celebrates independent landowners who would carve thousands of new holdings out of the inexhaustible west. "We have an immensity of land," he writes, "courting the industry of the husbandman. . . . Those who labour in the earth are the chosen people of God, if ever he had a chosen people, whose breasts he has made his peculiar deposit for substantial and genuine virtue."[11]

But here was Boone at the outset of a great exploration to double the American claim to territory. And Boone's Settlement provided conspicuous, living witness that the virtue and sacrifice of chosen husbandmen might count for nothing. It might not secure independent prosperity or hold it long. Was Clark silent on this manifest failure of American hopes? Probably he was simply much too busy to notice; he had a new river to pilot and new routines to establish at every moment on this particular day. Besides, what point would there be in affronting the president with such proof that this whole western conquest might be in vain? [12]

As we look at them after two centuries, Lyon, Girty, and Boone seem to emerge on the outskirts of St. Louis to challenge the departure of Lewis and Clark. Lyon seems to insist that the American democracy that had sent these explorers west was not always civil and not always at its best when civility was just another name for suppression. Poor rheumatic Girty cries out that conquest had already been bloody, dirty, cruel work that left its heroes ruined. Boone bears witness that the land beneath a newcomer's feet could slide out from the best efforts to hold it or prosper upon it.

But could Lewis, Clark, or anyone in their company have heard these old ghosts of the early republic or have heeded their warnings? The party pushed on anyhow. Two years later they returned, flushed with success and ready for the welcoming interest of merchants, scientists, politicians, family members, and common citizens. In their turn, however, the members of this expedition were growing older, and for many of them the end of this adventure marked the beginning of new hazards, disappointments, and even paths leading to sudden death.

"Some perverse urge in the modern historian makes him want to call back through time and tell these people what lies ahead, even if the news is somber." So Donald Jackson writes about this expedition, and he goes on to call out the names of member after member through two pages, foretelling their lives and losses once the journey is over. He writes a line or two for the figures who left even a footnote in later history, then closes with the others: "Bratton, Collins, Gibson, Hall, Howard, McNeal, Shields, Thompson, Warner, Windsor—drain your ardent spirits, put your hands to the oars tomorrow, and forget about fame. You will be names only, accompanied by brief snippets of biographical data in the pantheon of American explorers." [13]

But the "ardent spirits" of many would not be drained so easily. Some remain on the trail to the present day, haunting famous sites with legends cut deep into lasting markers, or hovering over the entire route with a shadow of evening melancholy.

Sergeant Charles Floyd comes immediately to mind, the one man who died on the journey west. By the best guess of modern science his appendix burst, and no procedure in the medicine of that time could have saved him. He was buried at the top of a bluff near what is now Sioux City, Iowa, "with the Honors of War much lamented" (*Journals* 2:495). A cedar post marked the site, and a nearby river was given Floyd's name. Later the bones were reinterred, and a one-hundred-foot obelisk now marks the spot. It is on a high hill overlooking the Missouri River—a marker appropriately like the Washington Monument, which stands near the Zero Milestone in the capital, the symbolic starting point of American history and geography.

Two members died more violently at the Three Forks, where the Jefferson, Madison, and Gallatin rivers come together to form the Missouri. Here the party had attained one of their primary objects by tracing the Missouri as far as they could and giving enduring names to these three tributaries. Here they also began the next stage of their work, the ascent and crossing of the Continental Divide. And here, not many years later, two of the men were killed and another ran for his life.

The invaluable hunter George Drouillard fell near this spot at the hands of hostile Blackfeet Indians. He had come back up to work at a Missouri Fur Company trading post here in 1810. Despite warnings from others, he and some Delaware Indian companions set out one day to check their traps. About two miles away they ran into trouble. But according to the reports of the men who found the bodies, Drouillard held out valiantly: "From the appearance of the scene of this attack it was apparent that Drouillard made a desperate defense. He seems to have used his horse as a breastwork, turning him so as to shield himself constantly from the enemy. It was but a short time until the horse was killed and he himself was the next victim. A most painful feature of this affair was that it took place within ordinary hearing distance of relief, but owing to a high wind prevailing at the time, the firing was not heard."[14]

A loud wind, a fall in action next to a dying horse, proximity to help at the Three Forks, swift death from surrounding Indians—these features make a fitting tableau for the death of a Lewis and Clark explorer. Drouillard, the son of a French-Canadian father and a Shawnee mother, lived always between two worlds in America. To be back at the Three Forks, he had chosen to invade the wilderness again and to work for European-American trapping interests, though he told one of his companions, "I am too much of an Indian to be caught by Indians."[15] Having shared deadly violence with Lewis and the Piegan Blackfeet of northern Montana in 1806, he knew the risks he could be taking. And so he went down, turning and turning with an animal forced between himself and death, until a howling wind carried off his last breath.

John Potts had died nearby some months earlier when he was trapping with John Colter along the Jefferson River. The earliest published account of that incident was taken down by John Bradbury in St. Louis in 1810, when Colter carried his tale back from the Yellowstone. Like Drouillard, Potts and Colter were well aware of their risks in trapping near hostile Indians. We have seen Colter getting special permission to go back west with a trapping party while the Corps of Discovery was heading homeward in 1806. Since then he had traveled over much previously unexplored territory, including the area now set aside as Yellowstone National Park. Early in 1808 he had also been wounded near the Gallatin River in a large battle between opposing Indian tribes. Knowing the danger, Potts and Colter stayed concealed by day, set their traps at night, and took them up very early. But one morning their luck ran out. Five or six hundred Indians appeared, commanded them to leave their traps, and beckoned them to come ashore.

As Colter told the story, Potts fell in a hail of arrows after he had leveled a rifle and brought down at least one Indian. Colter himself put up no resistance, but he was stripped naked and prepared for torture. Suddenly one of the chiefs devised a way of giving him a sporting chance—a head start followed by a run for his life. Drawing on every resource of cunning, strength, quick thinking, stamina, and wilderness experience, Colter escaped across hundreds of miles. Bradbury's account has to be quoted at length for its full effect:

> They now seized Colter, stripped him entirely naked, and began to consult on the manner in which he should be put to death. They were first inclined to set him up as a mark to shoot at; but the chief interfered, and seizing him by the shoulder asked him if he could run fast? Colter, who had been some time amongst the Kee-kat-sa, or Crow Indians, had in a considerable degree acquired the Blackfoot language, and was also well acquainted with Indian customs. He knew that he had now to run for his life, with the dreadful odds of five or six hundred against him,

and those armed Indians; therefore cunningly replied that he was a very bad runner, although he was considered by the hunters as remarkably swift. The chief now commanded the party to remain stationary, and led Colter out on the prairie three or four hundred yards, and released him, bidding him *to save himself if he could.* At that instant the horrid war whoop sounded in the ears of poor Colter, who, urged with the hope of preserving life, ran with a speed at which he was himself surprised. He proceeded towards the Jefferson Fork, having to traverse a plain six miles in breadth, abounding with the prickly pear, on which he was every instant treading with his naked feet. He ran nearly half way across the plain before he ventured to look over his shoulder, when he perceived that the Indians were very much scattered, and that he had gained ground to a considerable distance from the main body; but one Indian, who carried a spear, was much before all the rest, and not more than a hundred yards from him. A faint gleam of hope now cheered the heart of Colter: he derived confidence from the belief that escape was within the bounds of possibility; but that confidence was nearly being fatal to him, for he exerted himself to such a degree, that the blood gushed from his nostrils, and soon almost covered the fore part of his body. He had now arrived within a mile of the river, when he distinctly heard the appalling sound of footsteps behind him, and every instant expected to feel the spear of his pursuer. Again he turned his head, and saw the savage not twenty yards from him. Determined if possible to avoid the expected blow, he suddenly stopped, turned round, and spread out his arms. The Indian, surprised by the suddenness of the action, and perhaps at the bloody appearance of Colter, also attempted to stop; but exhausted with running, he fell whilst endeavouring to throw his spear, which stuck in the ground, and broke in his hand. Colter instantly snatched up the pointed part, with which he pinned him to the earth, and then continued his flight. The foremost of the Indians, on arriving at the place, stopped till others came up to join them, when they set up a hideous yell. Every moment of this time was improved by Colter, who, although fainting and exhausted, succeeded in gaining the skirting of the cotton wood trees, on the borders of the fork, through which he ran, and plunged into the river. Fortunately for him, a little below this place there was an island, against the upper point of which a raft of drift timber had lodged. He dived under the raft, and after several efforts, got his head above water amongst the trunks of trees, covered over with smaller wood to the depth of several feet. Scarcely had he secured himself, when the Indians arrived on the river, screeching and yelling, as Colter expressed it, "like so many devils." They were frequently on the raft during the day, and were seen through the chinks by Colter, who was congratulating himself on his escape, until the idea arose that they might set the raft on fire. In horrible suspense he remained until night, when hearing no more of the Indians, he dived from under the raft, and swam silently down the river to a considerable distance, when he landed, and travelled all night.[16]

Here is adventure upon adventure—like a prose translation from Homer or some other high epic of ancient combat. In fact there is so much vivid detail here that we must suspect Colter of at least practicing his telling all the way back to St. Louis. Hiram Chittenden puts it politely: Colter "succeeded in making himself accounted a confirmed prevaricator, and a cloud of doubt and ridicule hung over his memory until far later years proved the truth of his statements"—that is, his statements about western geography.[17] But a few more lines from Bradbury must be quoted, to show that at least this story could only have befallen a member of the Corps of Discovery:

Although happy in having escaped from the Indians, his situation was still dreadful: he was completely naked, under a burning sun; the soles of his feet were entirely filled with the thorns of the prickly pear; he was hungry, and had no means of killing game, although he saw abundance around him, and was at least seven days journey from Lisa's Fort, on the Bighorn branch of the Roche Jaune River. These were circumstances under which almost any man but an American hunter would have despaired. He arrived at the fort in seven days, having subsisted on a root much esteemed by the Indians of the Missouri, now known by naturalists as *psoralea esculenta*.[18]

These closing details about prickly pear and breadroot betray Bradbury's peculiar interests as a British botanist in America—with a deeper feeling for plant species than for violent adventures. But those particular plants are very familiar to readers of the journals. Prickly pear tore the feet of the men very often and cruelly, especially when they were toiling over the portage around the Great Falls. And for long periods the party had gone hungry in this part of the world and learned to survive on plants when there was no game. Breadroot—also called white apple, prairie turnip, ground potato, pomme blanche, or *pomme de prairie*—was new to science when Lewis and Clark recorded it in their journals. It was from a sample they brought back that Frederick Pursh described the plant and gave it its scientific name. What is more, the explorers mention it, or something like it, as a food first served to them by Teton Sioux, the Indians who challenged their passage into the Upper Missouri region.[19]

As a result of these violent deaths and other rough encounters, white trappers withdrew from the Three Forks region for decades. Danger from Indians also combined with the dry climate and forbidding distances of the Great Plains so that white settlements did not get far before the time of big railroads and the army forces that developed after the Civil War. But then stories of death and loss turned another way. A caption in the Yakima Nation Cultural Heritage Center in Toppenish, Washington, recalls an 1805 meeting along the Columbia River: "One day downriver from the East came strangers, white men and a black man in canoes. We received them as honored guests, as tradition would have us do. In a few days they departed downstream to the West. Life for our people would never be the same." Nearby are maps showing the diminution of Yakima land claims from huge tracts to smaller and smaller reservations.[20]

The same story was dramatized in the history of relations between white people and the Nez Perces. When Clark and his advance party emerged from the Lolo Trail in September 1805, they were starving and exhausted. Indians at Weippe Prairie welcomed and fed them, traced the route that lay ahead, and prepared to welcome the rest of their party. Over the course of the next few days they taught them a better method for building dugout canoes, furnished more food, and provided two guides to go with them down to the Columbia. Over the following seven months they kept their horses for them. When the explorers returned and were forced to camp among them, awaiting a spring thaw, they again kept up friendly relations, gladly receiving Clark's medications, which were among the few items the white men could offer in trade. Eventually they furnished three guides to lead the party back over the Lolo Trail. Over the next seventy years, the Nez Perces could boast that none of them had ever killed a white man. But in the 1850s and 1860s their lands were diminished by treaties. Then gold was discovered in nearby mountains, and Indians were ordered onto reservations to open the land to white development. Hin-mah-too-yah-lat-kekht, famous in American history as Chief Joseph, refused to be bullied and began to lead his people toward Montana and then to the Canadian border in 1877. They were pursued, attacked, and finally surrounded by army units, and Chief Joseph was taken prisoner when he trusted a flag of truce. A few of his followers made it to Canada, but he was eventually forced onto a reservation in the state of Washington.[21]

For the Nez Perces, too, white strangers had come and "life for our people would never be the same." At the outset of Chief Joseph's long march, he moved east over the same harsh Lolo Trail that had brought Lewis and Clark west to their first encounter with his people.[22]

In this sense, the coming of Lewis and Clark literally foreshadowed the going of the Nez Perces. And their chief's words still haunt this trail as a reproach to western American strife:

> The earth is the mother of all people, and all people should have equal rights upon it. You might as well expect the rivers to run backward as that any man who was born a free man should be contented when penned up and denied liberty to go where he pleases. If you tie a horse to a stake, do you expect he will grow fat? If you pen an Indian up on a small spot of earth, and compel him to stay there, he will not be contented, nor will he grow and prosper. I have asked some of the great white chiefs where they get their authority to say to the Indian that he shall stay in one place, while he sees white men going where they please. They can not tell me.[23]

Along the entire Lewis and Clark route, another Indian name remains engraved, painted, printed, carved, and repeated. Spelled Sacajawea, Sakakawea, or Sacagawea, it stands for one of the most famous women in American history and legend, whose original name as a child lies beyond our knowledge.[24]

What Sacagawea did on this journey is recorded in scattered entries. She seems to have died young in 1812 (*Letters* 2:638−39). One of her certain, undisputed accomplishments was teaching another member of the party to walk before the expedition ended. This was Jean Baptiste Charbonneau, also known as Pomp or Pompey, the child she bore in 1805, two months before the departure from Fort Mandan. After the expedition was over, William Clark kept up an interest in this boy's development. He was brought to St. Louis at the age of six and educated there. Prince Paul of Württemberg met him while exploring on the Missouri in 1823 and took him to Europe for many years. By 1829, when he returned, this young man of twenty-four was fluent in French, Spanish, German, and English; he later served as a guide and interpreter with exploring parties in the West,[25] and his name appears in the records of many western trapping and hunting parties and trading camps, where he served as a hunter, guide, trader, and very good cook. By the time of the gold rush he was in California; he left in 1866 to seek gold in Montana or Idaho and died in Oregon on the way. Thus the child who began life as a traveler into the Far West went on for over sixty years of purposeful travel and frontier life. One observer in the 1840s reported his reputation as "the best man on foot on the plains or in the Rocky Mountains." What better praise could there be for a child of the Corps of Discovery? [26]

Were there other children, too, whose lives began and took shape along the trail of this expedition? Rumors about children of York and numerous Indian women have been handed down over the years. All of them rest on hearsay and stereotyping of York as a black man with insatiable sexual drives. [27] Robert Betts rightly points out that many members of the party were treated for venereal disease during the expedition, but York was not among them. And the one child who grew up to claim an expedition father and pose for an early photographer asserted that he was the son of William Clark. This may have been a light-haired, blue-eyed Nez Perce who was taken prisoner as one of Chief Joseph's men in 1877. [28]

Sexual relations between the men and Indian women were allowed and anticipated in the medical supplies; they are recorded in the journals; and they were encouraged by many tribes as part of their rituals, trading practices, and customs for gaining power from impressive rivals. So it may well be that the party engendered babies who were born many months after they had moved on. If so, they have gone unrecorded, but they must have brought care to the women who bore them, and they must have suffered themselves if they lived long enough to notice their differences from all their close relatives. Some may have carried troubling questions into their old age if they survived to see the world turned upside down, like the man who was taken prisoner with Chief Joseph.

The most haunting story of all the members of the party is the tale of Meriwether Lewis's violent death. No matter how it is told or extenuated, it puts a grim ending to a long adventure that should have turned out differently. The shared command of two captains not only worked out well, it succeeded brilliantly and left Lewis and Clark still fast friends. The daily hazards of travel in rough, unknown country gave Lewis only one deep scar, from a hunting accident late on the return trip. Attacks and threats of attacks from fierce animals and hostile Indians were safely past. Lewis and Clark came back to enjoy celebrity, public rewards, and appointments to responsible posts in the new territory. And both were still young men; in 1806 Lewis was just thirty-two. But three years later he was dead, suddenly, of gunshot wounds. He had left a history of despondency, alcoholism, and erratic behavior. People as close to him as Clark and Jefferson could readily accept that he had killed himself.

Lewis died on October 11, 1809, at a remote farmhouse that served as an inn on the Natchez Trace in Tennessee, while he was en route to Washington from St. Louis. He had arrived at Grinder's Stand with two servants, taken over the main house by himself, and retired for the night. But around three in the morning Mrs. Grinder, the woman who was keeping the place while her husband was away, was roused by shots. According to her report, she and the servants came from nearby buildings to find Lewis still alive but mortally wounded by pistol shots to the head and chest. Major James Neelly, who had been detained in search of wandering horses, came on the scene "some time after, & had him as decently Buried as I could in that place" (*Letters* 2:468). Neelly's account, addressed to Thomas Jefferson on October 18, is the earliest source of these details. But others have confirmed this story, including Alexander Wilson, the ornithologist, who purposely visited Grinder's Stand in 1811 and interviewed the people who were there, and Major Gilbert Russell, an army officer who had detained Lewis for two weeks on his way east after learning of two earlier attempts at suicide.[29]

To his contemporaries, Lewis's sudden death was a shock. They and many later readers have had to strain to find reasons for a suicide. The young captain of intelligence, courage, and competence, who had so recently and successfully commanded the expedition, hardly matches the deranged, alcohol-dependent, erratic man described in reports of his final year. Jefferson, in a memoir written for the narrative *History* of the expedition, attributed Lewis's decline to "hypochondriac affections" or a "constitutional disposition," by which he meant a congenital mental disorder, inherited from his father, which vigorous activity suppressed but which came over him again "after his establishment at St. Louis in sedentary occupations" (*Letters* 2:591–92). In a private letter to Major Russell, Jefferson also speculated that this "hypochondria" was intensified by heavy drinking (*Letters* 2:575n, 748). To explain the heavy drinking, many researchers have combed the surviving documents and found evidence of disappointed courtship, overextended personal and public debts, severe problems and evasions of duty in administrating Upper Louisiana Territory as its governor, indolence about preparing the journals of the expedition for the press, and resulting strains in Lewis's personal relations with Jefferson. Malaria, other organic disorders, and psychiatric problems common to children who have lost a parent in their youth have also been adduced as sufficient (and blameless) ultimate causes of Lewis's strange behavior in his final months. And to some, the suicide explanation has remained so incredible that they have attacked the motives of Major Neelly and Mrs. Grinder and suspected them of being implicated in Lewis's murder.[30]

His death by violence remains an undisputed fact nevertheless. And no matter what its immediate cause may have been, its circumstances are bound to trouble anyone who comes to care for Lewis by reading his journals and letters. Its setting was sordid, its timing cruel.

Major Neelly was traveling with Lewis partly to protect him from others, partly to watch over his own behavior. Neelly was at that time the Indian agent for the Chickasaws, and the route they were taking lay through their country.

> On our arrival in the Chickasaw nation I discovered that he appeared at times deranged in mind. We rested there two days & came on. One days Journey after crossing Tennessee River & where we encamped we lost two of our horses. I remained behind to hunt them & the Governor proceeded on, with a promise to wait for me at the first houses he came to that was inhabited by white people; he reached the house of a Mr. Grinder about sun set, the man of the house being from home, and no person there but a woman who discovering the governor to be deranged, gave him up the house & slept herself in one near it. His servant and mine slept in the stable loft some distance from the other houses. The woman reports that about three o'Clock she heard two pistols fire off in the Governors Room. (*Letters* 2:467–68)

No matter how one takes these lines, as artless report or contrived cover story, they make a demeaning end for a man like Lewis. Again he travels through wilderness (he even "proceeds on"), but now he has to be led and managed. Again he finds shelter in a land of Indians and strangers, but he acts or is treated as if not fit for any human company. Again he and another army officer share deliberations and agree to part for a time, for good reasons, trusting each other to get on safely along the trail. But by the next dawn, all has gone awry. Lewis bungles even as a marksman. "He had shot himself in the head with one pistol & a little below the Breast with the other." And Lewis, the journal keeper who often filled his pages with excited discovery, now has precious little to say. "When his servant came in he says; I have done the business my good Servant give me some water. He gave him water, he survived but a short time" (*Letters* 2 : 468). One wants his death to be a fitting conclusion to his life, but it reads as a travesty of Lewis's days on the trail—an incongruous, discontinuous perversion of his career at its height.

To make matters worse, there is evidence right here to show that Lewis was not wholly out of his senses. He was traveling to Washington very purposefully to complete unfinished business directly related to the western expedition. "I have got in my possession," Neely goes on, "his two trunks of papers (amongst which is said to be his travels to the pacific Ocean) and probably some Vouchers for expenditures of Public Money for a Bill which he said had been protested by the Secy. of War; and of which act to his death, he repeatedly complained" (*Letters* 2 : 468). It is not clear from these lines whether one trunk contained the expedition journals and the other contained vouchers for territorial expenditures, but certainly Lewis was carrying a heavy load of documents. The journals were his promise of enduring fame; the vouchers were his proofs for clearing himself from immediate defamation.

The voucher problem was a legacy of the expedition, too. Following Jefferson's instructions, Lewis and Clark had persuaded Indian chiefs to come down the Missouri and travel to Washington to meet the president directly. Among these ambassadors was Sheheke, a Mandan chief who came aboard the party's boats just as John Colter was heading back west and the Charbonneau family was settling again at the Mandan villages. Sheheke and his family did go on to Washington in 1806, but returning them home proved very difficult. The way was blocked by new hostility on the part of Sioux and Arikara peoples; the latter were upset over the fate of their own chief, who had gone to Washington in 1805 and died there the following April. Nathaniel Pryor of the original Corps of Discovery was charged with returning Sheheke to his people in 1807, but his armed party of forty-eight men was forced to turn back (*Letters* 2 : 414, 432–38). In 1809 Lewis signed a bill for 7,000 dollars and later bills in smaller amounts to pay the Missouri Fur Company of St. Louis for safely completing this task. But here he ran into big trouble. By the time these bills reached Washington, Jefferson had left office and President Madison had appointed a new secretary of war. This new officer, William Eustis, not only questioned the propriety of hiring a private company to complete this public commission, but he notified Lewis on July 15 that his bills were not being honored (*Letters* 2:456–57).

The letter from Eustis was such a jolt to Lewis that he resolved instantly to go to Washington and explain himself in person. His reply of August 18 states this plan and goes into detail about several distresses Lewis was feeling. He feared that his whole reputation was at stake and that it was crucial to reach Washington with this reply "in time to prevent any decision relative to me"—presumably a sudden dismissal from his office. He promised to bring all his papers, to show not only his financial probity but also his unswerving loyalty to the United States. (The 1807 trial of Aaron Burr for treason was still fresh in memory; Burr had been conspiring to detach western lands by raising military forces there and invading Mexican territories.) Lewis protested that the refusal to honor his bills had brought him to the point of personal bankruptcy. He tried to explain why unexpected developments on the frontier had required such recent large outlays for returning the Mandan chief (*Letters* 2:459–61).

Was Lewis so utterly distracted and undermined by a harsh change in administrations that he was finally driven to his death? Or is his letter evidence of a mind still circumspect and a will still strong and well prepared for any challenge to a young man's public honor? Or could it be that a distracted, erratic, self-destructive spirit rode east in the same body with a purposeful, earnest, and upright self-defender? The evidence is ambiguous enough to support the latter enigmatic possibility—and that might explain, too, why a decisive marksman like Lewis took ineffectual aim when he turned his pistols on himself.

But without better witnesses or proofs we can never know. The evidence is so confusing that it will long be contended. William Clark went on successfully in St. Louis, lived almost another thirty years, married, had many children, held high public offices, survived controversies, and retained the respect of many administrations in the East and many Indians in the West. His bright career makes Lewis's early death look all the darker. Men like these two, who had seen so much of America and taken such firm strides across it, should have prospered together and made joint achievements through many years.

But Lewis died by violence. That violence, whatever its sources, was tainted by dishonor. And that dishonor not only touched Lewis personally but also extended from the cold calculations of his new superiors in Washington to the harsh realities of changing forces on the upper Missouri. Reviewing the story of his death a few years ago, Paul Russell Cutright quoted a line from *Hamlet* as the title of his article: "Rest, rest, perturbèd spirit." Cutright provides an accurate citation: act 1, scene 5, line 182. But he might have done well to explain further: these are the prince's words to a very troubling ghost. Like George Rogers Clark, Daniel Boone, Simon Girty, Charles Floyd, and many others, Lewis marched into the wilderness young and was broken before he grew old. Unlike them, he lived to write out scores of paragraphs of new perception and understanding. For a few short years he saw the West as no one else could, before or after him, and he left a rich legacy. But his pages end with stains of blood and tears.

Chapter 12   The Rockies by Moonlight

In the course of their travels to the Far West, Lewis and Clark sometimes looked to the moon to determine where they were standing on the earth. Once, in January 1805, they observed a total eclipse. Lewis wrote: "I had no other glass to assist me in this observation but a small refracting telescope belonging to my sextant, which however was of considerable service, as it enabled me to define the edge of the moon's immage with much more precision that I could have done with the natural eye." He timed the stages of the eclipse with his chronometer and so calculated the latitude of the Mandan villages anew, and for a time he pondered some corrections to earlier maps (*Journals* 3:273, 275n). Much later, these men of science scoffed at a different claim about lunar observations. Clark saw a medicine man among the Wallula Indians and was told that he could foretell things: "He had told of our Comeing into their Country and was now about to Consult his God the moon if what we Said was the truth &c. &c" (*Journals* 7:181). To men who could define the edge of the moon's image with modern instruments, the idea of deriving lunar prophecies seemed preposterous. That distant satellite cast no charms or enchantments in its pale light, but steady, useful beams. If they looked upward, these explorers used lenses to correct and enhance what Lewis called "the natural eye." A supernatural eye was none of their concern. To them the moon was no longer the legendary power it had been to people over the centuries—a symbol of the changeable, waxing, waning, unpredictable nature of life in this "sublunary" world. Instead it had become a wholly predictable, remote index of time and space—a body like the fixed stars, on which reliable calculations could be made and analyzed from any point on this planet.

Almost two centuries later, we see the moon differently ourselves.

The Rockies by Moonlight

Within vivid memory, the United States and the former Soviet Union landed rockets on the moon's sparkling surface and brought back sightings and information from newer instruments. Another Meriwether Lewis and William Clark, named Neil Armstrong and Edward Aldrin, put on special suits and left a small landing rocket on July 20, 1969, to step out, collect samples, and make observations on the spot. Dozens of full-color photographs of Earth as a bright blue orb in the black universe have become commonplace since that time, along with hourly satellite assessments of the weather around the globe. We have become used to looking back at ourselves from a lunar orbit.

From this perspective, how tiny, frail, crude, and clumsy Lewis and Clark must seem—crawling westward a few miles each day; daunted by river currents, steep trails, and seasonal changes; anxious for many weeks about the sufficiency of their food, horses, and canoes. And yet, when set next to the Apollo program that sent men suddenly across hundreds of thousands of miles, how much richer they were, too—how much more independent, resourceful, and reflective than even the best of the astronauts could be.

In many ways the Apollo flights reenacted the exploration of the Corps of Discovery. Once again a president initiated a bold excursion into unknown space, in competition with a great foreign empire. Again the resources of modern science were summoned and tested. Again a special military corps was selected and disciplined to support the work of a few outstanding officers. Again young men were sent to reach the limit of conceivable exploration, through a barrier of anxious ignorance and doubt—not to the edge of the new continent, this time, with the chance of happening upon Eldorado, the lost tribes of Israel, mastodons, or Welsh Indians; but to the outermost sphere of the planet, with the chance of being bombarded by cosmic rays or freak microbes and being engulfed forever in the ultimate source of romance, tides, lunacy, and green cheese.

In the end, the astronauts even went through some atavistic rituals that recalled Lewis and Clark. With great difficulty they set up an American flag on the hard surface of the Sea of Tranquillity. In that scant atmosphere, a normal cloth flag would have drooped, so they brought along a metal framework to stretch out a bright rectangle of red, white, and blue—a specially designed emblem with a prefabricated fluttery curl. But what could such an emblem mean? The United States had recently ratified the Outer Space Treaty against territorial claims in space, and there was no imminent possibility of exploiting the moon by settlement or industrial development. This odd flag was only a token of token conquest. And it was an act of strange futility to bring stripes and especially stars out into space—stripes for thirteen colonies in an age that disavowed colonialism; stars for fifty states, the American history of expansion over the surface of another globe, now condensed to be driven into a tiny posthole. The astronauts also collected samples to bring back, though that tiresome effort could probably have been accomplished better by automated equipment with calibrated shovels or borers. They ate. They slept. They went through the motions of inhabiting a place. In mid-journey they communicated directly with the president. But unlike Lewis and Jefferson, Armstrong and Richard Nixon had no ties of personal acquaintance. Their exchanges were void of scientific significance and were evidently scripted for public performance.

As everyone could see, these newfangled explorers might reach the moon, but they would not touch it. They were sheathed and encumbered in protective space suits, with faces masked behind reflective shields. And the surfaces they imprinted were arid and lifeless as well. There was nothing for them to see or engage with, no exuberance of foliage, nothing wild and wily to hunt, no countervailing intelligence to encounter. The only form of life was what they had brought—the rhythms of breath and pulsing blood that moved with them inside their apparatus and were instantly recorded and monitored back in Houston, Texas.

Altogether the astronauts were harnessed and constrained as much as they were supported by the enormous intricacies of their project. Countless interconnections of circuits, mechanisms, and contingency provisions were matched by countless disciplines of selection, training, loyalty, and circumspection. It had taken centuries for human beings to learn how to lift themselves off the earth with balloons or kites or wings attached to engines. It had taken decades of intensive work since then to develop rockets with computerized guidance systems, interlocking stages, heat resistant shielding, electronic communications, and adequate provisions for life and comfort beyond the atmosphere. To stay in control of such equipment, the pilots had mastered many complexities of engineering, aeronautics, and data transmission. They had also learned very well the protocols of living under the scrutiny of a bureaucratic national government and an eagerly probing international press corps. Once they were under way they were either too busy or too regimented to make many spontaneous remarks or observations. Besides, the modern technology of rockets had also produced telecommunications so rapid that it made most commentary superfluous. The cameras that went with the astronauts showed most of what they could see at the same time they were seeing it.

No one, therefore, could redigest this adventure. It occurred immediately and simultaneously before millions of viewers. A thrill shared around the planet was part of the experience. Norman Mailer, the celebrated American novelist, had received a large advance to write a book on the moon landing, but stage after stage he found himself baffled. He had advantages for getting as close to the action as any journalist could: his own background as a student of engineering, years of practiced observation in politics and American zaniness, celebrity and aggressiveness for pushing through prohibited doors. But the astronauts were kept cordoned from acquaintance—behind plate glass or other equally antiseptic barriers. The flight occurred for Mailer, as for even the highest officials and experts, on television screens and in a steady exchange of numerals, acronyms, and binary-coded signals. It became a flat, ongoing, predictable, and hence boring wait for an incident, for hours and days at a stretch. The writer caught himself looking elsewhere, to the eyes of officials glinting through tired masks of flesh, to the slouches and impatient gestures of fellow reporters. Miller posed a deep question at the heart of the book he finally wrote: "Was the voyage of Apollo 11 the noblest expression of a technological age, or the best evidence of its utter insanity?"[1] He amassed evidence to support both possibilities and suffered months of headache trying to decide.

During the course of earlier space flights the men in the rocket ships had had little to say worth repeating. In fact, astronauts had become notorious for the clumsy banality of their instantaneous reports, and Apollo 11 was not much different. "It feels good, buddy! It's great sport!" (Gordon Cooper in orbit, May 15–16, 1963). "Everything outside is about like we predicted" (Michael Collins, after stepping out into space from the Gemini 10 flight, July 1966). "It's not green cheese. It's made of American cheese" (Frank Borman after circling the moon on Christmas Eve, 1968). Neil Armstrong was carefully prepared to pronounce a Great Quotation when he stepped off the last rung onto the moon's surface: "That's one small step for a man, one giant leap for mankind." But Buzz Aldrin a few moments later said only, "Beautiful, beautiful, beautiful." Helen Bevington quoted these lines and compared them playfully with lines of poetry that might have said more in few words. But she admitted, too, that no living poets had risen to the challenge of recomposing the moon landing very well, and that when she saw rockets lift off, her own language fell into cliché. Later astronauts may even have felt a pressure to observe a very old literary convention—to seem democratically humble by becoming manifestly inarticulate. "Whoopee, man! Holy cow! Son of a gun! Ho, ho, ho, hey!" (Charles Conrad and Alan Bean of Apollo 12). Were they consciously or unconsciously trying to sound like frontiersmen again? "We is here, man, we is here," said Gene Cernan on the last moon landing in 1972. Then he sang: "Oh, bury me not on the lone prairie."[2]

People had dreamed for ages of ascending to the heavens and looking back upon the earth as a scene of trivial strife. But for Christians and earlier pagan visionaries, that kind of experience lay beyond this life in a realm of inspired dreams or blissful death. With the invention of aircraft and rockets, a different kind of imagining became possible. People could actually look back at Earth from on high and relate to it still as home.[3] At the end of the twentieth century, however, that experience was still new, still disorienting even for the most sophisticated members of what the 1960s called the "jet set." Architects were still building homes and office buildings that were meant to impress pedestrians, even though people commonly sped past them in their cars or swept over them in airplanes. Church buildings still went up with pointed steeples, though the neighborhoods around them were beginning to rely on satellite dishes for messages from above. Dozens of flights every day passed smoothly over the Rockies, and their hundreds of passengers could look down in comfort at those high barriers to pioneers and railroads.

But what did one see from such elevation? On a clear day, not majesty so much as creases and slopes of dull-colored rock and endless forest. On many other days, just cloud, a layer of gray or white that wearied the eye with glare. To escape from narrow bounds and mount upward into heaven did not always result in the supernal joy that centuries past had promised. It could result instead in disillusionment, in a feeling of insignificance. In the course of a few decades, millions of bored passengers had looked out over tracts of bungalows and factories from city to similar city and washed down their packaged meals with some liquor less than ambrosial.

A few months before the moon landing Lyndon Johnson had given voice to this bewilderment in his State of the Union Address of 1968. "Let me speak now," he said, "about some matters here at home":

> Tonight our Nation is accomplishing more for its people than has ever been accomplished before. Americans are prosperous as men have never been in recorded history. Yet there is in the land a certain restlessness—a questioning.
>
> The total of our Nation's annual production is now above $800 billion. For 83 months this Nation has been on a steady upward trend of growth.
>
> All about them, most American families can see the evidence of growing abundance: higher paychecks, humming factories, new cars moving down new highways. More and more families own their own homes, equipped with more than 70 million television sets.
>
> A new college is founded every week. Today more than half of the high school graduates go on to college.
>
> There are hundreds of thousands of fathers and mothers who never completed grammar school—who will see their children graduate from college.
>
> Why, then, this restlessness?[4]

It is immediately noteworthy in these lines that the president measured prosperity and good in terms of the conquest of distance in America. He and his speech writers evidently hoped to touch a common chord in people from coast to coast by pointing to cars and highways and television sets; they expect that everyone has known aircraft and private automobiles for a long time and automatically thinks of the United States as a continental nation held together by these familiar connections of technology. But upward, upward, further upward: that is Johnson's theme. Prosperity is rising with productivity and growth. Paychecks are higher. Higher numbers of students are climbing higher in higher education. Yet all is not well. "Why, then, this restlessness?" Why, indeed?

I watched this address in a common room at Cornell University in my final year of climbing toward a Ph.D. There was no single answer there to the president's hurt questioning but plenty of evidence that he had not touched a common chord. Rather, he had hit a nerve. Many around me were primed to hurl remarks back at that television screen.

By January 1968 hundreds of thousands of American troops had been lifted high and carried through the air across the Pacific to Vietnam. Global strategists had confidently looked down and calculated the interrelations of nations in Southeast Asia and around the Pacific rim. Military experts had predicted swift victory from concentrated air attacks on a tiny, backward nation. And yet after many years none of this high-flown intelligence had made much difference. North Vietnam was as far from defeat as ever; the United States was merely demoralized from fighting with cruel futility against people who were supposed to be simple, backward peasants. Meanwhile there had been years of conspicuous violence at home. Johnson had come into office in 1963 after the shocking assassination of a younger, more glamorous president. Since then city after city had erupted with riots and protests. "All about them" the president said, "most American families can see the evidence of growing abundance." But many looked out on bleak, endless stretches of squalor. The new cars on the new highways were passing through urban wastelands. The seventy million television sets furnished glimpses of gunshots, bombings, and protest marches every evening at suppertime. Faster travel and rapid communications did not necessarily put people at ease. Nor did education. College students were provoked to ask questions, not just contentedly earn more, drive farther, and watch more situation comedies. Their questions probed a gap between the lofty assurances of public authorities and the manifest chaos and cruelty of life at ground level.

And yet behind those well-known discontents of the late 1960s there was also a depth of history, a current of discontent that ran deep and obviously in America over a century earlier and that can be traced back, too, to times before Lewis and Clark. The terms Johnson chose to use had been rehearsed by Alexis de Tocqueville in the 1830s. They stand out in a chapter of *Democracy in America* entitled "Why the Americans Are Often So Restless in the Midst of Their Prosperity." "In America I have seen the freest and best educated of men in circumstances the happiest to be found in the world," Tocqueville writes; "yet it seemed to me that a cloud habitually hung on their brow, and they seemed serious and almost sad even in their pleasures." He discusses the problem at some length:

> It is odd to watch with what feverish ardor the Americans pursue prosperity and how they are ever tormented by the shadowy suspicion that they may not have chosen the shortest route to get it.
>
> Americans cleave to the things of this world as if assured that they will never die, and yet are in such a rush to snatch any that come within their reach, as if expecting to stop living before they have relished them. They clutch everything but nothing fast, and so lose grip as they hurry after some new delight.
>
> An American will build a house in which to pass his old age and sell it before the roof is on; he will plant a garden and rent it just as the trees are coming into bearing; he will clear a field and leave others to reap the harvest; he will take up a profession and leave it, settle in one place and soon go off elsewhere with his changing desires. If his private business allows him a moment's relaxation, he will plunge at once into the whirlpool of politics. Then, if at the end of a year crammed with work he has a little spare leisure, his restless curiosity goes with him traveling up and down the vast territories of the United States. Thus he will travel five hundred miles in a few days as a distraction from his happiness.
>
> Death steps in in the end and stops him before he has grown tired of this futile pursuit of that complete felicity which always escapes him.
>
> At first sight there is something astonishing in this spectacle of so many lucky men restless in the midst of abundance. But it is a spectacle as old as the world; all that is new is to see a whole people performing in it.[5]

How very modern this passage sounds; how odd that it should appear in Tocqueville rather than any of several dozen popular books about American discontents in the twentieth century. Tocqueville attributes the American restlessness chiefly to abundance itself and to a cast of mind that believes in the good things of this world as the only quest worth pursuing. The repeated words here are terms for haste, hurry, frenetic effort to grasp and keep grasping for more. To this foreign observer, rapid travel and its resulting overview of the earth were not the cause so much as the symptom of the American's fretful brow. And yet he goes on to list two other causes. One is "a social state in which neither law nor custom holds anyone in one place"—in other words, the novel openness of American democratic society. The other is the creed of human equality. This, he writes, has led again and again to frustration and disillusionment, because even those who attain what they seek have to observe that many others get it too. There can be no distinction worth much, no power, no excellence that can endure:

> When all prerogatives of birth and fortune are abolished, when all professions are open to all and a man's own energies may bring him to the top of any of them, an ambitious man may think it easy to launch on a great career and feel that he is called to no common destiny. But that is a delusion which experience quickly corrects. The same equality which allows each man to entertain vast hopes makes each man by himself weak. His power is limited on every side, though his longings may wander where they will. . . .
>
> When men are more or less equal and are following the same path, it is very difficult for any of them to walk faster and get out beyond the uniform crowd surrounding and hemming them in.
>
> This constant strife between the desires inspired by equality and the means it supplies to satisfy them harasses and wearies the mind.[6]

Here, if President Johnson had known of it, was an answer to his question. But it is an answer to undermine and explode the notion that progress ever upward should lead to happiness.

Behind Tocqueville loom other figures, too, that challenge and qualify his pronouncements. How, after all, did Americans of the 1830s find themselves living on a continent free of class restrictions, abounding in wealth, and sharing a belief in equality? They, too, must have had restless forebears, explorers and adventurers from Europe and Asia who crossed to America and left their old ways behind. Was there not an earlier deep restlessness behind the particular phenomenon of American restlessness? Is there perhaps a genetic disposition in our species that makes many of us incurable hunters and gatherers? Must we ever seek new discoveries to supplant holdings that do not satisfy?

By 1969, anyhow, the age-old urge to reach for the moon had become a literal project of American industry. And much seemed to depend on its success: confirmation of American ingenuity, power, wealth, and special destiny; vindication of American military cleanliness and honor, after years of napalm bombings in Asia and the bullying of other nations with threats from the air. For a few days everyone seemed to share a single anxiety for a safe landing and return.

Then it was accomplished. But what did it prove? What restlessness did it allay? As months and then years passed, it was still hard to say. Moon samples came back for intense analysis. Thousands of photographs and electromagnetic signals were cataloged and studied. But the romance of the moon landings faded away. There was no further to go with them. They stopped in 1972. By the science of the time, there could be no new launching of men or women to farther planets or stars. Landings on the moon were a triumph, but they also marked a limit. The astronauts came back down to earth and grew old like everyone else. Twenty years later, no one speaks of sending chosen heroes into space to set their boots on mysterious rocks.

Against the hard glitter, inconceivable size, and incomprehensible data of the Apollo expeditions, Lewis and Clark look almost innocent and refreshing. Their journey, too, was an act of the mind. What is more, it was an act that can still be traced best in the records of the explorers themselves. After their return they continued to work directly with the material they had gathered. Clark in particular pressed on to synthesize it in a single, large, detailed map of the entire American West. He completed this map sometime in 1810 and saw it through to engraving and publication in Biddle's *History* of the expedition in 1814. By this means Clark made himself a kind of astronaut, or pilot through space; for he ascended to a high new point of view over the American continent, cleared away many clouds of misunderstanding, and enabled his generation to see all of America in great detail for the first time.

Geographers have continued to praise many features of Clark's cartography. He made mistakes, perpetuated some myths, and allowed distortions in regions where he had not traveled himself. But compared to all earlier maps of western America, his map made great advances. Clark introduced the courses of the Columbia and Missouri rivers, newly determined by his own experience. He showed that the Rockies were not a single or simple barrier, but a series of mountain ranges, quite distinct from the Cascades and Coastal ranges and covering a large area of the American interior. He brought out the existence of subordinate systems such as the Black Hills. He showed new regions such as the Great Columbian Plain. He forced later explorers and travelers to think in different dimensions and give up some old delusions. Demolished was the idea that one could make a simple portage, mount a single ridge, and look westward to see the Pacific.[7]

To compose this final, comprehensive map, Clark had resources not only in the expedition journals but also in maps he and others had been making over many years. His own detailed maps, made on the trail, overlapped one another to cover almost all of the places he and Lewis explored. Over sixty of them were found among Clark family papers in New York City in 1903, in time for most of them to be reproduced in Thwaites's edition of the *Original Journals* (1904–5). Those maps are now in the Western Americana holdings at Yale University; they are also reproduced and discussed in the atlas volume of the current Moulton edition of the *Journals*. In addition to this preparation and experience, Clark drew on the maps and information of others. He put his map together in St. Louis, where he remained in touch with trappers, traders, and other explorers. John Colter's information went into this work, and so did George Drouillard's—including a map prepared in 1808 from Drouillard's information but drawn and annotated mainly by the hand of Meriwether Lewis (*Journals* 1:12). For areas that had not been directly seen by white explorers, Clark incorporated information he and others had gathered from Indians. Areas along the Mississippi, Arkansas, and Rio Grande rivers were explored by Zebulon M. Pike in 1805, 1806, and 1807; the results were published in 1810. Clark drew on this information too. For example, he put the caption "Highest Peak" next to what is now called Pike's Peak in Colorado.[8]

Clark's master map went on to two different histories after he completed it and forwarded it to Biddle. Most obviously, it went on directly to an engraver for publication. In the process, it was slightly altered: among other things, the northern and southern portions were left out so that the relevant and more accurate details were emphasized along the Lewis and Clark trail. But upon publication the engraved version became the standard of western knowledge for over a generation. In the words of an expert on western cartography: "This 1814 map was the progenitor of many later maps, and one of the most influential ever drawn, its imprint still to be seen on maps of Western America. . . . [It] was a map of towering significance. It remained so for thirty years, until men had been through the area many times, and until the region had been mapped by many persons. This was a great map, a milestone of mapping in its time, and countless placenames it gave to the face of America remain today as an ineradicable cultural heritage."[9]

That was the public outcome of Clark's masterpiece. But the original map was also returned to Clark in 1816; he reported to Jefferson that it had come back to him in St. Louis (*Letters* 2:624). There it continued to grow and change under his hand as he learned yet more from other Indians, explorers, and adventurers.[10] It was not only a memento of the Corps of Discovery but also an ongoing mural of living memory and discovery, which no modern reproduction can quite recapture. Gary Moulton explains that "numerous words and geographic features [are] faintly written in pencil," and these can hardly be made out in the reduction of a sheet of 51 × 29 in. to fit even the oversize pages of an atlas volume.[11]

Reading or viewing either final version remains an absorbing experience. In part this is because of the ordinary conventions of mapmaking and map reading. We peer down onto something like a picture of the topography of a region, but in a pleasing way it is not a picture at all. It does not have confusions of cloud or of hazy natural coloring. There are no distortions of receding distances or distractions of extraneous detail. And we can be everywhere or nowhere at once. We can move at a glance from the mouth of the Columbia to the fine curve on the Grand Detour of the Missouri and then slip west in another instant to hover over the Yellowstone and count its tributaries. But in part the reading of these maps is a result of Clark's own sense of scale and significance. The maps are large, but the features and notations are small. One has to keep one's nose close to the surface and not try to pull away to get a panoramic view. To make out the words and the precise details they describe, one must lean forward and become surrounded or engulfed by the wide extent of the rest of the route.

In this way these maps remain close to Clark's experience both during and after the expedition. They reflect his untrained but highly developed art as a mapmaker, one who took pains to make many smaller maps and then remained true to them as he fitted together a large one. They also reflect his sense of a living country. The notations mark not just static features but also points of history and development. "Old Mandan Village," reads a jotting by the Upper Missouri; "appears to have been fortified." Further north is Fort Mandan, "Wintering Post of Messrs. Lewis and Clark in 1804 and 1805." Along the Yellowstone: "Here Capt. Clark made Canoes to descend the River." Further south a dotted line: "Colter's Route in 1807."

And from Clark, the ongoing superintendent of Indian affairs, comes a vivid sense that this was a fully inhabited country. Lightly noted on his own map but plainly printed on the engraved version are names of Indian peoples and estimates of their numbers: "Chinnook *400 Souls*"; "Cho-pun-nish *8000 Souls*"; "Ricaras *3000 Souls.*"

Altogether these maps hold Clark and his reader close to the texture of the journals. What is seen at last from above still shows what was learned and observed over puzzling miles. It still holds that immediate authority and that enduring personal interest and even reverence. Of how many exploration documents can such praise be made? Lewis and Clark overcame the West with their skills as explorers and came over it again by their ingenuity and insight as geographers. But they did not rise so high that they lost sure touch with that earth. They remained in it and of it, as it remained in and of them, for years after their return. And it is this double sense of a land both grand and intricately surprising that they have passed on in their records and their maps, as well as their famous deeds.

Perhaps their work occurred in the last decades when such direct and obvious discovering was possible—the kind that could fill in large blank spaces on a continental map of America. Their own travels and observations marked out a new route across from sea to sea. After them and James Cook and other explorers of their time, all the major continents were known to science, at least in outline. Within a century they would all be mapped in detail. And after them would come observers equipped with new technology to make notations more rapidly and coldly: from a steamboat deck or a railroad line, through a camera lens or with instruments mounted in aircraft or satellites. After them, it would be harder to trace the act of discovery. Expert perceptions now seem to require expert preparation by others before they can be understood. Observant walking and jotting seem to produce discoveries only in much more confined areas.

But one must hedge a paragraph like the foregoing with a qualifying "perhaps," for such is the nature of science and discovery. A perception wholly new is often a radical challenge to what has long seemed obvious and settled. Many discoveries in science and geography have completely altered our understanding of North America within the past century. One example is the modern geological theory of continental drift, derived from ideas proposed by Alfred Wegener in 1912. Another is the argument that the modern Columbia River gorge was carved by flooding from an enormous ice-trapped lake at the end of the last age of glaciation. Like Wegener before him, J Harlen Bretz was harshly criticized in the 1920s when he posited a flood unlike any other on earth to explain the scablands of eastern Washington. But his theory is now widely accepted.[12] Of course, these discoveries had to be confirmed and elaborated with some sophisticated further studies, which included aerial and satellite photographs and measurements from deep under the sea. But the fact remains that they began with commonplace observations of the earth's surface and the contours of the continents. It was persistent intelligence—like Lewis and Clark's—not inscrutable machinery or calculations, that brought them about. And they are now readily understandable, too, easily diagrammed and explained to beginning students or tourists along the Columbia gorge.

In addition, the world seems to disclose unlikely changes even when scientists or explorers do not actively pursue them. One of the most beautiful, symmetrical mountains in the Cascade range was named by George Vancouver in 1792, sighted by Lewis and Clark in 1805, and later thoroughly mapped and measured. That was Mount St. Helens. But we now have to write "was" because in 1980 its volcanic core erupted suddenly and blew its top off. Other, more subtle changes continue to come into notice, just as wild animals and plants continue to flicker unexpectedly into sight before hikers and campers around the world. Despite the notion that science might master nature, nature has led science a merry chase for the past century. The mastery of nature, in the old Linnaean-Jeffersonian sense of the complete cataloging and mapping of the universe, has had to give way to perplexity before phenomena that resist names, categories, metaphors, or consistent models of any kind. Examples are familiar to everyone who has sampled quantum physics or molecular biology. At the end of the twentieth century many have begun to wonder whether science itself is a misleading structure of thought. Here, for example, are some words from Daniel Botkin, a well-respected researcher in ecology:

> Once we realize that we are part of a living system, global in scale, produced and in some ways controlled by life, and once we accept the intrinsic qualities of organic systems—with their ambiguities, variabilities, and complexities—we can feel a part of the world in a way that our nineteenth-century ancestors could not, but our ancestors before them did. We can leave behind the metaphors of the machine, which

are so uncomfortable psychologically because they separate us from nature and are so unlifelike and therefore so different from ourselves, and we can arrive, with the best information available for us in our time, at a new organic view of the Earth, a view in which we are a part of a living and changing system whose changes we can accept, use, and control.[13]

Botkin ends with ideas of use and control, but in the context from which these words are taken his emphasis is definitely on acceptance, understanding, and recognition of inescapable limits in our understanding.

Some of those limits are immediately at hand. A good example takes us back to the passage with which this chapter opened, where Lewis noted seeing the moon and defining its image much better with an optical instrument than he could have done "with the natural eye." There is a long, persistent, and still baffling problem about how people see the moon differently with their eyes and with instruments. It is called the moon illusion. The moon appears larger near the horizon than it does when seen overhead, yet its measured dimension (the angle of vision it subtends) is identical in both situations. The experience of seeing the moon differently at different hours has been so evident and puzzling that it has provoked explanations since ancient times. Aristotle and Ptolemy seem to have argued that the distortion of the sun and other objects near the horizon was caused by refraction of light through the atmosphere. But in the seventeenth century exact measurements completely undermined this idea by showing that the size of the moon does not really vary at all. Yet the moon illusion has persisted and been hard to refute to people who still experience it all over the world. To many the moon also seems closer when it is near the horizon, in defiance of accepted theories of size and distance perception. By 1985 there were eight major explanations of this illusion, based on optics, psychology, and neurology—in other words, eight ways of pointing out quirks and defects in human powers of observation "with the natural eye." Four years later these conflicting explanations, with commentaries, were enough to fill a hefty and inconclusive book.[14]

Looking at the moon turns out to be a very complicated business. What is one to trust—one's own experience, often shared with family and neighbors? the readings of impersonal instruments? contentious but well-reasoned discussions of why the eye at night sees differently when looking to a horizon or into the depths of the sky? Or are these the most pertinent questions? We all see the moon through myths and histories, as well as through eyes and lenses. Even though the astronauts have walked around on it, it remains an untouchable mirror of the sun's light and the earth's shape, a great measure of rhythmic changes, a singular spectacle when full or in eclipse. It seems unlikely that we will exhaust it as a focus for discovery.

Moreover, our human moon-watching may still be millennia behind the observational powers of another, much simpler organism. The common chambered nautilus (*Nautilus pompilius,* Linnaeus) is well known for its wonderfully spiraled shells made up of successively larger chambers. As the animal grows, it secretes a new wall at intervals and so creates a shell that builds round and round in a graceful curve. The size of each successive chamber is larger, but its shape is the same as the others because the curve follows a very precise line. It can be described in a simple mathematical formula and precisely traced on graph paper; it makes what is called a logarithmic spiral, one of many equiangular spirals to be found in nature.[15] Recent research concerning the nautilus also shows that fine growth lines within each of its chambers seem to correspond with days, and chamber walls appear regularly at intervals of about thirty lines—one every cycle of the moon. What is more, fossils of ancient nautiloids show that chamber sequences have been growing, from nine lines per chamber for fossils 420 million years old to the thirty-line chambers of our time. This evidence reinforces other biological and astronomical data to suggest that the moon was once much closer to the earth and made more rapid revolutions in its orbit.[16]

No one suggests that the nautilus sees the moon very acutely, calculates its cycles, and records them. "The prominent stalked eyes are uncomplicated," says a brief modern description. "A comparison with a simple pinhole camera comes to mind."[17] Besides, this mollusk lives in the depths of the far Pacific. No one has yet hit upon an explanation of how it has come to record the moon's cycles in its shell, in fact to seal them in dark chambers lined with pearly nacre. Still, it not only does that but also anticipates other achievements of modern science. Long, long before Robert Fulton, this organism had mastered the techniques of submarine navigation. It has a long tube, or siphuncle, extending back to its innermost chamber, through which it can control its fluid content and so rise or sink. In fact, Fulton called

his first submarine a "mechanical *Nautilus*"—the name that was repeated for the first nuclear-powered submarine in modern times. And
to propel themselves, these animals squirt out jets of fluid, as early
steamboat inventors like Fitch and Rumsey labored to do effectively.
Somehow, steadily and unthinkingly, the chambered nautilus has been
rising and sinking in the deep for millions of years, recording month
after month and leaving good records, still pleasing to the eye as well
as challenging to modern minds.

In the mid-nineteenth century Oliver Wendell Holmes celebrated
this "ship of pearl" in lines that were once widely read in schools and
diligently memorized:

> Year after year beheld the silent toil
> > That spread his lustrous coil;
> > Still, as the spiral grew,
> He left the past year's dwelling for the new,
> Stole with soft steps its shining archway through,
> > Built up its idle door,
> Stretched in his last-found home, and knew the old no more.

Thus the poet tried in his way to see into a phenomenon of nature
and to match it with writings that might spread *his* "lustrous coil."
The idea of time as a series of chambers or shining archways is com-
forting to take in and hold and recite; so is the promise of moving on
and on to larger chambers, the reward for steady advancement. And
the nautilus, a sea animal from depths like those of outer space or
eternity, makes an irresistible symbol for the grandest longings, in
Holmes's final stanza:

> Build thee more stately mansions, O my soul,
> > As the swift seasons roll!
> > Leave thy low-vaulted past!
> Let each new temple, nobler than the last,
> Shut thee from heaven with a dome more vast,
> > Till thou at length art free,
> Leaving thine outgrown shell by life's unresting sea![18]

Are the writings of Lewis and Clark an outgrown shell? It might
seem so. With them the United States moved into a realm twice its
previous size. With them science made the firm connection across the
long-sought Northwest Passage. Close after them came steamboats,
railroads, and all the clanking apparatus of modern industry. These

explorers seemed to seal off the era of Thomas Jefferson as they carried its ideals to a far extreme.

But their lines are far more intricate and lively than the regular ridges of a simple being. Again and again they saw subtle possibilities in commonplace occurrences, what to others might have seemed ordinary sights and uneventful daily happenings. And in the end their stories reflect a deep awareness of loss in the course of seeming progress, of bewilderment in the midst of triumph. For these reasons Lewis and Clark's journals still challenge us to recognize the wilderness that is all around us here and now, and to face it with intelligent courage.

Notes

Chapter 1: Discovery and Serendipity

1. See also Donald Jackson, *Among the Sleeping Giants: Occasional Pieces on Lewis and Clark* (Urbana: University of Illinois Press, 1981), 7.

2. Paul Russell Cutright provides a thorough discussion of the complicated history of the specimens or "booty" after the end of the expedition in *LCPN,* 349–92.

3. Clark's map is discussed more fully in chapter 12. The central accomplishments of Lewis and Clark as geographical explorers are also discussed at length in John Logan Allen, *Passage through the Garden: Lewis and Clark and the Image of the American Northwest* (Urbana: University of Illinois Press, 1975) and Donald Jackson, *Thomas Jefferson and the Stony Mountains: Exploring the West from Monticello* (Urbana: University of Illinois Press, 1981).

4. Samuel Eliot Morison, *The European Discovery of America: The Northern Voyages, A.D. 500–1600* (New York: Oxford University Press, 1971), 3. Readers of footnotes will be rewarded to learn that I first came upon this passage serendipitously—by looking up *serendipity* in the *Oxford English Dictionary.*

5. See Tzvetan Todorov, *The Conquest of America,* trans. Richard Howard (1984; New York: Harper Perennial, 1992), 3–50; Pauline Moffitt Watts, "Prophecy and Discovery: On the Spiritual Origins of Christopher Columbus's 'Enterprise of the Indies,' " *American Historical Review* 90 (1985): 73–102; and Stephen Greenblatt, *Marvelous Possessions: The Wonder of the New World* (Chicago: University of Chicago Press, 1991), esp. 73–85. Greenblatt remarks that "Columbus's whole life is marked by a craving for something that continually eluded him, for the kingdom or the paradise or the Jerusalem that he could not reach" (81), and he asserts that in his final writings the explorer believed himself to be the chosen king of the Promised Land (85). Many detailed studies of Columbus are currently appearing to mark the five hundredth anniversary of his first voyage. For

a preliminary expert survey of this new work, see the special "Columbian Encounters" issue of *William and Mary Quarterly,* 3d ser., 49 (April 1992).

6. Katherine Lee Bates, "America the Beautiful," in *A Treasury of the Familiar,* ed. Ralph L. Woods (New York: Macmillan, 1943), 71–72. Morison's passage about the motives for discovery, quoted earlier, contains lines about "a land of pure delight" from Isaac Watts, *Hymns and Spiritual Songs,* book 2, no. 66, a hymn under the rubric "A prospect of heaven makes death easy"; these verses aim to palliate death by opening a vision of the afterlife. Bates's hymn, however, seems to celebrate life here on earth or an afterlife in the American future. The chorus is aptly quoted in the title of a popular historical novel about the family of William and George Rogers Clark: James A. Thom, *From Sea to Shining Sea* (New York: Ballantine Books, 1984). And Bates herself claimed a westering inspiration in these verses; according to the *Dictionary of American Biography,* supplement 1, the opening lines came to her during a visit to Pike's Peak in 1893.

7. Wilmarth S. Lewis et al., eds., *Horace Walpole's Correspondence,* 48 vols. (New Haven, Conn.: Yale University Press, 1937–83), 20:407–8.

8. Theodore G. Remer, *Serendipity and the Three Princes* (Norman: University of Oklahoma Press, 1965); James H. Austin, *Chase, Chance, and Creativity: The Lucky Art of Novelty* (New York: Columbia University Press, 1978); Gilbert Shapiro, *A Skeleton in the Darkroom: Stories of Serendipity in Science* (San Francisco: Harper and Row, 1986); Royston M. Roberts, *Serendipity: Accidental Discoveries in Science* (New York: John Wiley & Sons, 1989).

9. A full modern translation of the 1557 Italian version, *Peregrination of the Three Young Sons of the King of Serendippo, Translated from the Persian Language into Italian by M. Christoforo Armeno,* is provided in Remer, *Serendipity,* 51–163. A much condensed version appears in Austin, *Chase, Chance, and Creativity,* 195–200.

10. *Samuel Johnson: Selected Poetry and Prose,* ed. Frank Brady and W. K. Wimsatt (Berkeley: University of California Press, 1977), 97.

11. Modern science seeks to account for natural events without recourse to occult or providential causes. Austin's *Chase, Chance, and Creativity* allows that there is such a thing as serendipity and traces examples of it in the author's own research experience, but Austin goes on to explain serendipity itself as a special kind of psychological or intellectual preparation by the researcher. He describes four varieties of chance, three of them conditioned by the activity or personality of the investigator; it is only from these three that valid discoveries arise. More recently, Robert Scott Root-Bernstein has thoroughly discussed many famous examples of serendipity cited in the past (including the discoveries of penicillin and X-rays), to show that in every case

the mind and energies of the discoverer had been at work to make accidents likely to occur and be fruitful. In *Discovering* (Cambridge, Mass.: Harvard University Press, 1989), Root-Bernstein argues that good science results from very playful sagacity, but never from independent intrusions of mere chance or accident. I should acknowledge here that I have found Root-Bernstein's discussion of this subject very stimulating.

12. Robert W. Tucker and David C. Hendrickson, *Empire of Liberty: The Statecraft of Thomas Jefferson* (New York: Oxford University Press, 1990), 88–93.

13. Alexander Hamilton, "Purchase of Louisiana," *New-York Evening Post,* July 5, 1803; reprinted in *Fame and the Founding Fathers: Essays by Douglass Adair,* ed. Trevor Colbourn (New York: W. W. Norton, 1974), 265, 266.

14. Robert K. Merton, *Social Theory and Social Structure,* rev. ed. (Glencoe, Ill.: Free Press, 1957), 12. On later pages (96, 103), Merton recasts this definition to read "the discovery, by chance or sagacity, of valid results which were not sought for"—thus making a common but crucial disjunction (chance *or* sagacity) between Walpole's strictly joined criteria. But he reunites them in a later formulation—"the serendipity pattern: an unexpected and anomalous finding elicited the investigator's curiosity, and conducted him along an unpremeditated by-path, which led to a fresh hypothesis" (108)— which is modified further in a later chapter (229). Merton notes that he has engaged on a long study of the term *serendipity,* its origins, usage, and diffusion into common parlance (104n), but it seems to squirm and wriggle in his hands as much as anyone's.

Chapter 2: The American Sublime

1. Thomas Jefferson, *Notes on the State of Virginia,* ed. William Peden (1954; New York: W. W. Norton, 1972), 19. Further references are cited by page number in the text.

2. James Madison to Thomas Jefferson, Aug. 12, 1786, in Julian P. Boyd and Thomas Cullen, eds., *The Papers of Thomas Jefferson,* 23 vols. to date (Princeton: Princeton University Press, 1950–), 20:230.

3. Thomas Jefferson to Horatio G. Spafford, May 14, 1809, in Andrew A. Lipscomb and Albert Ellery Bergh, eds., *The Writings of Thomas Jefferson,* 20 vols. (Washington, D.C.: Thomas Jefferson Memorial Association, 1903– 4), 12:279–81.

4. Ibid., 13:xlvi.

5. Josiah Quincy, *Cleminole* No. 7 (March 17, 1804), quoted in Linda K. Kerber, *Federalists in Dissent: Imagery and Ideology in Jeffersonian America* (Ithaca, N.Y.: Cornell University Press, 1970), 177.

6. Garry Wills, *Inventing America: Jefferson's Declaration of Independence* (Garden City, N.Y.: Doubleday, 1978), 259–72.

7. Thomas Jefferson to Maria Cosway, October 12, 1786, in Boyd and Cullen, *Papers*, 10:447.

8. Longinus, *On Great Writing*, trans. G. M. A. Grube (New York: Library of Liberal Arts, 1957), 4. Further references are cited by page number in the text.

9. Original descriptions of these devices are quoted in Elizabeth Wheeler Manwaring, *Italian Landscape in Eighteenth Century England* (1925; London: Cass, 1965), 182, 186.

10. Ibid., 95.

11. James Thomson, *The Castle of Indolence*, canto 1, stanza 38, quoted from *The Complete Poetical Works of James Thomson*, ed. J. Logie Robertson (London: Oxford University Press, 1908), 265.

12. Manwaring, *Italian Landscape*, 107, 196 (including John More quote).

13. William Wordsworth to Sir George Beaumont, August 28, 1811, quoted in Martin Price, "The Picturesque Moment," *From Sensibility to Romanticism*, ed. Frederick W. Hilles and Harold Bloom (New York: Oxford University Press, 1965), 288.

14. Immanuel Kant, *The Critique of Judgment*, trans. James Creed Meredith (Oxford: Clarendon Press, 1952), 110–11.

15. Quoted in Samuel H. Monk, *The Sublime: A Study of Critical Theories in XVIII Century England* (1935; Ann Arbor: University of Michigan Press, 1960), 211.

16. William Wordsworth, *A Guide through the District of the Lakes*, quoted in Price, "Picturesque Moment," 288.

17. Thomas Burnet, *The Sacred Theory of the Earth*, 6th ed., 2 vols. (London, 1726), 1:188–89, quoted in M. H. Abrams, *Natural Supernaturalism: Tradition and Revolution in Romantic Literature* (New York: W. W. Norton, 1969), 101. The classic discussion of Burnet's theories and their influence on English literature is Marjorie Hope Nicolson's *Mountain Gloom and Mountain Glory* (Ithaca, N.Y.: Cornell University Press, 1959).

18. William Wordsworth, *The Fourteen-Book Prelude*, ed. W. J. B. Owen (Ithaca, N.Y.: Cornell University Press, 1985), 6.597–606.

19. Ibid., 6.625–41.

20. Benjamin Smith Barton, "A Description of the Falls of Niagara," *Philadelphia Medical and Physics Journal* 1 (1804): 39, quoted in Elizabeth McKinsey, *Niagara Falls: Icon of the American Sublime* (New York: Cambridge University Press, 1985), 89.

21. James Thomson, *The Seasons: Autumn*, ll. 773–80, in *Poetical Works*, 160–61.

22. Alexander Wilson, "The Foresters: A Poem Descriptive of a Pedestrian

Journey to the Falls of the Niagara," ll. 2,061–72, quoted in McKinsey, *Niagara Falls*, 40.

23. McKinsey, *Niagara Falls*, 48, 89–90. The Wilson plate is reproduced on page 49.

24. Two versions of *Falls of Niagara* exist, at the Metropolitan Museum of Art in New York City and in Williamsburg, Virginia. For color plates see Alice Ford, *Edward Hicks: His Life and Art* (New York: Abbeville Press, 1985), 57; and Eleanor Price Mather and Dorothy Canning Miller, *Edward Hicks: His Peaceable Kingdoms and Other Paintings* (Newark, Del.: University of Delaware Press, 1983), 202–3 and plate I.

25. Boyd and Cullen, *Papers*, 15:177. Actually, Trumbull's expressed ideals closely coincide with Kant's discussion of the moral dimensions of the sublime. Here is Trumbull on Washington's resignation from the army after the close of the Revolution, in *Autobiography, Reminiscences and Letters of John Trumbull from 1756 to 1841* (New Haven, Conn.: B. L. Hamlen, 1841), 429–30: "What a dazzling temptation was here to earthly ambition! Beloved by the military, venerated by the people, who was there to oppose the victorious chief, if he had chosen to retain that power which he had so long held with universal approbation? The Caesars, the Cromwells, the Napoleons, yielded to the charm of earthly ambition, and betrayed their country; but Washington aspired to loftier, imperishable glory—to that glory which virtue alone can give, and which no power, no effort, no time, can ever take away."

For comparison, here is Kant on the dynamic sublime, in the paragraph following the one about natural scenery quoted earlier: "Eternal nature is . . . estimated in our aesthetic judgement as sublime . . . because it challenges our power (not one of nature) to regard as small those things of which we are wont to be solicitous (worldly goods, health, and life) and hence to regard its might (to which in these matters we are no doubt subject) as exercising over us and our personality no such rude dominion that we should bow down before it, once the question becomes one of our highest principles and of our asserting or forsaking them" (*Critique of Judgment*, 111).

26. See Helen A. Cooper, ed., *John Trumbull: The Hand and Spirit of a Painter* (New Haven, Conn.: Yale University Art Gallery, 1982), 206–30, esp. 210; McKinsey, *Niagara Falls*, 55–76.

27. See Ford, *Edward Hicks*, 46–57, 118–19. Mather and Miller list four early versions of *The Peaceable Kingdom* showing the Natural Bridge arching over the treaty vignette (*Edward Hicks*, 95–98 and plate II) and two later canvases (1845 and 1847) in which the bridge appears in the right background, apart from the treaty scene (144, 150). They also illustrate the development of the treaty vignette from copies of a painting by Benjamin West (30–34).

28. Wallace Stevens, "The American Sublime," *Collected Poems* (New York: Alfred A. Knopf, 1954), 130–31.

Chapter 3: Confronting the Bear

1. Francis Bacon, *The New Organon,* aphorism 1.129, in Sidney Warhaft, ed., *Francis Bacon: A Selection of His Works* (Toronto: Macmillan of Canada, 1965), 373–74.

2. Elizabeth L. Eisenstein, *The Printing Press as an Agent of Change,* 2 vols. (Cambridge: Cambridge University Press, 1979), 1:20–21.

3. These instruments are fully described in Silvio A. Bedini, "The Scientific Instruments of the Lewis and Clark Expedition," *Great Plains Quarterly* 4 (Winter 1984): 54–69. Seafarers and land explorers used very different methods of calculating longitude. Lewis and Clark's methods have been explained recently in a seminar paper by Arlen J. Large, "How Far West Am I?: The Almanac as an Explorer's Yardstick," The Center for Great Plains Studies, Lincoln, Nebraska, April 1992.

4. Bedini, "Scientific Instruments," 63–65.

5. Ruby El Hult, *Guns of the Lewis and Clark Expedition* (Tacoma: Washington State Historical Society, 1960), 2. The most extensive discussions of the party's firearms have been written by Carl P. Russell, beginning with a survey he made for the National Park Service, reprinted as "The Guns of the Lewis and Clark Expedition," *North Dakota History* 27 (January 1960): 25–34, and expanded in his later books *Guns on the Early Frontiers* (Berkeley: University of California Press, 1962) and *Firearms, Traps, and Tools of the Mountain Men* (New York: Alfred A. Knopf, 1967). In the latter book, Russell notes that Lewis ordered slings for this rifle, though rifles issued later did not have swivels. More recently, the rifles and other guns of the expedition have been discussed and illustrated in Louis A. Garavaglia and Charles G. Worman, *Firearms of the American West, 1803–1865* (Albuquerque: University of New Mexico Press, 1984).

6. Warhaft, ed., *Francis Bacon,* 373.

7. Henry Adams, *The Education of Henry Adams,* ed. Ernest Samuels (Boston: Houghton Mifflin, 1973), 486. Further references are cited by page number in the text.

8. John Milton, *Complete Poems and Major Prose,* ed. Merritt Y. Hughes (New York: Odyssey Press, 1957), 123.

9. No. 159, in *The Spectator,* ed. Donald F. Bond, 5 vols. (Oxford: Clarendon Press, 1965), 2:122.

10. Notes dictated by William Wordsworth to Isabella Fenwick in 1843, quoted in W. J. B. Owen, ed., *Lyrical Ballads 1798,* 2d ed. (London: Oxford University Press, 1969), 135.

11. Milo M. Quaife, ed., *The Journals of Captain Meriwether Lewis and Sergeant John Ordway, Kept on the Expedition of Western Exploration, 1803–1806* (Madison: State Historical Society of Wisconsin, 1916), 116.

12. Ibid., 123.

13. Quoted in John Warkentin, ed., *The Western Interior of Canada: A Record of Geographical Discovery, 1612–1917* (Toronto: McClelland and Stewart, 1964), 23. In his prose journal for August 20, 1691, Kelsey described a "great sort of a Bear which is Bigger then any white Bear & is Neither White nor Black But silver hair'd like our English Rabbit" (24).

14. A. Irving Hollowell's dissertation "Bear Ceremonialism in the Northern Hemisphere" contains a bibliography that runs to over ten printed pages in *American Anthropologist*, n.s., 28 (1926): 1–175. Hallowell notes that the hunted bear is almost always named as a person, often as a grandfather, old man, or uncle, and addressed with respect and even apologies (43–61).

15. Paul Schullery, ed., *American Bears: Selections from the Writings of Theodore Roosevelt* (Boulder: Colorado Associated University Press, 1983), 10–12.

Chapter 4: Extending George Washington's Errand

1. James Thomas Flexner, *George Washington: The Forge of Experience, 1732–1775* (Boston: Little, Brown, 1965), 44–45.

2. Douglas Southall Freeman, *George Washington: A Biography,* 7 vols. (New York: Charles Scribner's Sons, 1948–57), 1:6.

3. Patricia Seed, "Taking Possession and Reading Texts: Establishing the Authority of Overseas Empires," *William and Mary Quarterly,* 3d ser., 49 (1992): 183–209, quotations at 205, 206–7.

4. Patricia Nelson Limerick, *The Legacy of Conquest: The Unbroken Past of the American West* (New York: W. W. Norton, 1987), 100.

5. *The Diaries of George Washington,* ed. Donald Jackson et al., 6 vols. to date (Charlottesville: University Press of Virginia, 1976–), 1:18.

6. Flexner, *Washington,* 89.

7. Ibid., 336.

8. Ibid., 289–303; see also Freeman, *Biography,* 3:408–9; 7:486.

9. *Dictionary of American Biography,* s.v. "Clark, George Rogers"; Lowell H. Harrison, *George Rogers Clark and the War in the West* (Lexington: University Press of Kentucky, 1976); Hugh F. Rankin, *George Rogers Clark and the Winning of the West* (Richmond: Virginia Independence Bicentennial Commission, 1976).

10. John Logan Allen, *Passage through the Garden: Lewis and Clark and the Image of the American Northwest* (Urbana: University of Illinois Press, 1975), 27, 119.

11. Alexander Mackenzie, *Voyages from Montreal, on the River St. Lawrence, through the Continent of North America, to the Frozen and Pacific Ocean,* 2 vols. (London, 1801), 411, quoted in Donald Jackson, *Thomas Jefferson and the Stony Mountains: Exploring the West from Monticello* (Urbana: University of Illinois Press, 1981), 95.

12. Jackson, *Jefferson,* 223–67.

13. Ibid., 25–78.

14. Ibid., 117–21.

15. Dumas Malone, *Jefferson and His Time,* 6 vols. (Boston: Little, Brown, 1948–81), 4:43–44.

16. Ibid., 4:40.

17. Jefferson to Benjamin Smith Barton, February 27, 1803, *Letters* 1:17; similar letters are printed in *Letters* 1:18–21.

18. Charles A. Miller, *Jefferson and Nature: An Interpretation* (Baltimore: Johns Hopkins University Press, 1988), 10–11.

19. Allen, *Passage through the Garden,* esp. 169–70, 225, 243, 249–50. Allen notes (136–37) that Jefferson's (and the world's) knowledge of the Missouri region beyond St. Louis took up a single erroneous page in his report to Congress of November, 1803, entitled "An Official Account of Louisiana."

20. Miller, *Jefferson and Nature,* 138–39; Boyd and Cullen, *Papers,* 6:581–616, including maps of several successive plans; quotation at 6:592.

21. Miller, *Jefferson and Nature,* 23–55. Michel Foucault provides a more elaborate general analysis of Enlightenment taxonomical thinking in *The Order of Things: An Archaeology of the Human Sciences* (New York: Vintage, 1970), esp. 125–65.

22. These lists are discussed further in chapter 8. They are treated as a part of Jefferson's complex of attitudes toward Indians in Bernard Sheehan, *Seeds of Extinction: Jeffersonian Philanthropy and the American Indian* (Chapel Hill: University of North Carolina Press, 1973), 54–58.

23. Ronda cites two accounts: Olin D. Wheeler, *The Trail of Lewis and Clark, 1804–1904,* 2 vols. (New York: G. P. Putnam's Sons, 1904), 2:311–12, for an interview between George Bird Grinnell and Wolf Calf, who claimed to be the youngest warrior of the party; and James H. Bradley, "The Bradley Manuscript," Montana Historical Society *Contributions* 8 (1917): 135.

Chapter 5: Ingesting America

1. A recipe for this soup is given in E. G. Chuinard, *Only One Man Died: The Medical Aspects of the Lewis and Clark Expedition* (Fairfield, Wash.: Ye Galleon Press, 1979), 160–61. Further information, including another soup

recipe, is provided in Steven Harrison, "Meriwether Lewis's First Written Reference to the Expedition—April 15, 1803," *We Proceeded On* 9 (Nov. 1983): 10–11.

2. Chuinard, *Only One Man Died*, 222.

3. If it seems odd or primitive that whole peoples depended so heavily on a single resource—salmon or buffalo—for their subsistence, one should bear in mind that the French boatmen who pulled Lewis and Clark upstream had been carried west themselves by a large, modern Canadian economy based on beaver pelts and that the highly civilized Thomas Jefferson, who planned this expedition, had once had his governor's salary fixed at sixty thousand pounds of tobacco (see Dumas Malone, *Jefferson and His Time*, 6 vols. [Boston: Little, Brown, 1948–81], 1:315).

4. See W. Raymond Wood, "Slaughter River: Pishkun or Float Bison?" *We Proceeded On* 12 (May 1986): 11–14.

5. Lewis to Henry Dearborn, January 15, 1807, *Letters* 1:369. For Clark's contrasting letter to Charbonneau in 1806, extending appreciative support, see *Letters* 1:315–16.

6. See Chuinard, *Only One Man Died*, 360–61; see also *LCPN*, 223–24, with citations to other sources.

7. Later Lewis noted that "Indians of this coast" went to sea and took whales with harpoons (*Journals* 6:407).

8. The phrase is Lewis's, from another of his descriptions of Coastal Indians (*Journals* 6:436).

9. I am grateful to Lori Fraser, a former student of mine at Mount Allison University, for briefly but insistently questioning this passage in a senior seminar in 1990–91.

10. See Owen Beattie, "Elevated Bone Lead Levels in a Crewman from the Last Arctic Expedition of Sir John Franklin (1845–1848)," in *The Franklin Era in Canadian Arctic History*, ed. Patricia D. Sutherland, Archeological Survey of Canada Paper No. 131 (Ottawa: National Museum of Man, 1985), 141–48; see also London *Times* (Oct. 26, 1988): 5. In *Unraveling the Franklin Mystery: Inuit Testimony* (Montreal: McGill-Queen's University Press, 1991), David C. Woodman explicitly rejects lead poisoning as a major contributing factor to the collapse of the expedition and argues that the primary cause of the crewmen's deaths was a food problem—scurvy or vitamin C deficiency (336–38).

Chapter 6: Signals of Friendship

1. Ronda recounts the *Tonquin* incident in *Astoria and Empire* (Lincoln: University of Nebraska Press, 1990) and concludes that it was caused by the stupid, overbearing behavior of the ship's captain. But he also mentions that

"the captain did not rig the usual boarding nets commonly used in the maritime fur trade to prevent surprise attack" (236).

2. On the idea of Welsh Indians generally, see Bernard DeVoto, *The Course of Empire* (Boston: Houghton Mifflin, 1952), 68–73, and John Logan Allen, *Passage through the Garden: Lewis and Clark and the Image of the American Northwest* (Urbana: University of Illinois Press, 1975), 207n. The search for lost Israelites was suggested to Lewis by Benjamin Rush (*Letters* 1:50).

3. W. P. Clark, *The Indian Sign Language* (1885; Lincoln: University of Nebraska Press, 1982), 412.

4. Garrick Mallery, "Sign Language among North American Indians," *First Annual Report of the Bureau of Ethnology, 1879–80* (Washington, D.C., 1881), 535, cited in John E. Rees, "The Shoshoni Contribution to Lewis and Clark," *Idaho Yesterdays* 2 (Summer 1958): 6.

5. Rees, "Shoshoni Contribution," 6.

6. Ibid., 7n.

7. Samuel Johnson, *Diaries, Prayers, and Annals,* ed. E. L. McAdam, Jr., with Donald and Mary Hyde (New Haven, Conn.: Yale University Press, 1958), 81.

8. See the introductions by Merle W. Wells in two books by Brigham D. Madsen: *The Lemhi: Sacajawea's People* (Caldwell, Id.: Caxton, 1979), 28; and *The Northern Shoshoni* (Caldwell, Id.: Caxton, 1980), 20.

Chapter 7: Reading the Birds

1. For illustrations and discussion, see Georges Bataille, *Lascaux, or the Birth of Art,* trans. Austyn Wainhouse (Lausanne: Skira, 1955), 113–18.

2. Kevin R. McNamara, "The Feathered Scribe: Discourses of American Ornithology before 1800," *William and Mary Quarterly,* 3d ser., 47 (1990): 210–34.

3. Ibid., 214, quoting the preface to John Ray, *The Ornithology of Francis Willughby* (London, 1678), A4r, A2v.

4. David Scofield Wilson provides a sensitive and amply illustrated discussion of Catesby and his ways of seeing in *In the Presence of Nature* (Amherst: University of Massachusetts Press, 1978), 123–85.

5. Carolus Linnaeus, *A General System of Nature,* trans. William Turton, 10th ed. (London, 1802–6), 1:144, quoted in McNamara, "Feathered Scribe," 227. The outline of Linnaeus's system and its relations to science in early America are briefly surveyed by Raymond Phineas Stearns in *Science in the British Colonies of America* (Urbana: University of Illinois Press, 1970), 526–33.

6. McNamara, "Feathered Scribe," 219.

7. Ibid., 228.

8. Thomas Jefferson, *Notes on the State of Virginia,* ed. William Peden (1954; New York: W. W. Norton, 1972), 66–70.

9. McNamara, "Feathered Scribe," 229.

10. Charles Coleman Sellers, *Mr. Peale's Museum: Charles Willson Peale and the First Popular Museum of Natural Science and Art* (New York: W. W. Norton, 1980), 162.

11. Sellers, *Mr. Peale's Museum,* 187–88. Surviving items given to the museum from this expedition are illustrated on pages 172–83; they are now preserved at the Peabody Museum at Harvard University.

12. William Wordsworth, "The Green Linnet," *Poems, in Two Volumes, and Other Poems, 1800–1807,* ed. Jared Curtis (Ithaca, N.Y.: Cornell University Press, 1983), 229–30.

13. Samuel Taylor Coleridge, *Biographia Literaria,* ed. James Engell and W. Jackson Bate, 2 vols. (Princeton: Princeton University Press, 1983), 2:148–49.

14. Wordsworth, "The Green Linnet," 230. Coleridge makes some slips in quoting these stanzas in the discussion noted earlier.

15. Lauren Brown, *Grasslands,* Audubon Society Nature Guides (New York: Alfred A. Knopf, 1985), 543.

16. Whitehouse's journal for September 18 reports Lewis's killed bird as "a bird of pray resembling the European magpy" (Thwaites 7:59). Ordway also writes that Lewis's party killed "one curious Bird of a blackish & greenish coullour Black Bill & a verry long tail—resembling a bird that we call a magpy" (Milo M. Quaife, ed., *The Journals of Captain Meriwether Lewis and Sergeant John Ordway* [Madison: State Historical Society of Wisconsin, 1916], 132–33).

17. Paul Russell Cutright, "A History of Lewis's Woodpecker and Clark's Nutcracker," *We Proceeded On* 10 (May 1984): 9–15. On the methods of preserving birds, Cutright cites Edwin Morris Betts, ed., *Thomas Jefferson's Garden Book,* in *Memoirs* 22 (Philadelphia: American Philosophical Society, 1944), 95. The journal passages on preserving birds are in Thwaites 5:70–71, 75–76. See also *LCPN,* 26, 379, 384–85, 391–92; Sellers, *Mr. Peale's Museum,* 24–25, 199 (on Peale's methods). On a visit to the Museum of Comparative Zoology at Harvard in November 1991, I was informed that the specimen of Lewis's woodpecker cannot now be seen without special permission.

18. In *LCPN,* 100–101, Cutright cites two articles by Edmund C. Jaeger: "Does the Poor-will Hibernate?" *Condor* 50 (1948): 45–46; and "Further Observations on the Hibernation of the Poor-will," *Condor* 51 (1949): 105–9. Jaeger ("Further Observations," 108) credits Hopi and Navaho observers with noting this bird's peculiar habits before he studied them.

McNamara notes that the torpidity of birds was a topic of interest in ancient Greece and had been debated in the eighteenth century in the *Philosophical Transactions* of the Royal Society ("Feathered Scribe," 229n).

19. Virginia C. Holmgren, "Birds of the Lewis and Clark Journals," *We Proceeded On* 10 (May 1984): 23–26.

20. McNamara, "Feathered Scribe," 210.

21. Holmgren, "Birds," 19, citing entries of June 4 and 5, 1804.

22. Annie Heloise Abel, ed., *Tabeau's Narrative of Loisel's Expedition to the Upper Missouri,* trans. Rose Abel Wright (Norman: University of Oklahoma Press, 1939), 88–89.

23. The passing reference is in *Journals* 3 : 293. Cutright asserts that Lewis and Clark "went into detail about its behavior. It surprised them with its tameness, since it often came within two or three feet of them to snatch away pieces of meat while they were skinning a deer or buffalo" (*LCPN* 84). But these words seem to repeat a passage from Alexander Wilson's *American Ornithology,* based on reports from an unnamed hunter, not details provided directly by Lewis or Clark. Wilson writes that on the expedition "the magpie was found to be far more daring than the jay, dashing into their very tents, and carrying off the meat from their dishes. One of the hunters who accompanied the expedition informed me, that they frequently attended him while he was engaged in skinning and cleaning the carcass of the deer, bear or buffalo he had killed, often seizing the meat that hung within a foot or two of his head" (*American Ornithology,* 5 vols. [Philadelphia, 1810–14], 2 : 79, quoted in Raymond Darwin Burroughs, *The Natural History of the Lewis and Clark Expedition* [East Lansing: Michigan State University Press, 1961], 247–48).

24. Jean Myron Linsdale, "American Magpie," in *Life Histories of North American Jays, Crows, and Titmice,* ed. Arthur Cleveland Bent, U.S. National Museum Bulletin 191 (1946; New York: Dover Books, 1964), 133–55; Derek Goodwin, *Crows of the World* (Ithaca: Cornell University Press, 1976), 171–81; Morris D. Johnson, *Black and White Spy: The Magpie* (Dickinson, N.D.: Professional Printing, 1988).

25. William Blake, *The Marriage of Heaven and Hell* (1793), plates 14, 7, in *Blake: Complete Writings,* ed. Geoffrey Keynes (London: Oxford University Press, 1966), 154, 150.

26. Percy Bysshe Shelley, "To a Skylark," in *Percy Bysshe Shelley: Selected Poetry,* ed. Neville Rogers (Boston: Houghton Mifflin, 1968), 369.

Chapter 8: Finding Words

1. Elijah H. Criswell, *Lewis and Clark: Linguistic Pioneers,* University of Missouri Studies 15 (Columbia: University of Missouri, 1940): 32. In 1991

a photographic reproduction of this scarce book was issued by the Headwaters Chapter of the Lewis and Clark Trail Heritage Foundation.

2. Ibid., ccxi.

3. Michel Foucault, *The Order of Things: An Archaeology of the Human Sciences* (New York: Vintage, 1973), 82.

4. K. M. Elisabeth Murray, *Caught in the Web of Words: James Murray and the Oxford English Dictionary* (New Haven, Conn.: Yale University Press, 1977), 300, 235.

5. Ibid., 221–22.

6. Clark's Memorandum Book of 1798, quoted in Jerome O. Steffan, *William Clark: Jeffersonian Man on the Frontier* (Norman: University of Oklahoma Press, 1977), 15.

7. Steffan, *William Clark,* 43–51.

8. Biddle's notes were presented to the American Philosophical Society in 1949 and were first published in *Letters* 2:497–545; for later letters between Biddle and Clark see *Letters* 2:550–54, 562–64, 568.

9. Seymour Dunbar quoted in Robert B. Betts, "'we commenced wrighting &c': A Salute to the Ingenious Spelling and Grammar of William Clark," *We Proceeded On* 6 (Nov. 1980): 10–12.

10. Bernard DeVoto, ed., *The Journals of Lewis and Clark* (Boston: Houghton Mifflin, 1953), vii.

11. Walter H. Marx, "A Latin Matter in the Biddle 'Narrative' or 'History' of the Lewis and Clark Expedition," *We Proceeded On* 9 (Oct. 1983): 21–22. Marx provides the first full translation of Biddle's Latin. In his own notes, Biddle recorded another sexual adventure in French (*Letters* 2:503).

12. Bob Saindon, "The Lost Vocabularies of the Lewis and Clark Expedition," *We Proceeded On* 3 (July 1977): 4–6.

13. I follow the order of words in a photocopy of one of Jefferson's printed forms, item 2051 in John F. Freeman, *A Guide to the Manuscripts Relating to the American Indian in the Library of the American Philosophical Society* (Philadelphia: American Philosophical Society, 1966), 225. A "facsimile" of this form is reprinted in Thwaites (7: following 408), but its tabulations are out of order and many terms are repeated.

14. Kim R. Stafford, *Having Everything Right* (New York: Penguin, 1986), 7.

15. Bernard W. Sheehan, *Seeds of Extinction: Jeffersonian Philanthropy and the American Indian* (Chapel Hill: University of North Carolina Press, 1973), 54–55.

16. Betts, "'we commenced wrighting,' " 10.

17. The origins and early promulgation of Visible Speech are briefly surveyed in Robert V. Bruce, *Bell: Alexander Graham Bell and the Conquest of Solitude* (Boston: Little, Brown, 1973), 39–43. Its influence eventually af-

fected the development of the telephone, the *Oxford English Dictionary*, and Shaw's creation of Eliza Doolittle in *Pygmalion*. The photograph of Bell at the Bell National Historical Site in Baddeck, Nova Scotia, is captioned "Alexander Graham Bell in Brantford, Ontario, dressed in Mohawk reglia" and identified as "Nat. Geog. Soc. neg no. 156500 AB." Bell was initiated in 1871, but the photograph was taken in 1876.

18. Milo M. Quaife, ed., *The Journals of Captain Meriwether Lewis and Serjeant John Ordway, Kept on the Expedition of Western Exploration, 1803–1806* (Madison: State Historical Society of Wisconsin, 1916), 95n; *Journals* 2:366–68.

19. A restoration of this special car is part of the permanent display at the Montana Historical Society in Helena. See also *F. Jay Haynes: Photographer* (Helena: Montana Historical Society Press, 1981), plate 83, p. 106.

20. Robert B. Betts, "'The wrightingest explorers of their time': New Estimates of the Number of Words in the Published Journals of the Lewis and Clark Expedition," *We Proceeded On* 7 (Aug. 1981): 4–9.

21. Criswell, *Lewis and Clark,* cxxxviii–cxxxix.

22. W. Kaye Lamb, ed., *The Journals and Letters of Sir Alexander Mackenzie,* Hakluyt Society extra series no. 41 (Toronto: Macmillan, 1970), 262, 264; Charles Coleman Sellers, *Mr. Peale's Museum: Charles Willson Peale and the First Popular Museum of Natural Science and Art* (New York: W. W. Norton, 1980), 206–8 (the broadside is reprinted on p. 208); *Oxford English Dictionary,* s.v. "grizzly" (which cites Gass's *Journal,* 221). According to Sellers, when the grizzly bear displayed by Peale was killed, its haunch was sent to Thomas Jefferson.

23. Criswell, *Lewis and Clark,* cxxviii.

24. Ibid., cxxvii–cxxviii.

Chapter 9: The Rhythms of Rivers

1. Jefferson to Robert R. Livingston, April 18, 1802, in *The Writings of Thomas Jefferson,* ed. Paul Leicester Ford, 10 vols. (New York: Putnam, 1892–99), 8:144–45.

2. Dumas Malone, *Jefferson and His Time,* 6 vols. (Boston: Little, Brown, 1948–81), 1:16.

3. Charles A. Miller, *Jefferson and Nature: An Interpretation* (Baltimore: Johns Hopkins University Press, 1988), 227–29.

4. Some of the pervasiveness of river life in the Lewis and Clark experience has been dramatized in the musical play *Riversong* (lyrics by Tim Rarick, music by Tom Cooper), which was first performed at the Renton (Washington) Civic Theatre. I saw a performance by the Idaho Repertory Theatre in August 1990.

5. Mark Twain, *Life on the Mississippi,* from *Mississippi Writings,* ed. Guy Cardwell (New York: Library of America, 1982), 283–84. Further references are cited by page number in the text.

6. John Logan Allen, *Passage through the Garden: Lewis and Clark and the Image of the American Northwest* (Urbana: University of Illinois Press, 1975), 196.

7. Ibid., 196.

8. Twain's problems in seeing as both a pilot and a passenger are at the heart of Leo Marx's influential book *The Machine in the Garden: Technology and the Pastoral Ideal in America* (New York: Oxford University Press, 1964), but Marx mentions the development of steamboats only in passing.

9. James Thomas Flexner, *Steamboats Come True,* rev. ed. (Boston: Little, Brown, 1978).

10. Ibid., 126.

11. Washington's diary for September 7, 1784, quoted in Flexner, *Steamboats,* 66.

12. Jefferson to Joseph Willard, March 24, 1789, in Julian P. Boyd and Thomas Cullen, eds., *The Papers of Thomas Jefferson,* 23 vols. to date (Princeton: Princeton University Press, 1950–), 14:698–99. In the same paragraph Jefferson also praises Thomas Paine for his invention of an iron bridge—another great advance in mastering rivers. Jefferson concludes by exhorting Willard (who was then president of Harvard and corresponding secretary of the American Academy of Arts and Sciences) in terms that anticipate his enthusiasm for the Lewis and Clark expedition: "What a feild have we at our doors to signalize ourselves in! The botany of America is far from being exhausted; it's Mineralogy is untouched, and it's Natural history or Zoology totally mistaken and misrepresented. . . . It is for such institutions as that over which you preside so worthily, Sir, to do justice to our country, it's productions, and it's genius. It is the work to which the young men, whom you are forming, should lay their hands."

13. Dumas Malone, *Jefferson and His Time,* 6 vols. (Boston: Little, Brown, 1948–81), 2:281–85.

14. Flexner, *Steamboats,* 66.

15. Henry Adams, *History of the United States during the Administrations of Thomas Jefferson and James Madison,* 9 vols. (New York: Charles Scribner's Sons, 1891–96), 1:68–70.

16. Jonathan Swift, *Gulliver's Travels and Other Writings,* ed. Louis A. Landa (Boston: Houghton Mifflin, 1960), 108.

17. Cedric Ridgely-Nevitt, "The *Steam Boat,* 1807–1814," *American Neptune* 27 (1967): 10–11. This article is a thorough review of what is known about the design of Fulton's original Hudson River boat.

18. The accurate date of this voyage and the accurate name of the vessel, *North River Steam Boat* (not *The Clermont*), are untangled from the errors repeated in many sources in Donald C. Ringwald, "First Steamboat to Albany," *American Neptune* 24 (1964): 157–71.

19. Donald Jackson, *Voyages of the Steamboat Yellow Stone* (New York: Ticknor & Fields, 1985), surveys the history and design of this boat. On its 1832 voyage it carried the artist George Catlin, whose paintings are the earliest visual record of many scenes Lewis and Clark had described in their journals.

20. Adams, *History*, 4:135.

21. Ibid., 9:173. The steamboat was "the chief technological means by which the wilderness was conquered and the frontier advanced," according to a more recent economic historian, Louis C. Hunter, in *Steamboats on the Western Rivers* (Cambridge, Mass.: n.p., 1949), quoted in Jackson, *Voyages,* xiv–xv.

Chapter 10: Themes for a Wilderness Epic

1. Frank Bergon, ed., *The Journals of Lewis and Clark* (New York: Viking, 1989), x. William Gilpin (1813–94) was the first territorial governor of Colorado and author of *Mission of the North American People* (1873).

2. Robert B. Betts, *In Search of York* (Boulder: Colorado Associated University Press, 1985), must now be supplemented by a more recently discovered cache of Clark letters, being edited at the Filson Club in Louisville, Kentucky. According to James J. Holmberg, the curator of manuscripts at the Filson Club, these letters show that Clark treated York harshly after his return, separated him from his wife and family, hired him out to a severe master in Kentucky, and threatened him with beatings or sale to a slave trader when he became refractory. Holmberg presented a preliminary report on these letters at the meeting of the Lewis and Clark Trail Heritage Foundation in Louisville on August 7, 1991.

3. Samuel Johnson, *Lives of the English Poets*, ed. George Birkbeck Hill, 3 vols. (1905; New York: Octagon, 1967), 1:170. I have modernized some spellings.

4. John Dryden, *Poetical Works*, rev. ed. by George R. Noyes (Boston: Houghton Mifflin, 1950), 252.

5. The pressure to produce an epic worthy of early America is recounted in detail in John P. McWilliams, Jr., *The American Epic: Transforming a Genre, 1770–1860* (New York: Cambridge University Press, 1989), esp. 15–93.

6. William Shakespeare, *Antony and Cleopatra* 5.2.82–83, 91–92, in

The Riverside Shakespeare, ed. G. Blakemore Evans (Boston: Houghton Mifflin, 1974), 1383.

7. Eric A. Havelock, *Preface to Plato* (Cambridge, Mass.: Harvard University Press, 1963).

8. M. H. Abrams et al., eds. *The Norton Anthology of English Literature,* 4th ed., 2 vols. (New York: W. W. Norton, 1979), 2:1110–11.

9. Ibid., 1:1395.

10. These editorial principles are explained in Bernard DeVoto, ed., *The Journals of Lewis and Clark* (Boston: Houghton Mifflin, 1953), v–x; and Bergon, *Journals,* xvii.

Chapter 11: Ghosts on the Trail

1. Quoted in J. Fairfax McLaughlin, *Matthew Lyon: The Hampden of Congress* (New York: Crawford, 1900), 500. A more recent biography is Aleine Austen, *Matthew Lyon: "New Man" of the Democratic Revolution, 1749–1822* (University Park: Pennsylvania State University Press, 1981), but McLaughlin prints many original documents in full.

2. I follow the brief but colorful account of Lyon at this time in John C. Miller, *Crisis in Freedom: The Alien and Sedition Acts* (Boston: Little, Brown, 1951), 102–11.

3. *Annals of Congress,* 6th Congress, 2d session (1801), 1033.

4. McLaughlin, *Matthew Lyon,* 398.

5. Douglas Leighton, "Simon Girty," in *Dictionary of Canadian Biography,* ed. Frances G. Halpenny et al., vol. 5 (Toronto: University of Toronto Press, 1983), 346. For a more detailed account of the Girty family I have also consulted Consul Willshire Butterfield, *History of the Girtys* (Cincinnati: Clarke, 1890).

6. In a note to his edition of *The Field Notes of Captain William Clark, 1803–1805* (New Haven, Conn.: Yale University Press, 1964), 29, Ernest Staples Osgood quotes a letter by Girty, written much later in 1804, in which he longed to see family members near Pittsburgh. Osgood also notes an influx of many tribes to the St. Louis area after it was transferred to the United States in 1804. But neither of these circumstances explains this western journey.

7. Samuel Johnson, *Selected Poetry and Prose,* ed. Frank Brady and W. K. Wimsatt (Berkeley: University of California Press, 1977), 63.

8. George Gordon, Lord Byron, *Don Juan,* ed. Leslie A. Marchand (Boston: Houghton Mifflin, 1958), 259.

9. Timothy Flint, *Biographical Memoir of Daniel Boone,* ed. James K. Folsom (New Haven, Conn.: College and University Press, 1967), 187, 177.

10. George Imlay, *A Topographical Description of the Western Territory of North America* (London, 1793), 337.

11. Thomas Jefferson, *Notes on the State of Virginia,* ed. William Peden (1954; New York: W. W. Norton, 1972), 164–65.

12. Just a few years later, however, John Bradbury traveled up the Missouri with the overland expedition to Astoria. On March 17, 1811, the leader Wilson Price Hunt "pointed out to me an old man standing on the bank, who, he informed me, was Daniel Boone, the discoverer of Kentucky." But Bradbury had expected such an encounter; he bore a letter of introduction from Boone's nephew, and he went ashore and had a conversation with the seventy-seven-year-old man, who claimed to have "lately returned from his spring hunt, with nearly sixty beaver skins." John Bradbury, *Travels in the Interior of America in the Years 1809, 1810, and 1811,* 2d ed. (1819), ed. Reuben Gold Thwaites (1904; Lincoln: University of Nebraska Press, 1986), 43.

13. Donald Jackson, *Among the Sleeping Giants: Occasional Pieces on Lewis and Clark* (Urbana: University of Illinois Press, 1987), 9–10.

14. Hiram M. Chittenden, *The American Fur Trade of the Far West,* 2 vols. (1902; Stanford, Calif.: Academic Reprints, 1954), 1:143. Another, slightly more gruesome account is in Thomas James, *Three Years among the Indians and Mexicans* (1846; Lincoln: University of Nebraska Press, 1984), 46.

15. James, *Three Years,* 46.

16. Bradbury, *Travels,* 45–47.

17. Chittenden, *American Fur Trade,* 2:722.

18. Bradbury, *Travels,* 47.

19. Clark mentions "ground potatoes" served to him on September 26, 1804 (*Journals* 3:117, 119). Paul Russell Cutright identifies this food as *psoralea esculenta* (*LCPN* 91). Gary Moulton calls it *apios americana* but notes that this species is no longer found this far north (*Journals* 3:120). Curiously, Cutright never mentions this latter plant, though it is clear that Lewis took time to describe both species elsewhere in the journals (2:223, 4:125–26). Of course, it is not at all certain what plant or plants Colter ate; we can only be sure that this rough trapper did not call his food *psoralea esculenta.*

20. It is always risky to quote museum displays or captions, which may change. This caption is quoted in Gerald W. Olmsted, *Fielding's Lewis and Clark Trail,* Fielding Travel Books (New York: William Morrow, 1986), 238. When I visited this display in June 1990, I found the caption but in a slightly different place from the display Olmsted describes.

21. Ronda, 157–60, 221–37; Dee Brown, *Bury My Heart at Wounded Knee: An Indian History of the American West* (New York: Holt, Rinehart

& Winston, 1970), 316–30. I copy the spelling of the chief's Nez Perce name from Alvin M. Josephy, Jr., *The Nez Perce Indians and the Opening of the Northwest* (New Haven, Conn.: Yale University Press, 1965). Josephy translates it as "Thunder Traveling to Loftier Mountain Heights" and explains that it was the name of this chief's mother's brother (447).

22. Ralph S. Space, *The Lolo Trail: A History of Events Connected with the Lolo Trail since Lewis and Clark* (Lewiston, Idaho: Printcraft Printing, 1970), 45–47.

23. Chief Joseph, "An Indian's View of Indian Affairs," *North American Review* 128 (1879): 432. This entire manifesto (pp. 415–33) traces the history of the Nez Perces from their first encounter with French-speaking traders to the aftermath of their 1877 defeat.

24. Numerous memorials, including five statues, six paintings, two rivers, two lakes, and four mountains, are listed in Harold P. Howard, *Sacajawea* (Norman: University of Oklahoma Press, 1971), 193–96. Others are listed in Ella E. Clark and Margot Edmonds, *Sacagawea of the Lewis and Clark Expedition* (Berkeley: University of California Press, 1979), 155–57.

25. *Journals* 3:291n; Charles G. Clarke, *The Men of the Lewis and Clark Expedition* (Glendale, Calif.: Arthur H. Clark, 1970), 148.

26. W. M. Boggs, "Manuscript on Bent's Fort, 1844–45," ed. LeRoy R. Hafen, *Colorado Magazine* 7 (Mar. 1930), quoted in Howard, *Sacajawea,* 173. Irving W. Anderson, "A Charbonneau Family Portrait," *American West* 17 (Mar./Apr. 1980): 4–13, 58–64, provides a thorough, brief review of accurate information about these family members, with a list of source documents.

27. Robert B. Betts, *In Search of York* (Boulder: Colorado Associated University Press, 1985), 68–72.

28. Ibid., 71. Betts reports that the photograph was taken by William Henry Jackson, and a copy is in the Iconographic Collections of the Wisconsin Historical Society. An illustrated, unsigned article on the subject is "What Are the Facts?" *Montana: The Magazine of Western History* 5 (Summer 1955): 36–37.

29. Wilson's account was published in the *Port Folio* in 1812 and is reprinted in Elliot Coues, ed., *History of the Expedition under the Command of Lewis and Clark,* reprint ed., 3 vols. (New York: Dover Books, 1965), 1:xliv-xlvi. Russell's report of earlier attempts was first printed in *Letters* 2:573–74.

30. The extensive discussions of Lewis's death were surveyed by Paul Russell Cutright in "Rest, Rest, Perturbèd Spirit," *We Proceeded On* 12 (Mar. 1986): 7–16. That discussion has been recently and vigorously attacked in E. G. Chuinard, "It Was Murder," *We Proceeded On* 17 (Aug. 1991): 4–11; (Nov. 1991): 4–10; and 18 (Jan. 1992): 4–10. James E. Starrs, a professor

of forensic sciences at George Washington University, has recently proposed to exhume Lewis's remains in an attempt to resolve this issue. His proposal was announced at the August 1992 meeting of the Lewis and Clark Trail Heritage Foundation.

Chapter 12: The Rockies by Moonlight

1. Norman Mailer, *Of a Fire on the Moon* (1969; New York: Grove, 1985), 382.

2. Helen Bevington, *Beautiful Lofty People* (New York: Harcourt Brace Jovanovitch, 1974), 186–92.

3. Kim R. Stafford, *Having Everything Right* (New York: Penguin, 1987), 11–21.

4. *Public Papers of the Presidents of the United States: Lyndon B. Johnson, 1968–69*, 2 vols. (Washington, D.C.: U.S. Government Printing Office, 1970), 1:27.

5. Alexis de Tocqueville, *Democracy in America*, 2 vols. (1835, 1840), ed. J. P. Mayer, trans. George Lawrence (1966; New York: Anchor, 1969), 2:536.

6. Ibid., 2:537.

7. John Logan Allen, *Passage through the Garden: Lewis and Clark and the Image of the American Northwest* (Urbana: University of Illinois Press, 1975), contains a full discussion of these advances with illustrative maps (375–94).

8. Ibid., 376. Donald Jackson, *Thomas Jefferson and the Stony Mountains: Exploring the West from Monticello* (Urbana: University of Illinois Press, 1981), briefly discusses Pike's explorations and his jealousies toward Lewis and Clark (242–67).

9. Carl Irving Wheat, *Mapping the Trans-Mississippi West*, 5 vols. (San Francisco: Institute of Historical Cartography, 1957–63), 2:58–59. Wheat quotes and cites further expert praise on these points from the chief cartographer of the National Archives: Herman R. Friis, "Cartographic and Geographic Activities of the Lewis and Clark Expedition," *Journal of the Washington Academy of Sciences* 44 (Nov. 1954).

10. Allen, *Passage through the Garden*, 382.

11. *Journals* 1:23n, 24. The reproduction in *Journals* is about half-size. A full-size reproduction was published by the Yale University Library in 1950, but many of its features are very faint too.

12. Philip B. King, *The Evolution of North America*, rev. ed. (Princeton: Princeton University Press, 1977), 6–7; J Harlen Bretz, H. T. U. Smith, and George E. Neff, "Channeled Scabland of Washington: New Data and Interpretations," *Geological Society of America Bulletin* 67 (1956): 957–1049;

J Harlen Bretz, "The Lake Missoula Floods and the Channeled Scabland," *Journal of Geology* 77 (1969): 505–43.

13. Daniel B. Botkin, *Discordant Harmonies: A New Ecology for the Twenty-first Century* (New York: Oxford University Press, 1990), 189.

14. Maurice Hershenson, ed., *The Moon Illusion* (Hillsdale, N.J.: Laurence Erlbaum Associates, 1989).

15. H. E. Huntley, *The Divine Proportion: A Study in Mathematical Beauty* (New York: Dover Books, 1970), frontispiece and 100–102, 164–68.

16. Peter G. K. Kahn and Stephen M. Pompea, "Nautiloid Growth Rhythms and Dynamical Evolution of the Earth-Moon System," *Nature* 275 (1978): 606–11. I was led to this paper by a discussion of it in Botkin, *Discordant Harmonies,* 187–88.

17. Bernhard Grzimek, *Grzimek's Animal Life Encyclopedia,* vol. 3: *Mollusks and Echinoderms* (New York: Van Nostrand Reinhold, 1974), 195.

18. Oliver Wendell Holmes, "The Chambered Nautilus," ll. 15–21, 29–35, in *A Treasury of the Familiar,* ed. Ralph L. Woods (New York: Macmillan, 1943), 416–17.

Index

The following abbreviations are used: GW for George Washington, LCE for Lewis and Clark Expedition, ML for Meriwether Lewis, TJ for Thomas Jefferson, and WC for William Clark. In subentries these abbreviations represent last names: WC stands for Clark; GW, for Washington.

Index

Index

Grizzly bears: claws of, 53, 63; encountered by LCE, 52–53, 56, 59, 64–67, 165–67; feeding habits, 66–67; mating of, 147; named, 165–66; observed before LCE, 64, 165, 253n13; personified, 65, 67, 253n14

Guns and gunpowder. *See* Firearms; Inventions

Hailstorms, 67–68
Hall, Hugh, 215
Hamilton, Alexander, 20, 198
Hamilton, Henry, 76
Havelock, Eric, 199
Haynes, F. Jay, 164–65
Hemingway, Ernest, 190–91
Hicks, Edward: *The Falls of Niagara,* 46–47; *The Peaceable Kingdom,* 47–50, 251n27
Hidatsa Indians, 20, 65, 94, 105–7, 116
History of LCE (1814), 5, 57, 81, 158–61, 168, 237–38
Hollowell, A. Irving, 253n14
Holmes, Oliver Wendell, 244–45
Holmgren, Virginia C., 149–50
Homer: epic poems of, 190, 195–200, 219
Horses: as food, 98, 104; needed by LCE in Rocky Mountains, 120, 124
Howard, Thomas Proctor, 215
Hudson River, 75, 172–73, 180, 187–89
Hunt, Wilson Price, 264n12

Imlay, George, 213
Indian languages: Blackfeet, 217; Chinook, 164; LCE and, 110–11, 115, 161–62, 166, 168; Mohawk, transcribed by A. G. Bell, 163; Ojibwa, 162; Shoshone, 119, 123–25; signing, 98, 116–18, 123; vocabulary lists, 115, 161–62
Indians: aid LCE, 18, 20–21, 25, 39–40, 93, 94, 98–100, 108, 115, 220, 238; in American Revolution, 211–13; assimilation of, 193–94, 200–201; children of, 221–22; and WC's map, 238, 240; cooking methods, 98–100, 102–3; courage of, 63, 65, 90, 126–27, 130; customs and beliefs of, 10, 61–62, 87, 105–7, 108, 123, 228; diplomacy of, 88–90, 113–14; diseases of, 99–100; distrusted, 114–15, 127, 130–32; hunt-

ing practices of, 65, 94–95, 105–6, 161; in paintings, 45, 48–49; property of, respected by LCE, 112–13; in Seven Years' War, 73, 75; sexual customs, 95, 111, 133, 161, 222; smoking of, 99, 111, 123, 127, 154–55; visit Washington, D.C., 112, 225–26; violent encounters with, 76, 88–90, 216–21. *See also* Indian languages; names of individual tribes

Instruments: of LCE, 54–55, 68, 228
Invention: in language, 168
Inventions, revolutionary: Henry Adams on, 58–59; aircraft, 232–36, 240; automobile, 233–34; Bacon on, 53–54; chronometer, 54, 228; electronics, 230–31; gunpowder, 53–58, 186–87; internal combustion engine, 185; iron bridge, 189, 261n12; jet propulsion, 183, 244; magnetic compass, 53–54; modern metallurgy, 54; printing, 53–54, 56–57; optical lenses, 54; paddle wheels, 185; railroads, 58, 189, 240; rocketry, 229–32; satellites, 229, 232, 240–41; screw propeller, 185; sextant, 54; steam power, 58–59, 185; steamboats, 58–59, 178–91; stirrup, 54; submarines, 187, 243–44; telegraph, 58–59, 163; telescope, 54, 117, 228; television, 233–34; Visible Speech, 162–63, 259n17

Jackson, Donald, 80, 92, 203, 215
James River, 75
Jefferson, Thomas: Declaration of Independence, 82–83; election of 1800, 209–10; instructions to LCE, 4–5, 9, 54–59, 79, 83–84, 86–87, 111–12, 115, 148, 162; and ML, 27, 80–81, 160, 223–24; Monticello, 29–31, 83, 87; Natural Bridge, 28–30, 45; *Notes on the State of Virginia,* 27–30, 44, 79, 83, 139, 149, 172, 214; peace medals, 125–26; plans LCE, 78–80, 92; scientific correspondents of, 4, 43, 139–40, 147, 161; scientific knowledge of, 82–87, 139, 141, 161–62, 183–84, 241, 261n12; and steamboats, 181, 184; on the sublime, 27–31, 40; and the West, 19–20, 77–80, 83–86, 172, 214